T H E   Y E A R

Y E L L O W S T O N E

B U R N E D

THE YEAR

YELLOWSTONE

BURNED

A TWENTY-FIVE-YEAR PERSPECTIVE

JEFF HENRY

Foreword by BOB BARBEE

TAYLOR TRADE PUBLISHING

Lanham • Boulder • New York • London

Published by Taylor Trade Publishing
An imprint of The Rowman & Littlefield Publishing Group, Inc.
4501 Forbes Boulevard, Suite 200, Lanham, Maryland 20706
www.rowman.com

Unit A, Whitacre Mews, 26-34 Stannary Street, London SE11 4AB, United Kingdom

Distributed by NATIONAL BOOK NETWORK

British Library Cataloguing in Publication Information Available

Library of Congress Cataloging-in-Publication Data
Henry, Jeff.
  The year Yellowstone burned : a twenty-five-year perspective / Jeff Henry ; foreword by Bob
Barbee.
    pages cm
  ISBN 978-1-58979-903-5 (pbk. : alk. paper) — ISBN 978-1-58979-904-2 (electronic) 1. Forest
fires—Yellowstone National Park. 2. Forest fires—Environmental aspects—Yellowstone National
Park. 3. Fire ecology—Yellowstone National Park. 4. Yellowstone National Park. I. Title.
  SD421.32.Y45H46 2015
  634.909787'5—dc23   2014046126

♾™ The paper used in this publication meets the minimum requirements of American National
Standard for Information Sciences—Permanence of Paper for Printed Library Materials, ANSI/
NISO Z39.48-1992.

Printed in the United States of America

This book is dedicated with the most sincere gratitude to all the family and friends who helped me survive my illnesses of the last four years. Quite simply and without any question whatsoever I would not have gotten through it without your help, this book never would have been written, and I would not be around today.

It would require all the space in an entire book to list the names of everyone who helped me—there were at least 78 different people who stepped up to take care of my roof shoveling obligations in Yellowstone during the winter of 2010–2011, for one example. But there are several individuals to whom I must express an extra special thank you. My father and mother, Jack and Roberta Henry, perhaps deserve the most credit of all. My brother Scott Henry also deserves special credit, as does my daughter Mariah Gale Henry. Another thank you should go out to my extended family—a terrific collection of aunts, uncles, and cousins.

I extend another special dedication and thank you to Jenny Wolfe of Yellowstone National Park, who quite literally saved my life in March of 2012. In addition to out-and-out saving my life in the spring of that year, Jenny was an immeasurable source of help and support through many difficult months that were simultaneously more than challenging in other areas of her life.

Special mention is also warranted for George and Kathryn Bornemann and their children Gus and Sonya, as well as to Dale Fowler, Crystal Cassidy, Lisa Culpepper, Amy Beegel, Mike Bryers, Herb Vaughn, Kyle Barrus, Doug Hilborn, Virgia Bryan, Tom Robertson, Dan and Jill Tompkins, Max Brenzel, Ashea Mills, Pat and Ginger Povah, Arden Bailey, Erica Hudgings, Paul Vucetich, the management of Yellowstone General Stores, the 2010–2011 employees of Old Faithful Snow Lodge, and to all the attendees of the extraordinarily touching benefit auction that was conducted in my behalf on March 4, 2011 in West Yellowstone, Montana.

I also would like to mention former Yellowstone National Park ranger Mike Robinson. Mike allowed me to use some of his experiences in the great 1988 fires in this book. He also contributed greatly to the protection of the park he loved through the many years of his service as a ranger. I had the privilege of knowing Mike and working with him on occasion during our years in Yellowstone. He was a great guy, and his untimely death in an auto accident in November of 2013 was tragic in the extreme.

To all the people listed here, and to many others—thank you.

Foreword

Superintendent Bob Barbee during the 1988 fires. Barbee was superintendent of Yellowstone National Park from 1983 through 1994. © Jeff Henry/Roche Jaune Pictures, Inc.

THERE WERE twenty five thousand individuals who played some role in the great Yellowstone fires of 1988 and an equal number of stories. Jeff Henry was one of those people, and his story is to be found in this book.

Over a quarter of a century has passed and the Yellowstone fires still challenge the psyche. They were the greatest single event in our national parks history. They were, in a word, epic. There have been numerous attempts to describe the fires. While many are adequate and some good, none of them quite "got it."

Finally someone has written a book that is both riveting and accurate. It is the "real deal." Jeff leads us through a tour de force of fire and man in the west then illustrates the growth of the 1988 fires with maps and his splendid photography. Far from only a detailed account of logistics, Jeff moves from fire to fire and weaves a coherent narrative brought to life with capsulated stories.

Firefighting is an enterprise filled with jargon. Here it is either avoided or described with a lucid explanation. Jeff Henry was there from beginning to end. He spikes his narrative with personal anecdotes and leaves the reader secure in the knowledge that here is someone who knows what he is talking about

I can sum up the now historic Yellowstone fires of 1988 as: Unpredictable—Unpreventable—Uncontrollable, and Unimaginable!

Bob Barbee
Yellowstone Superintendent, 1983–1994

Acknowledgments

A GREAT MANY people helped me put together this book.
Ann Rodman and Lorenzo Fracastoro of the National Park Service Spatial Analysis Center in Yellowstone produced the maps that are the backbone of the book, and I can't thank them enough for their efforts and suggestions.

I have to thank Bob Barbee, superintendent of Yellowstone at the time of the 1988 fires, for writing the foreword to my work.

I also have to thank a large number of people who granted interviews to me, usually to relate the experiences they had during the 1988 fires, but in many cases to elucidate about fire in general for me, and to comment on conclusions I had made about the great Yellowstone fires. These people include, but are not limited to: Joan Anzelmo, Lee Whittlesey, Les Inafuku, Dawn Inafuku, Ann Marie Chytra, Kathleen O'Leary, Roger Santala, Dana Boroughs, Chris Gastrock, Jill Waters, Mike Bader, Bob Jackson, Dave Poncin, Sr., Dave Poncin, Jr., Mike Adkins, Mike Bryers, Emma Fuller, Bill Blackford, Jim Peaco, George Bornemann, Dan Tompkins, Les Brunton, Bob Duff, Toni Duff, Rick Bennett, Karen Bennett, Bonnie Whitman (Gafney), Katie Holsinger, Mark Marschall, Dan Krapf, Mike Robinson, Joe Fowler, Dale Fowler, George Helfrich, John Lounsbury, Jim Sweaney, Elenor Clark (Williams), Tom Robertson, Dan Tompkins, Darren Kisor, Dave Thomas, Mike Krebs, Patrick Povah, Paul Schullery, Dave Mattson, Jamie Jonkel, Mark Haroldson, Rich Jehle, Roy Renkin, Beth Casey, Ray Fenio, Kerry Gunther, Randy King, Larry Lahren, Jerry Brekke, Mark Watson, Dan Beadle, Amy Beegel, Roger Cooke, Edna Cooke, Barry Wolfe, Patrick Hoppe, Thomas Williams Munro, Tor Pederson, Jack Altemus,

Ralph Glidden, Kay King, Phil Cilwick, Glen Dixon, Rick Hoeninghausen, Gene Ball, Mike Keller, Diane Papineau, Carrie Holder, Greg Dahling, Dub Kennedy, Matt Higgins, Arden Bailey, Erica Hudgings, Eleanor Clark.

For providing illustrations for me to use in the book, I would like to direct special thanks to Jim Peaco, Dan Krapf, Mark Marschall, John Lounsbury, Dawn Inafuku, Thomas Williams Munro, Mike Krebs, Dan Beadle, Ann Marie Chytra, Roger Cooke, Edna Cooke, Bonnie Gafney (Whitman), Rich Jehle, Roy Renkin, Ray Fenio, Katie Holsinger, Kathy Peterson, Nancy Glazier, Mike Bader.

Paul Vucetich helped me greatly with the technical side of things in putting the book together.

I owe a special debt of gratitude to Dave Poncin, Sr., who was incident commander on two of Yellowstone's biggest fires in 1988, was a heck of a nice guy then and an even nicer guy now. He provided great amounts of time for interviews and also provided great amounts of special inside information.

A special note of thanks is due to Lee Whittlesey and Paul Schullery, who generously furnished much good information about fire history in Yellowstone, information for which they had put in much hard work to find.

One final addition to this list of acknowledgments is a sincere thank you to all the friends and family members who helped me pull through the last three years. Especially important in pulling me through the dark times was my daughter, Mariah Gale Henry. The efforts you all made on my behalf were as memorable, and much more touching, than the memories of the great Yellowstone Fires of 1988.

Introduction
Yellowstone Has Always Had Fires

YELLOWSTONE HAS always had fires. At least it has since the glaciers of the last ice age melted off the Yellowstone Plateau about 14,000 years ago. The very first European American visitors to the area, the fabled mountain men of the early nineteenth century, frequently noticed the effects of fire on the landscape, and on occasion observed wildfires actively burning. In the scanty records of the fur trade are found fairly frequent notations about fire in the Rocky Mountain region in general, and in some cases the Yellowstone region in particular.

The famous author Washington Irving, like many others of his own time and ever since, was greatly enamored with the perilously romantic lives led by the fur trappers, and spent a good portion of his career writing about them. In several of his writings about the mountain men, Irving made note of wildfires. In the 1849 edition of his book *The Adventures of Captain Bonneville*, for example, Irving related that in 1836 Captain Benjamin Bonneville and the party he was leading found themselves surrounded by "one vast conflagration; which swept over the long grass in billows of flame, shot up every bush and tree, rose in great columns from the groves, and sent up clouds of smoke that darkened the atmosphere." Bonneville and his men, who were on a foray to explore the West and its fur trading possibilities, attempted "to avoid this sea of fire," but the farther they went the more they found themselves surrounded by the huge fire, which "seemed to embrace the whole wilderness." The captain added an astute observation of fire behavior when he noted that the flames burned quickly through the grasslands of lower elevations, but "took a stronger hold amid the wooded glens and ravines of the mountains." In these heavier fuels, the wildfire "sent up sheets of flame, and clouds of lurid smoke, and sparks and cinders that in the night made them resemble the craters of volcanoes." A little later the

Fire was an integral part of the scene in Yellowstone, long before humans appeared in the area. © Nancy Glazier

flames gradated into even larger displays and became "towering columns of fire," and were further described as "stupendous sights . . . combined with rushing blasts caused by the rarefied air, which whirled forth the smoke and flames in impetuous wreaths."

These fiery adventures of Captain Bonneville, as told through Washington Irving, occurred in Oregon, several hundred miles west of today's Yellowstone National Park. But there are many similarities in the habitat between the area where Bonneville was nearly engulfed and Yellowstone, especially in terms of fire regime, and Bonneville himself noted that not only was he traveling during the "season of fire," he was also encountering "one of the phenomena of the western wilds," indicating that wildfires were commonly seen by the mountain men in their travels.

Much closer to home in the Yellowstone area is the place name "Burnt Hole," which was the name the mountain men applied to the Hebgen Lake basin, along the Madison River just north of the present-day town of West Yellowstone, Montana, and just west of today's Yellowstone National Park. A "hole," in the parlance of the trappers, was a valley ringed by mountains, and the Burnt Hole was a place that had been blackened by a forest fire during their time, or perhaps just before their arrival on the scene. The name appears in several records of the fur trade, including the journals of Osborne Russell, Joe Meek, and Warren Angus Ferris. The latter was a trapper who operated in the Rocky Mountains from 1830 to 1835, and he recorded in his journal that the Burnt Hole was so named because the "district was observed to be wrapped in flames some years since. The conflagration that occasioned the

A wildfire in the coniferous forests of the northern Rockies, such as those sometimes encountered by the early-day mountain men. © Jeff Henry/Roche Jaune Pictures, Inc.

A regenerating forest in the Yellowstone area, similar to the Burnt Hole of the mountain men, the area known today as the Hebgen Lake Basin. © Jeff Henry/Roche Jaune Pictures, Inc.

name must have been of great extent, and large forests of half-consumed pines still evident the ravages." An interesting footnote in the context of Yellowstone National Park history is that later in the nineteenth century the name metamorphosed to "Firehole" and migrated from its original placement on the Madison to the river flowing through the remarkable geyser basins in the western portion of the world's first national park—the stream we know as the Firehole River.

In common with all humans since the domestication of fire, the mountain men also directly set fires to the landscape, both intentionally and unintentionally. On occasion the trappers probably set fires on purpose to drive game, or perhaps with the intention of altering the range to affect future distribution of game animals. History does not record such use of fire in the immediate Yellowstone area, but there is at least one example of a campfire in the area of today's park that accidentally escaped from some mountain men and ran off through the forest. On August 28, 1839, after he had been wounded in a surprise attack by Blackfeet Indians along Pelican Creek near its inlet into Yellowstone Lake, trapper Osborne Russell took refuge in a wooded site near today's Fishing Bridge. Russell noted in his journal that he and his "companions threw some logs and rubbish together forming a kind of shelter from

Lewis and Clark on the Upper Missouri River, a painting by Roger Cooke that depicts a scene shortly before the explorers stashed their dugout canoes by sinking them in a pond to protect them from prescribed fires set by Indians. Courtesy of Edna Cooke

the night breeze," but unfortunately for the defeated trappers the logs and rubbish apparently were too close to their campfire, because "in the night it took fire (the logs being pitch pine)," and "the blaze ran to the tops of the trees."

Of course the experience of the Rocky Mountain trappers was but a snapshot when compared to the experiences of Native Americans, who had been in the area for around 13,000 years before the mountain men showed up. It is hard to overstate just how important fire was to North America's first human inhabitants—lithic technology and fire were the two principal underpinnings of the Indians' lifeway. In addition to domestic fire for heat, light, and cooking, Indians used fire as a tool to manage their environment. When intentionally set, Indian fires were usually intended to improve grazing for herbivores by clearing away old plant growth and opening the way for new. On March 6, 1805 in his journal, for instance, with his usual creative spelling and capitalization Captain William Clark observed "a Cloudy morning & Smokey all Day from the burning of the plains, which was Set on fire by the *Minnetarries* [a tribe of local Indians] for an early crop of Grass as an endusement for the Buffalow to feed on."

Clark's discerning observation was made on the plains of what is now North Dakota, a long way east of today's Yellowstone, but Clark and his partner Captain

Meriwether Lewis continued to notice additional evidence of prescribed burns set by Indians as they journeyed west in the spring and summer of 1805. Along the upper forks of the Jefferson River, almost immediately west of Yellowstone National Park, Lewis recorded that "the Indians appear on some parts of the river to have destroyed a great proportion of the little timber which there is by setting fire." So pervasive was Indian fire that when it came time for Lewis and Clark to cache the dugout canoes they had used to ascend the Missouri and Jefferson rivers, and which they hoped to use to descend the same rivers the following summer, they "sunk them in the water [of a pond] and weighted them down with stone . . . hoping by this means to guard against . . . the fire which is frequently kindled in these plains by the natives."

Without any question, Indians also had campfires that escaped and burned into the surrounding countryside, and they also set fires for reasons other than range management. As the best source for providing a glimpse into native life before it was irrevocably changed by contact with European Americans, I again refer to Lewis and Clark. On June 25, 1806 in the Rocky Mountains west of today's Missoula, Montana, the explorers' Indian guides "entertained us with Setting the fir trees on fire. they have a great number of dry limbs near their bodies which when Set on fire create a very Sudden and emmence blaize from bottom to top of those tall trees. they are a boutifull object in this Situation at night. . . . the nativs told us that their object in Setting those trees on fire was to bring fair weather for our journey."

Any number of other European Americans who traveled in the American West in the wake of Lewis and Clark left additional accounts of Indians using fire for a variety of purposes, all of which had profound implications for the environment. One such traveler was the widely traveled Belgian missionary, Father Pierre J. DeSmet, who recognized additional aspects of the spiritual importance of fire in Indian life when he wrote, "Fire is, in all the Indian tribes I have known, an emblem of happiness and good fortune. It is kindled before all their deliberations."

Another early-day traveler who left an account of Indians using fire, in this case as a weapon of war, was mountain man Joe Meek. Recorded in *The River of the* West, by **Frances Fuller Victor**, on September 9, 1835, Meek was camped with a number of other trappers along the valley of the Madison River a short distance downstream from today's Quake Lake when they were attacked by a party of about eighty Blackfeet Indians. After the battle had reached a stalemate the Indians set fire to grass that surrounded a stand of timber where the trappers had forted up, in an attempt to burn the white men out. Meek recorded that "the fire quickly spread to the grove, and shot up the pine trees in splendid columns of flame, that seemed to lick the face of heaven." The Indians closed on the trapped trappers, using the flames and smoke to cover their advance, and for a time things looked grim for the fur men.

Osborne Russell, who was also present, described the situation in his *Journal of a Trapper* as "the most horrid position I was ever placed in[. D]eath seemed almost

A photo of a grass fire sweeping into the trees of an adjacent forest, as happened when Black-feet Indians set fire to burn out a party of mountain men along the Madison River in 1835. This particular scene was also along the Madison, and shows the North Fork Fire burning along the slopes above the river near the Cougar Creek trailhead in August of 1988. © Jeff Henry/Roche Jaune Pictures, Inc.

inevitable." But the trappers were a "game party," according to Meek, and more than just game, they also had the presence of mind to start a backfire to burn out fuel in front of the fire started by the Blackfeet. Russell's version of the battle has it that "all hands began immediately to remove the rubbish around the encampment and setting fire to it to act against the flames that were hovering over our heads: this plan was successful beyond our expectations[.] Scarce half an hour had elapsed when the fire had passed around us and driven our enemies from their position."

So, as often happens in the world of fire, the blaze the Indians kindled backfired against them, and the trappers survived. This battle between fur trappers and the Blackfeet happened just downriver from the Burnt Hole of the mountain men, and only about 20 miles west of the boundary of present-day Yellowstone National Park. Among other things, it is a rock solid account of the use of an intentional backfire set to save people caught in front of an advancing larger fire, and it happened 114

Lost explorer Truman Everts accidentally set fire to the forest south of Yellowstone Lake after he became separated from his comrades in the early autumn of 1870. Unknown artist, image appeared in Truman Everts's "Thirty-Seven Days of Peril," *Scribner's Monthly*, November 1871.

years before smokejumper Wagner Dodge used the technique to save himself (and tried to save others in his crew) in Montana's disastrous Mann Gulch Fire of 1949 (the story of which was famously chronicled in Norman Maclean's book *Young Men and Fire*). Some sources erroneously credit Dodge with pioneering the technique of the "escape fire," but not only did Russell, Meek, and their fellows use it in 1835, there are also a number of other accounts of Indians using similar measures to survive fast-moving grass fires on the windy Great Plains, including one left by James Fenimore Cooper in his 1827 book *The Prairie*.

For the purposes of this book, the anecdote involving trappers and Blackfeet in the Madison Valley is noteworthy because it happened very close to today's Yellowstone in a habitat identical to much of that found in the park, and it indicates that early September of 1835 must have been dry and forests were obviously in a burnable condition at the time. By extension, it is also an indication of the ecological effects of fire—the environmental consequences of the fire set by the Blackfeet in the early autumn of 1835 must have persisted for a long time after the battle smoke had cleared. Thus the fire serves as a microcosm of how Indian fires of all types, whether intentionally or unintentionally set, had widespread and lasting effects on the environment.

Unfortunately, references of Indian use of fire specific to what is now Yellowstone National Park are hard to find. One of the few was left by Walter Washington

DeLacy, who in September 1863 led a party of gold prospectors into what is now Yellowstone National Park. As DeLacy and his group approached Yellowstone from the south as they were leaving Jackson's Big Hole, they saw horse tracks, "and the mountains ahead seemed to be on fire. We might, therefore, expect to find Indians."

DeLacy did not elaborate as to why he made the jump from noticing horse tracks in front of him and wildfire in the distance and then concluded that the two phenomena must be related. He could, of course, have been correct that there was indeed an association between the horse tracks, the fire, and natives. But even if Indians were the cause of the fire he was seeing, there is no evidence given that might explain why the Indians had set the fire, not even whether the fire was intentional or unintentional.

Another early visitor to Yellowstone who recorded a scene that might have involved Indians and fire, this one from the era of official exploration, was Lieutenant Gustavus C. Doane. The cavalry officer was in charge of the military escort accompanying the Washburn Expedition of 1870, in late August of that year, when he noticed that Mount Everts, just south of the present North Entrance to the park, "had been recently burned off to drive away the game, and the woods were still on fire in every direction." Doane did not elaborate as to why he thought the fire on Mount Everts had been set to "drive off the game," or even whether he thought it had been set by Indians or by white men. By August of 1870 the latter were fairly common in Yellowstone, especially in the northern part of what is now the park, through which gold miners traveled on their way to and from the mines in the Cooke City area. Most likely, however, Doane was implying that the fire had been set by Indians, and was also presuming that the fire he saw had been set as part of a hunting strategy. If so, this probably reveals more about Doane's biases than it does about Indians and their use of fire.

Indians using fire to drive game was something white people could comprehend, and records of such use go back at least as far as Thomas Jefferson. In 1813 Jefferson noted that Indians in Virginia had used fire kindled in large circles to corral game, and that the technique had been used in his home state during his lifetime (he was born in 1743). Whites probably could grasp the idea of natives using fire to drive game more readily than they could conceive of Indians using fire for more sophisticated reasons, such as for purposes of spirituality or range management. Because of its unpredictability, many contemporary sources actually doubt that Indian use of fire to drive game was all that common.

Another vignette involving official explorers and fire in Yellowstone comes from the same Washburn Expedition of 1870 that included Lieutenant Gustavus Doane. The Washburn party was camped in heavily wooded country south of Yellowstone Lake on September 9, 1870 when one of its members became separated from the group. Truman C. Everts was a career bureaucrat with no wilderness experience when he became lost that autumn, and in addition to being inept, he was also myopic. The hapless Everts lost his horse and almost all of his equipment early in his separation, and then blundered from one misadventure from another. One of the few items remaining in his possession after his horse bolted was an opera glass, which Everts was able to use to make fire by focusing the rays of the sun on tinder. While camped near the West Thumb on Yellowstone Lake a few days after he became lost, however, Everts kindled a fire and built a "bower of pine boughs."

As happened to trapper Osborne Russell thirty-one years earlier on the other side of Yellowstone Lake, Everts apparently built his bower too close to his fire, and sometime in the night the comforting warmth of the campfire morphed into a terrifying conflagration in the surrounding forest. Everts lost most of the few items remaining in his meager kit, and he also burned his left hand and had his "hair singed closer than a barber would have trimmed it." In *Lost in the Yellowstone*, the account Everts left of his ordeal, he added a good description of how quickly fire can spread in Yellowstone's coniferous forests when conditions are ripe for burning:

> The grandeur of the burning forest surpasses description. An immense sheet of flame, following to their tops the lofty trees of an almost impenetrable pine forest, leaping madly from top to top, and sending thousands of forked tongues a hundred feet or more athwart the midnight darkness, lighting up with lurid gloom and glare the surrounding scenery of lake and mountains, fills the beholder with mingled feeling of awe and astonishment. I never before saw anything so terribly beautiful. It was marvelous to witness the flash-like rapidity with which the flames would mount the loftiest trees. The roaring, cracking, crashing, and snapping of falling limbs and burning foliage was deafening. On, on, on traveled the destructive element, until it seemed as if the whole forest was enveloped in flame. Afar up the wood-crowned hill, the overtopping trees shot forth pinnacles and walls and streamers of arrowy fire. The entire hill-side was an ocean of glowing and surging fiery billows. Favored by the gale [Everts earlier had noted that it was a windy night], the conflagration spread with lightning swiftness over an illimitable extent of country, filling the atmosphere with driving clouds of suffocating fume[s], and leaving a broad and blackened trail of spectral trunks shorn of limbs and foliage, smoking and burning, to mark the immense sweep of its devastation.

Everts was a good writer, but he must have been a slow learner in the realm of the wilderness. A few weeks later in his solitary ordeal that lasted thirty-seven days, Everts kindled another campfire that similarly escaped into the surrounding forest sometime during the night. This second escaped campfire was near Tower Falls, and it "burned a large space in all directions" while Everts slumbered. Fortunately for the lost man, Everts did not suffer bodily injury in the second fire he caused, and he was rescued a short time later, albeit in a dangerously wasted condition, by two frontiersmen named George Pritchett and "Yellowstone Jack" Baronett who had been sent to search for him.

Blackfeet Burning the Crow Buffalo Range, by Charles M. Russell, is another painting that shows Indians setting fire to a plains environment. In this depiction the title makes it certain that this is a case of one tribe burning the range of another in an effort to deprive their enemies of prey.

Another early-day frontiersman in the Yellowstone area, this one named Richard "Beaver Dick" Leigh, was born in England but spent a large portion of his life in the upper Snake River country a short distance south and west of Yellowstone National Park. In his painfully spelled writings, he left several accounts that offer glimpses into the subject of Indians and fire. In September of 1875 he noted that "there is a large fire burning from the head of camos [Camas] creek to the north fork a distance of 24 mills [miles] the Banock indans pased hear yesterday it is them set the fire out for thay genrly do when thay go thrue this way to Buflo."

This passage from Beaver Dick's diary refers to a district west of Henry's Lake called the Camas Meadows, through which the great Bannock Indian Trail passed on its way between the Snake River Plain and the buffalo country east of the Rocky Mountains. Tribes like the Bannock and the Shoshone seasonally made the trip from their country west of the Rockies to buffalo ranges along the lower Yellowstone River and its tributaries after about 1840, when bison along the Snake River disappeared, and the late 1870s, when the days of free-ranging Indians in the Yellowstone area came to an end.

The Indians to whom Leigh referred apparently set fires along the trail during their passage, perhaps from carelessly left campfires, or possibly with conscious intent to promote the growth of fresh vegetation for their horses to eat (and possibly to attract game to the vicinity of the trail) on their return journey from the buffalo plains. Either way, the Indians' fires would have had a major impact on the environment along the trail. Given that a few miles east of the Camas Meadows the Bannock Trail passed through Yellowstone National Park, it seems reasonable to assume that the Indians left similar fires there in the wake of their passage. And it is very interesting to note that Leigh wrote that the Indians "genrly" set fire to the surrounding country when they passed by on the trail, seemingly indicating that they did it as a regular matter of course.

Beaver Dick Leigh mentioned another fire in the upper Snake River country just two weeks later than the one he observed in the area around Camas Meadows. This one was burning "most of the snake river cuntry," and because of its extent, Leigh thought that its aftermath would "drive a big porchan [portion] of the game to other whintering grounds this year." In this case, Leigh did not give any indication as to the origin of the fire, but at the very least it tells us that 1875 must have been a dry year, with burnable conditions extending at least into early October. If this latter fire was set by Indians, and it did indeed mean that wildlife would be compelled to move elsewhere to find suitable winter range, then it could have been an example of a range fire set to force wildlife to another district, rather than as "an endusement," in Captain Clark's words, for them to move to burned over areas that had sprouted nutritious regrowth. This was a common use of fire by the Indians, too, designed either to move wildlife closer to a tribe's home area or to move the animals away from the home areas of enemy tribes. Such fires were typically set in the autumn, too late in the growing season for vegetation to regenerate before the onset of winter.

Of course it was shortly after 1875 that Indians in the Yellowstone area were fully confined to reservations, and their impact on the environment of the area greatly diminished. In short order, however, their role with fire in the landscape was largely replaced by the actions of white newcomers. In 1878 Beaver Dick Leigh made another observation regarding fire in the upper Snake River country, but this time it referenced white men instead of Indians. Noticing smoke in the distance from his home in the northern portion of Pierre's Hole (what we now call the Teton Basin, on the west side of the Teton Range), Leigh went to investigate its cause. Nearing the source of the smoke "i caushesley aproached were [where] the fire started I [saw] that wight men had been camped here with 3 horses[.] trapers [trappers] or prospector and the wind had started the big fire that is burning from thare camp fire[.] thare is over a hundred miles of cuntrey burned of now from this fire and still a burning it jumped the midle fork and is burning north and East." So either prospectors or trappers had started the wildfire when their campfire escaped into the surrounding forest, and again, 1878 must have been a dry year. Leigh also makes note of the direction the fire moved—to the north and east—typical movements in line with the Yellowstone area's prevailing southwesterly winds.

In keeping with the arrival of white people in growing numbers in the area, in 1877 Yellowstone Park Superintendent Philetus Norris lamented that the park was inadequately protected during his time, and not only were there deleterious impacts from poaching and vandalism, there had also been destructive impacts from the "careless use of fire." In seeming ignorance of the regenerative powers of Yellowstone's fire-adapted forests, Norris thought that fires were doing "irreparable injury in all the explored portions of the park." In view of the fact that Norris thought that the damage was being done in the "explored portions of the park," he probably was referring to neglected campfires from travelers touring the park as a source of ignition for the destructive blazes.

In addition to wildfires spawned by the campfires of careless tourists, a problem mentioned by several other early-day park managers besides Philetus Norris, Yellowstone Park in its infancy was frequently plagued by malicious fires. These fires were set by disgruntled frontier settlers who were angered by the fact that they could no longer exploit Yellowstone's natural resources for utilitarian purposes. Again referring to the writings of Superintendent Norris, these were a "small but despicable class of prowlers who, in addition to kindling devastating forest fires," also poached animals and vandalized geothermal formations.

Another mention of maliciously set fires was by park superintendent David Wear, who left Yellowstone in 1886 when civilian management of Yellowstone was turned over to the United States Army, which then in turn was left in charge of Yellowstone for the next thirty-two years. In a message to incoming commandant Captain Moses Harris of the U.S. Cavalry, Wear warned that there was a certain "class of frontiersman, hunters, trappers, and squaw men," who among other retributive acts set spiteful fires within the park. When Harris and his troops arrived at park headquarters in Mammoth Hot Springs on the evening of August 17, 1886, the most commanding of these intentional fires was burning on the north side of Bunsen Peak, the side of the mountain facing Mammoth. It was thought that hostile residents in the nearby Montana community of Gardiner had set that particular fire.

A common thread through almost all of the early-day references to fire in Yellowstone seems to be a general ignorance of the subject. Norris, for example, thought that the destruction caused by wildfire was "irreparable," implying that he was unaware that burned forests have the capacity to regenerate. In still another record from Yellowstone's early days, this one from a tourist named M. Augustin Seguin, blame for a forest fire was placed on Indians engaged in hunting. In describing a scene along Obsidian Creek near Obsidian Cliff, Seguin wrote,

> A great sadness lies over all this valley, whose marshy bottom [probably what was later called Beaver Lake], filled with tall grasses, is surrounded as far as the eye can see by burned forests. Fire is, for the Indians, the most usual method of hunting; they set fire to a vast enclosed area and wait for the game by the way out. In this way they destroy hundreds of hectares for some bears or bison which they manage to kill.

Along with most other white observers of the time, Seguin seemed to be unable to conceive that Indians could use fire for any purpose other than hunting, such as

Montana entrepreneur Walter Cooper was surveying for a possible railroad route near the west boundary of Yellowstone National Park in 1881 when he encountered a large forest fire. He mentioned "small game with seared fur" in the record he left of his observations, probably something similar to this unfortunate porcupine who was badly burned by the North Fork Fire near Seven Mile Bridge in August of 1988. © Jeff Henry/ Roche Jaune Pictures, Inc.

for spiritual reasons or for purposes of range management, and most if not all early chroniclers seemed to be unaware that some fires could be caused by lightning. The lack of awareness of lightning as a potential source of ignition for wildfire probably had something to do with the fact that virtually all early-day explorers came from the eastern United States, where conditions are much more humid and wildfires much less common.

Seguin's visit to Yellowstone was in 1879, so it is somewhat doubtful that there were Indians left in the vicinity of Obsidian Cliff to have started that fire for any reason—by then most Indians in the area had been forced onto reservations away from Yellowstone. Another reference from 1879 also betrays the fact that early-day journalists usually did not consider lightning as a possible source of ignition for fires they saw burning, or were the cause of burned country they observed in the aftermath of fire. A Yellowstone traveler named S. W. Mitchell noted that two of his companions had left his party to check a salt lick near Trout Lake for game, "but this proved a failure, some one having carelessly set fire to the tract." It certainly is possible that someone could have "set fire to the tract," but Mitchell does not even mention the possibility of lightning, and he made no mention of any evidence he might have seen that led him to the conclusion he made regarding the fire's origin. In view of the fact that Mitchell noted that someone had "carelessly set fire," it would seem that he thought the person who started the fire was white. Because the site of the fire was along the heavily traveled corridor leading to the New World Mining District near Cooke City, and because it was 1879, that might very well have been the case.

All the observations ever made by whites regarding Indians use of fire are, of course, only a brief moment when compared to the long sweep that elapsed between the time the ancestors of the Indians arrived in North America and the time Europeans arrived 13,000 years later. And any accounts written by whites of Indian behavior serve as ultimate examples of the Heisenberg Principle, whereby observation of a phenomenon changes the nature of the phenomenon. By the time the very first whites arrived in the Yellowstone area, Indian lifeways already had changed because the influence of the newcomers had preceded them across the continent, and by the time most chroniclers arrived those changes had become radical. Attempting to discern the effect that Native Americans had on the landscape through their use of fire in Yellowstone, or anywhere else for that matter, involves quite a bit of guesswork.

That said, based on what is known about Indian use of fire elsewhere in the American West, it seems reasonable to assume that they intentionally burned the grasslands of Yellowstone's northern range on a frequent basis, perhaps with intervals of just a few years. This use of fire to manage rangeland had the effect of promoting new growth of grasses and forbs, and also to some extent probably kept nearby forests from encroaching into the open country.

In Yellowstone's higher country, which is mostly forested plateaus, prescribed burning by Indians was probably less of a factor. Habitats at higher elevations in Yellowstone tend to be relatively unproductive, and burning them would not have yielded much of an increase in biotic production to benefit natives. And the interval between the times when Yellowstone's higher, cooler forests *can* burn is prescribed more by nature than it is by humans, be they natives or nonnatives. It takes a long time for enough organic material to accumulate to sustain a fire in Yellowstone's high, cool forests, where growing seasons are short and soils are poor. And then, even when sufficient fuel has accumulated, weather conditions warm and dry enough to support widespread fire were historically rare.

Burning intervals in most of Yellowstone's coniferous forests were probably on the order of one to four centuries, regardless of any efforts made by humans to alter the cycle. In a very real sense, it can be said that for most of the fire cycle, forests in Yellowstone simply will not burn—at least not to any considerable extent—but in those rare times when the factors of fuel and weather combine to allow for combustion, burning can become almost inevitable, and this is regardless of anything humans can do to encourage fire during the off times or to suppress it during the times when burning conditions are prime.

By the early 1880s, Indians had been expelled from Yellowstone, and white trappers and prospectors had also come and gone. Official exploration had been accomplished, and the dawn of Yellowstone as a tourist destination was at hand. Emblematic of the early 1880s was a businessman from Bozeman named Walter Cooper. In the late summer of 1881 Cooper and two companions, Peter Koch and George Wakefield, set out to survey the Gallatin Canyon as a possible railroad route between Bozeman and the west side of Yellowstone National Park, then only nine years old. Not surprisingly, at the end of their railroad survey, Cooper and his companions tacked on a tour of the geyser basins along the Firehole River. On the one outing they not only surveyed for entrepreneurial opportunities in the Gallatin Canyon, but also spent time as tourists in Yellowstone, metaphorically bridging the era of official exploration and the era of tourism.

On the return from their sojourn in the geyser basins, however, Cooper and his companions noticed that it was "smoke and hazy ahead," and that they "must be approaching forest fire." The next day was August 27, 1881, and conditions had worsened: "Smoke awful. Horses nervous. Birds with seared wings flying past us. No red glow anywhere but heavy smoke. Traveled all day—choked with smoke, eyes smarting badly." And conditions deteriorated still further through the course of the day, as the party traveled north along a route approximating today's Highway 191. By evening Cooper recorded in his diary that they could "see red glow ahead," and that the party was "very nervous." Apparently because he was so "very nervous," Cooper made his journal entries on his saddle as he rode along, not taking the chance to stop and write.

On the 28th conditions were even worse, as the party noticed "fire creeping toward us from every direction; all around us." Because of the hot embers on the ground, their horses' feet were "very sore," as were the feet of a dog they had along on the trip. The party was apprehensive about approaching darkness, as Cooper wrote, "What this night will bring and tomorrow, we know not," but the next day the trio had their worst trial by fire. Probably still writing on the pommel of his saddle, Cooper recorded:

> Making all possible haste . . . . Observations hard to make. Traveled most of the night, let horse have their heads; they seem to know trail. Flames jump canyon from one side to the other. Spectacular sight, but an inferno. See small game with seared fur and bewildered deer and elk race by, plunging into timber and out again. Hardly pause for food . . . . Hot ashes falling everywhere. Noise of fire deafening. By late afternoon reached burned over section and find heat not as intense. Stench of smoke still awful. Coughing constantly; horses heave and choke and short winded, getting exhausted. We judge we have made fifty miles since two

A photo of a fire that burned adjacent to the Upper Geyser Basin in 1901. The perspective of the photo suggests it was taken in the vicinity of Old Faithful Geyser, looking down basin toward the fire that was burning on the ridge above Riverside Geyser. 1901 National Park Service

this morning. No feed left in either upper or lower basins [of the Gallatin River]. Timber practically burned out; nauseating sight . . . . One mountain completely bare of timber. Named it Baldy. Fire out here. Some smouldering patches still and hot ashes everywhere. Some places the largest trees still standing. One wonders how they escaped. Seems a miracle, also, we got out.

Riding through burning country for over 50 miles—it was a big fire. And Cooper's reactions are similar to those of others viewing such a big fire for the first time. The "deafening" noise, the choking smoke, the wonder at how a few trees were left unburned in an ocean of fire, the sense that Cooper and his companions were lucky to survive—all these observations are common for people seeing such a fiery phenomenon for the first time (or in subsequent observations, for that matter).

And it's interesting to consider Cooper's notes on wildlife and fire, and what they might say about the way interpretation is skewed by preconceived notions lurking behind the eye of the beholder. The notation about birds flying by with seared wings, for example, makes today's reader wonder about how much singeing a bird's wings could take and still allow the burned bird to fly. And why didn't the birds, being birds, take flight before the flames approached closely enough to singe their wings?

In addition, the entry about bewildered deer and elk fleeing in front of the flames—that one reminds today's reader of the posterized Smoky the Bear image of wildlife fleeing in wild panic, in front of wildfire burning in the forested background behind the madly dashing animals. In contrast, many Yellowstone observers of wildlife and fire in 1988, many of whom were much more likely to embrace the image of fire as a necessary and beneficial element of nature, frequently commented on just how nonchalant wildlife such as elk and bison seemed to be, even when they were seen in fairly close proximity to fire. The animals were seen to be placidly grazing, mating, and otherwise going about the normal business of life without much regard for the blazes that were flaring a short distance away. But in view of the fact that at least several hundred animals were killed outright by the searing flames and choking smoke of 1988, it's obvious that not all Yellowstone wildlife was able to remain nonchalant through the entire burning season, and to some degree their nonchalance might have been in the eyes of 1988 beholders.

Another National Park Service photo, this one showing a 1953 fire that was burning near White Lake. Park service records show that this fire burned 1,486 acres, and on this particular day it apparently exploded to the point where firefighters had to wade across the water in the middle distance to escape the flames. A close look at the photograph shows that the firefighters, who were all male in those days, had taken the time to shed their pants before entering the water. 1953 National Park Service

In amazingly short order, of course, Yellowstone's popularity boomed in the years after Walter Cooper's tour. Annual visitation grew from about 1,000 when Cooper made his trip in 1881 to over 144,000 when he died in 1924. Hotels, tourist camps, and transportation systems were established, and with the exception of a few short-lived downturns brought on by wars or the Great Depression, visitation grew rapidly, often totaling major leaps just from one year to the next.

In Yellowstone's early days, tourists started many fires in the woods with carelessly attended campfires. As a matter of fact, escaped campfires were such a problem in the park's early days that one of the first managerial directives issued by the U.S. Cavalry after they arrived in Yellowstone in 1886 stated that "camping parties will only build fires when actually necessary, and must carefully extinguish them when no longer necessary." As time went on and park management evolved, however, campers were concentrated in established campgrounds where their fires were much more likely to stay contained in dedicated fire pits.

Fighting fires started by careless campfires and other causes consumed much of the time and energy of the first troopers in Yellowstone right after their arrival in 1886, and concern for wildfires continued through the entire thirty-two-year tenure of the army in Yellowstone. There is a telling notation, for example, that Captain Moses Harris made in September of 1889. Captain Harris was the commander of the first army contingent to be assigned to Yellowstone, and he referenced a fire burning near Norris Geyser Basin that probably had been started by a poacher named William James. The latter had been caught trapping in the park, had consequently been expelled, and then in a letter to Harris had promised retribution. He apparently made good on his threats by setting fire to the piney woods north of Norris, after which he was caught and expelled from the park once again.

Another army document from 1888 noted that there were one hundred fires in the park that year, and yet another referenced that while there were fewer fires the next year, conditions must have been drier because the acreage burned was greater. A good passage from 1889 describes a fire that was burning above the Madison Canyon, and that was so large "it took an hour to walk around" its perimeter. The 1889 fire was also persistent—it required the efforts of 29 men, sustained over a period of three weeks, before it could be fully contained. The attitude of the cavalry toward fire was summed up by a document written shortly after the turn of the twentieth century that listed the need to protect the Yellowstone area from wildfire was as great as the need to protect it "from the vandalism of specimen hunters, and from depredations of poachers."

Concerns about wildfire continued after the National Park Service was created in 1916, and after it assumed full control of Yellowstone from the army in 1918. In the early years of the agency, fire was seen as a threat to tourism, which then as now, the organization saw as its lifeblood. Before 1968, the policy was that fire should be fought as the second highest park priority, behind only the protection

A 1976 photograph of elk grazing nonchalantly in front of the Arrow Fire along Obsidian Creek, offering a photo opportunity for park visitors and park service archivists alike. 1976 National Park Service

of human life, and the service-wide attitude toward fire was expressed in official statements like these:

> "Forest fires are our greatest danger to this park [in this particular case, Glacier]."
> "[The Park Service mission] as custodian is to preserve, unmarred by fire or other agency of destruction, the picture dedicated to public use and placed in its charges."
> "Fire and its consequences are the major causes of loss of forests usable for recreation."
> "Fire is today, without a doubt, the greatest threat against the perpetual scenic wealth of our largest national parks, which, bereft of their trees and foliage, would become haunts only of those interested in the study of desolation."

Some of the above statements were made as late as the late 1930s, so it is remarkable that by the late 1960s the National Park Service attitude toward fire had done an almost complete turnabout. Research developed in the intervening three decades had shown that fire was an integral element in natural ecosystems, and attitudes and policies toward fire began to change. In an academically fascinating transition, fire and its aftereffects went from something that was seen to mar the tourist experience to a phenomenon that actually enhanced a visitor's trip to a natural national park. A 1976 fire in Yellowstone, for example, was described by a park official thusly: "The herd of elk remained in the lush, green meadow below the fire throughout the afternoon and evening, giving park visitors a once-in-a-lifetime opportunity to easily view and photograph the elk against a natural fire backdrop."

That 1976 blaze in Yellowstone burned in early July along Obsidian Creek near the Grizzly Lake trailhead, and it was named the Arrow Fire. It was allowed to burn and was seen as a beneficial phenomenon because Yellowstone's fire policy had changed in 1972 to allow fires that had been naturally ignited by lightning, and that did not threaten human life or developments, to burn through their natural course. To be sure, that 1972 change in fire policy was at first implemented on only about 15 percent of the park's acreage, but in 1976 the policy was extended to virtually all of the park. In spite of the new latitude, only about 36,000 acres burned in Yellowstone during the 1972–1987 period. That was the acreage burned by a total of 368 fires that were started by lightning, of which 235 were allowed to burn under the new policy. Interestingly, 208 of those 235 permitted fires burned less than one acre each before they expired.

As an aside, it is also interesting to note that in the entire period between 1881 (only nine years after Yellowstone was created and the first year for which records are available) and 1971 (the last year before fire policy changed to allow at least some naturally occurring fires to burn) there was a total of only sixty-one large fires. Large fires in this case were defined as those that burned more than one hundred acres, and in total those sixty-one fires burned 113,784 acres. A little arithmetic shows that the per year average of burned acreage in Yellowstone was not that different during the period when fires were actively fought and for the sixteen-year period when they were largely allowed to follow their natural course. The largest fire in the park's history before 1988 was the Heart Lake Fire in 1931, which burned about 18,000 acres near the lake for which it was named. The Heart Lake Fire was fought as aggressively as the capabilities of 1931 would allow, and it offers an interesting anecdote illustrating how factors of fuel and weather go a lot further in determining what a fire will do than any human efforts that might be made to manage the situation. In writing his report in conclusion of the firefighting effort at Heart Lake, the commander in charge of the effort first took credit for himself and his men for bringing the Heart Lake Fire to bay, and then commented on how difficult it was to break down the fire camp in rainy weather and to pack out equipment over muddy trails.

As a young park employee I first arrived to work in Yellowstone in 1977, just one year after the park's policy had made the full transition to allow for naturally caused fires to burn on a monitored basis over almost all of the park's backcountry. I remember that wildfires in my early days in Yellowstone were rare events, and that even small fires consequently attracted a lot of attention when they did occur. I remember, for example, making a special trip from the Lake Area, where I worked that first summer, to the top of Lake Butte, from where I and some of my friends could watch a small smoker that was puffing up on the south side of Yellowstone Lake. In 1979 I remember making a similarly special trip from the Lake Area to the Chittenden Road on the north side of Mount Washburn, from where we had a good view of a fire burning in the Tower Creek drainage. My friends and I sacrificed quite a bit of sleep in the interest of watching that one, for we lingered long into the night to watch what we then considered a dramatic fire show as individual trees flared off in displays that firefighters like to refer to as "torching."

Again, in the summer of 1981, I remember using a day off from work to hike with a coworker to a fire that was burning on the side of Stonetop Mountain north of Pelican Valley. The fire was only smoldering coolly on the ground, quite close to the thermal area in the Sulfur Hills, the day my friend and I went there, but it made a lasting impression on us nonetheless.

Other than 1981, the early 1980s were moist in Yellowstone. That was also true for the mid-1980s, with average or above-average snow in the winters and, with the exception of 1985, adequate rains in summer. Consequently there was nothing in the way of significant fires during that time. The winter of 1986–1987 was exceptionally dry, to a record or near-record extent, but the following summer was abnormally wet. Again in the winter of 1987–1988 snowpack in Yellowstone was low, but not as exceptionally low as that of the winter before, and not as dry as a number of other recorded winters. Overall though, Yellowstone was drying out, and there was considerable talk among park observers that late winter and early spring of 1988 of how dry the park was and how much we were going to be at risk for fire the following summer. I distinctly remember a conversation I had with a crusty old veteran ranger, who had not only worked many years in Yellowstone but who also had grown up in nearby portions of Montana. My old friend, whose name was Gary Kennedy but who always went by his nickname Dub, summed up his view of the situation by saying simply, "Pretty soon the smoke's gonna be rollin'."

Deceptively, however, the spring of 1988 was abnormally wet, with about 155 percent of average precipitation in April and about 181 percent in May. On another personal note, from the early 1980s until the early 1990s I worked springs for the Interagency Grizzly Bear Study Team, searching for the carcasses of winterkilled ungulates and monitoring the bear use thereof in the geyser basins along the Firehole River. The job required me to be outside most all day most every day, and I remember that there were a great many times that spring that were snowy and/or rainy, and that my job was often a wet one.

The wet weather in the spring of 1988 was indeed deceptive, for in retrospect it could be noted that Yellowstone had totaled only about 76 percent of its average annual precipitation for the entire calendar year. Considering weather records from a representative site near Canyon, 1988 was the sixth driest year on record for the 1895–2012 period—for the calendar year, that is, not the hydrologic year that is usually considered to be from October 1 through September 30 of the following year. Most of those other five years of extreme drought were in the Dust Bowl era of the 1930s (including the driest of the lot, 1931, which not surprisingly was the year of the Heart Lake Fire).

In the view of many, the flush of moisture the park received in the spring of 1988 served only to grow a good crop of quick growing grasses and forbs, which in turn served as fine fuels to kindle and carry the fires that sparked to life very soon after the conclusion of spring.

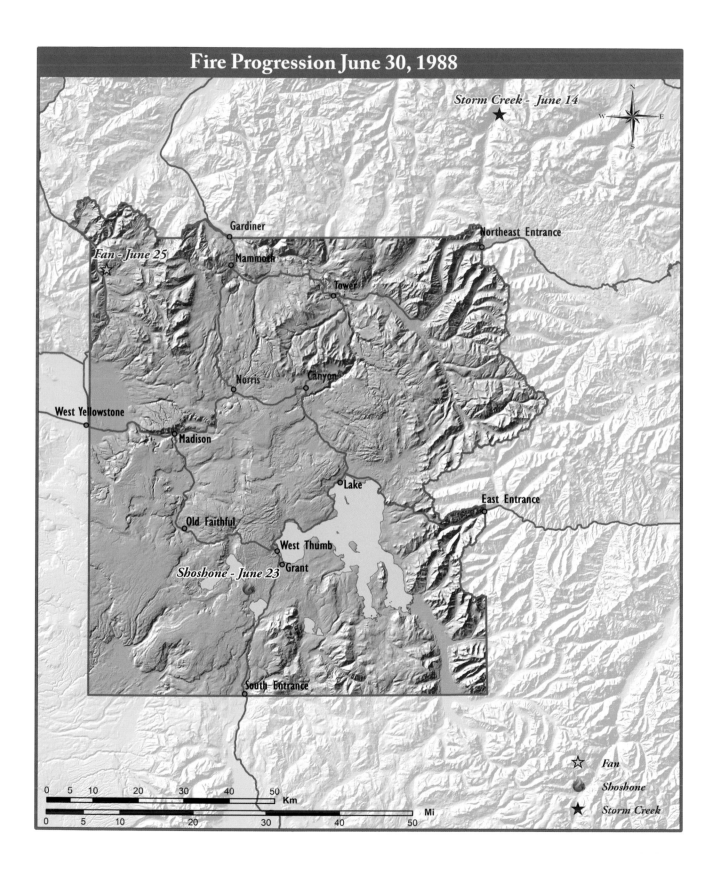

Fire Progression June 30, 1988

Storm Creek - June 14 ★

Gardiner
Northeast Entrance
Mammoth
Tower
Fan - June 25 ☆

Norris
Canyon

West Yellowstone
Madison

Lake
East Entrance

Old Faithful
West Thumb
Grant
Shoshone - June 23

South Entrance

0	5	10	20	30	40	50

Km

| 0 | 5 | 10 | 20 | 30 | 40 | 50 |

Mi

☆ *Fan*

🔴 *Shoshone*

★ *Storm Creek*

June 30, 1988

T HERE WERE several fires in the Yellowstone area that ignited before the Storm Creek Fire was sparked by lightning on June 14, 1988, but all the earlier fires went out before they amounted to much. The Storm Creek, on the other hand, did grow into a fire of consequence. It smoldered for more than two months, during which time it was largely forgotten because of dramatic events going on elsewhere in the area. It roared to life on August 19, however, and unexpectedly moved south against prevailing winds. Starting as it did almost due north of Yellowstone's Northeast Entrance and the resort towns of Silver Gate and Cooke City, Montana, its southward movement later in the summer evolved into a severe threat to those communities. The Storm Creek's starting point is marked by a star in the Custer National Forest, along the Stillwater River just a little east of due north from Yellowstone's northeast corner.

The Shoshone Fire is marked on this map by a star along the Lewis River between Shoshone Lake and Lewis Lake, just southwest of the West Thumb of Yellowstone Lake. In common with the Storm Creek Fire, it was ignited by lightning. Also like the Storm Creek Fire, the Shoshone smoldered for a time after it started on June 23, but in the case of the latter the incubation period was less than four weeks. It began to grow rapidly on July 20, and in another important respect that made it different from the Storm Creek Fire, it moved predictably in a northeasterly direction. In short order that movement made it a serious threat to the development at Grant Village.

The third fire of note to start in June of 1988 was the Fan Fire. Its starting point is marked by a star in the extreme northwestern corner of Yellowstone National Park, along Highway 191 and near the stream for which it was named, Fan Creek.

Shortly after it kicked up on July 1, 1988, the Fan Fire began to fill the gateway town of Gardiner, Montana, with a smoky haze. © Jeff Henry/Roche Jaune Pictures, Inc.

The Fan Fire started from a lightning strike on June 25. It smoked and smoldered for a few days until July 1, when it blew up and put on the first really impressive pyrotechnic display of the season.

On a personal note, I was working as a seasonal ranger for the National Park Service in 1988. I was stationed at Madison Junction that summer, but for the last week of June I was detailed to the Bechler area of the park to clear logs that had fallen into hiking trails over the course of the previous winter. I stayed in Bechler the whole week while I did that invigorating work and then drove home on Friday, which was July 1 that year. As I was driving through eastern Idaho on my way back to Madison, and especially as I neared the park's West Entrance in West Yellowstone, Montana, I could see a huge smoke column emanating from the Fan Fire to the north. An enormous thunderhead capped the smoke column. I had seen fires in Yellowstone before, during the summers of 1979, 1981 and other dry times, but never had I seen such a large, well-defined column that bespoke of such an awesome release of energy from the fire down below. I was transfixed, and immediately decided that I would use my upcoming weekend to drive to the area of the Fan Fire to have a closer look, and hopefully to be able to shoot some photos as well.

Back at Madison that evening I couldn't get the image of that smoke column and its gigantic, mushroom-shaped cloud out of my mind. Even from 30–40 miles away I had been able to see the angry boil of energy at the base of the column, and had marveled at the way the smoke whirled in a tornado-like spiral as it rose upward. How many BTUs must it take to create an expression like that in the sky? And this was only July 1, with the hottest, driest part of the summer and the bulk of the fire season yet to come.

That evening I phoned a friend of mine named Jim Sweaney, who at that time was a resource manager for the National Park Service in Yellowstone. For a total of eleven summers earlier in his career Jim had been a smokejumper—first for the Forest Service and then for the Park Service—and withal had a special interest in and a special knowledge of the subject of fire. I distinctly remember that Jim pointed out that in his estimation the Fan Fire had the potential to burn more acreage than the collective total of all the other fires that had been allowed to burn in Yellowstone since the park's fire policy had changed to accommodate naturally ignited fires in 1972.

Impressive stuff for sure, and indeed the Fan was the first fire to really pick up and make a major run that summer, and it did end up burning over 27,000 acres. It also menaced the town of Gardiner, Montana, for a time, and like the other major fires that year would not be completely extinguished until the lasting snows came in early November. The Fan also had the distinction of being one of the few fires that was successfully fought that summer, when it was contained before it could cross out of the northwestern corner of the park. All this was true, but at the time neither my friend Jim nor I nor anyone else could know how unprecedented the fire season of 1988 was to become—so much so that in retrospect, the Fan Fire would be only a relatively minor chapter.

Fire Progression July 2, 1988

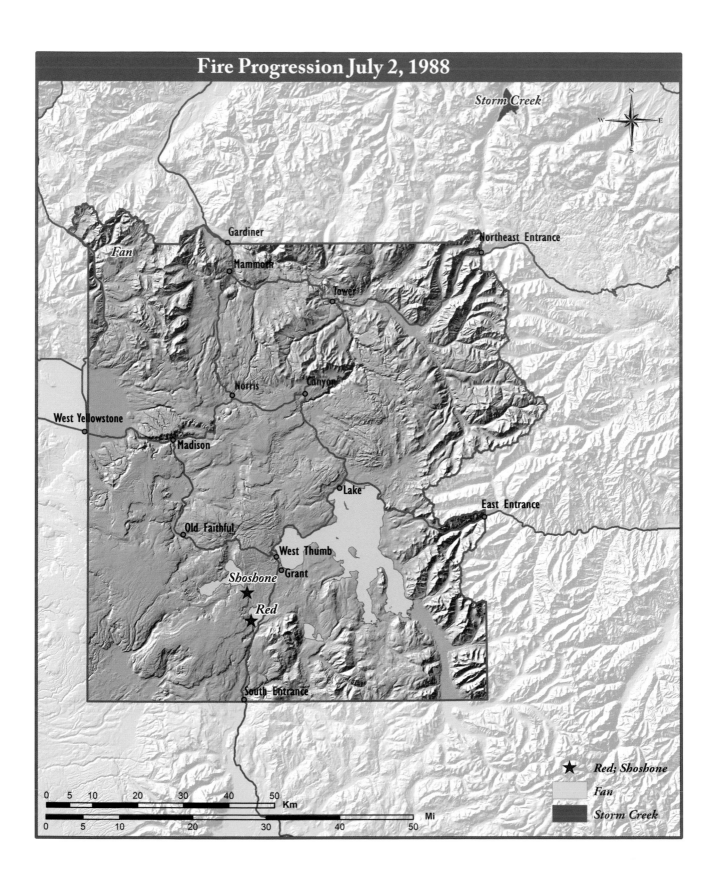

Storm Creek

Fan

Gardiner
Northeast Entrance

Mammoth

Tower

Norris
Canyon

West Yellowstone

Madison

Lake

East Entrance

Old Faithful

West Thumb

Grant

Shoshone

Red

South Entrance

★ Red; Shoshone

Fan

Storm Creek

| 0 | 5 | 10 | 20 | 30 | 40 | 50 | Km |

| 0 | 5 | 10 | 20 | 30 | 40 | 50 | Mi |

July 2, 1988

ON THIS MAP the growth the Fan Fire made on its run of July 1 is reflected in the yellow blotch on the map in the northwestern corner of the park. A pink blotch along the Stillwater River north of the northeastern corner of the park shows the growth of the Storm Creek fire, still only minor to that point.

The star marking the Shoshone Fire between Shoshone and Lewis Lakes indicates that the fire was as yet quite small. More portentously, a new star just south of the Shoshone Fire marks the beginning of the Red Fire, which was started by lightning on July 1. The Red Fire and the Shoshone Fire would eventually grow together and become so large that they would be given a hyphenated name, the Red-Shoshone Fire. Then, after several more fires ignited in the same part of the park, the Red and the Shoshone would be grouped together managerially with the new fires, and collectively they all would be known as the Snake River Complex. Before that point, however, the Shoshone Fire would make a major run at the Grant Village development, which in turn would be the first developed area in Yellowstone to be menaced by wildfire in the summer of 1988. And later in the summer, after the Red and the Shoshone had merged, they would make a second run at Grant Village, the second run happening on August 20.

I spent several days photographing the fire and the efforts to defend Grant Village in late July. While there and watching the tinder dry forest burn right up to the edge of the development, I couldn't help but marvel at the irony of how such a short time earlier in the season the same forest had been covered with snow and melt water.

In those days I worked each spring for the Interagency Grizzly Bear Study Team, before I began my summer season as a ranger for the National Park Service. My spring job for the Grizzly Team was to locate the carcasses of winterkilled ungulates and to keep track of how grizzly bears and other scavengers made use of the carrion.

A pair of photographs of roof-clearing work on the Yellowstone General Store at Canyon. The first photo shows the author sawing shallow snow into manageable blocks during the notoriously dry winter of 1987–1988. The second photograph shows roof clearing work in progress in almost the same location on the same roof, only in this photograph the snow is deep enough to dwarf a young cow bison that walked up on the general store over snow on the ground that was as deep as the eaves of the building. The second photo was taken in March of 2008, exactly twenty years after the first. As 1988 was not a year of record-low snow depth, neither was 2008 a record for maximum snow pack, but the two photos serve to illustrate how much snow pack can vary between years, with obvious implications for the degree of fire danger the following summer. © Jeff Henry/Roche Jaune Pictures, Inc.

In mid-May of 1988 three others and I were dispatched to Heart Lake, not far south of Grant Village, to survey that area for winterkills. At that time quite a few elk wintered in the Heart Lake Geyser Basin, and grizzly bears coming out of their dens scavenged meat from the elk that died there during the winter.

My coworkers, a group that included Dave Mattson, Jamie Jonkel, and Bill Bullard, and I began our trip at the Heart Lake trailhead on the South Entrance Road, followed the Heart Lake trail through the forest and over Paycheck Pass, and finally descended to the geothermal oasis along Witch Creek and the Heart Lake Geyser Basin. The trip was a tough one. The snowshoes we wore were not adequate to keep us on top of the spring-softened snowpack. Almost every step we broke through the three or four feet of supersaturated snow and punched all the way through to the muddy ground. Under the snow our snowshoes and boots sloshed around in standing meltwater that was anywhere from a few inches to a foot or more deep. Before every step we had to struggle to pull our snowshoes back up through to the slush to take the next stride forward. It was a cold, wet junket, and we were all relieved to make it to the bare ground around the Heart Lake thermals, with our relief dampened by the knowledge that in a few days we were going to have to turn around and make the same journey in the opposite direction to return to our vehicles at the Heart Lake trailhead. And then, just two months or so later, the same forest had dried out to the point where the Red and the Shoshone Fires were burning fiercely in the places that had been so cold and wet when we had made our spring trek to Heart Lake.

This anecdote about a slushy snowshoe trip to Heart Lake leads to an interesting point regarding 1988's snowpack in Yellowstone and the unimaginable fires of the following summer. The irony is that the year's snowpack was merely low, not record low. As a matter of fact, a check of two United States Department of Agriculture, automated snow monitoring stations that happen to be in the area of the Red and Shoshone Fires shows that there have been quite a few winters since 1981 when there was less snow than there was in 1988.

One of the stations is located on Two Ocean Plateau, about 25 miles southeast of Grant Village. Records for that station extend back to 1981, and since that year there have been ten winters that were dryer than 1988. This means that about one third of all recorded winters have had less snow ("snow water equivalent," as it is bureaucratically expressed) at that site than there was in 1988.

The other station is on West Thumb Divide, which is on the Continental Divide immediately south of Grant Village. Coincidentally, records there begin in 1988, and show that there have been six winters since that historic year that have been dryer, in this case amounting to about a quarter of the years since the recording station was installed. This, plus the fact that the spring of 1988 had above-average precipitation, and it becomes obvious that there were other factors involved in the weather equation that led to the great conflagrations of the following summer. Chief among those other factors was the extremely hot weather that developed early and then persisted throughout the entire summer, along with abnormally strong winds, and an almost complete lack of significant precipitation after the spring rains and snows ended.

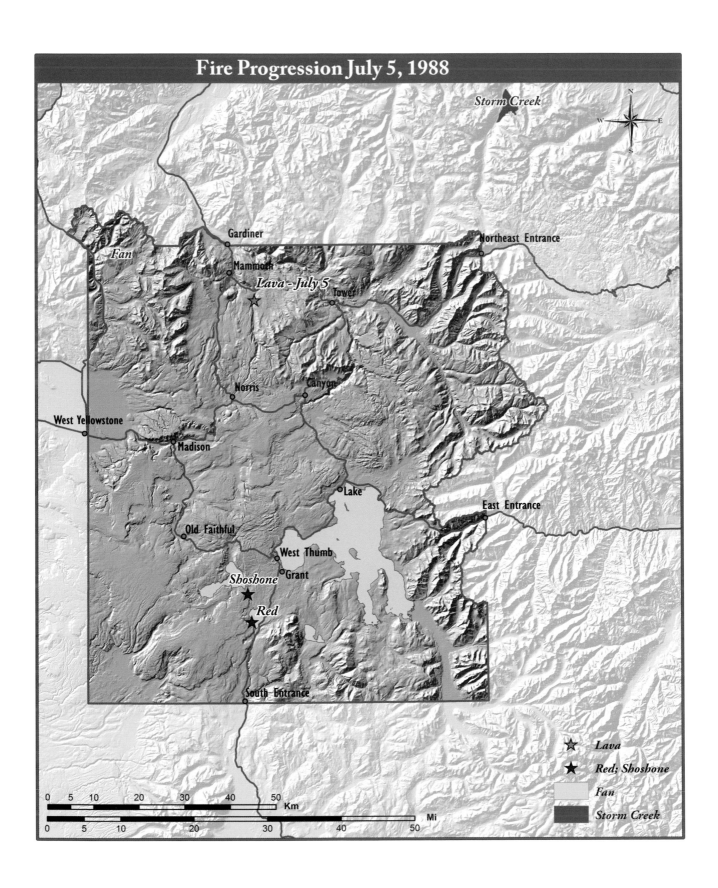

Fire Progression July 5, 1988

Storm Creek

Fan

Gardiner

Northeast Entrance

Mammoth

Lava - July 5

Tower

Norris

Canyon

West Yellowstone

Madison

Lake

Old Faithful

East Entrance

West Thumb

Grant

Shoshone

Red

South Entrance

	Km
0 5 10 20 30 40 50	
0 5 10 20 30 40 50	Mi

☆ Lava

★ Red; Shoshone

Fan

Storm Creek

July 5, 1988

THIS MAP shows the Red and the Shoshone Fires still in their nascent stages. It also shows the Fan Fire and the Storm Creek Fire at basically the same size as they were on the July 2 map.

The Lava Fire started on July 5. It shows as a star along Lava Creek, 7 miles southeast of Mammoth Hot Springs. As a lightning-caused fire, under Yellowstone's existing fire policy the Lava Fire was allowed to burn. After it started, however, the Lava burned so slowly that after a period of nine days it had grown to only two acres. Prime burning conditions existed on July 14, however, and several other fires in the Yellowstone area burned hotly and grew considerably in size. The Lava Fire itself did not blow up that day, but in view of the radical behavior displayed by some of the other fires on the 14th, and given that the 30-day forecast for the Yellowstone area called for a strong possibility of unusually hot and dry weather, park managers decided to suspend the natural fire policy and decreed that most of the existing fires in the park should be fought. Quite possibly because of its proximity to the developed complex at Mammoth Hot Springs, the Lava Fire was on the list of fires to be suppressed.

In 1988 Mike Bader was a coworker of mine in Yellowstone's ranger division. Mike is still a friend, and a man I greatly admire. While I did not work on the Lava Fire myself, my friend Mike did. One of his outstanding memories is from the site where the fire began. He remembers that the fire was caused by a "lightning strike on a massive Douglas fir and the blast blew shards of wood into the surrounding trees like shrapnel. The tree itself wasn't burned, but the supercharged shards started ground fire all around that spread." Of course Mike had no way of knowing it at the time, but his assignment to the Lava Fire was only the first of several fire details that would take him away from his home duty station at Canyon during Yellowstone's historic summer of fires.

The National Park Service (NPS) put a lot of emphasis on fighting the Lava Fire, partly because the same proximity to Mammoth that posed a threat to the development also made it more accessible for fire fighting efforts. Its nearness also rendered the fire and the efforts to control it more visible, which probably was another reason the NPS devoted so much time and effort to it. At times over one hundred firefighters were deployed on the Lava, and within a fairly short time the fire was contained at about seventy acres. This was in contrast to the much larger but more remote Clover-Mist Fire, which during the same time was growing toward 60,000 acres in size, but had a smaller number of firefighters assigned to it. The Lava also has the distinction of being one of the few fires successfully fought in the summer of 1988. The great irony is that later in the fire season the huge North Fork Fire, which was to start on July 22 in eastern Idaho, would reach the site of the Lava Fire and envelop the comparatively tiny latter fire in its maw, rendering the earlier success of the Lava firefighters irrelevant.

One of my own memories from this point in the summer of 1988 was from Mammoth Hot Springs. In early July the fires had not yet become all consuming in either their size or the attention they commanded from the Park Service, and time and effort could still be devoted to other issues of park management, such as removing what the service likes to call "hazard trees."

The iconic chapel at Mammoth Hot Springs was built by the United States Army in 1913, one of the last structures built by the troops during the thirty-two-year period when they looked after Yellowstone between 1886 and 1918, the latter being the year in which the National Park Service fully took over management of the world's first national park. The chapel was and still is surrounded by a number of large limber pines that are older and at least as deserving of reverence as the building itself. The trees were unusually large for their species, probably having benefited from decades of irrigation water applied to Mammoth's green lawns. By 1988, however, several of the old limber pines had died. Some of the dead trees were leaning toward the chapel, while others leaned toward other buildings in the neighborhood, and it was obviously just a matter of time before they came crashing down. Because of the size of the trees, they would have done major damage if that had been allowed to happen.

I was stationed at Madison Junction that summer, which is in a different administrative district than Mammoth, but I was known for my expertise with a chainsaw and I was detailed to Mammoth to take down the limber pines around the chapel. The trees were really big for Yellowstone, three or four feet in diameter, and correspondingly taller than Douglas firs with the same girth, pretty much the only other species in the area that can attain such a diameter. Running the chainsaw to directionally fell, limb, and then cut up the old trees left a part of my mind free to ponder the philosophical implications of what I was doing, removing venerable elements of nature in the interest of protecting works of humans.

Afterward, I counted the growth rings on the stumps, as I always do when I cut down trees. At this point, more than twenty-five years after the fact, I can't

Close-up of the trunk of a lodgepole pine that has been attacked by pine bark beetles. The tree unsuccessfully tried to flush the bugs out of its cambium with a rush of sap, as can be seen by the trickles running down the tree from the holes the beetles bored on their way in. © Jeff Henry/Roche Jaune Pictures, Inc.

remember exactly how old they were, but I do remember that by my standards they were by very old, having sprouted long before Americans of European descent appeared on the Yellowstone scene. I also distinctly remember wondering whether the big limber pines had died simply because they were old, or whether they might have lived even longer had it not been for Yellowstone's warming and drying climate. Based on the observation that quite a few of the trees had died at more or less the same time, I figured the latter was the more likely.

Indeed, the immediate cause of death of the old trees was the pine bark beetle, a tiny insect that feeds on the cambium layer of various species of pine. A vigorous pine can sometimes survive an attack of pine beetles, but if the bugs are too many or a tree too stressed by heat and drought, the tree will die. The limber pines at Mammoth were just a small handful of the millions of pines the beetles had killed in Yellowstone in the years leading up to 1988. Stark skeletons of the beetle-killed trees were visible throughout the park, and the dead wood was soon to provide dry fuel to the spectacular fires for which the summer will always be remembered.

Fire Progression July 10, 1988

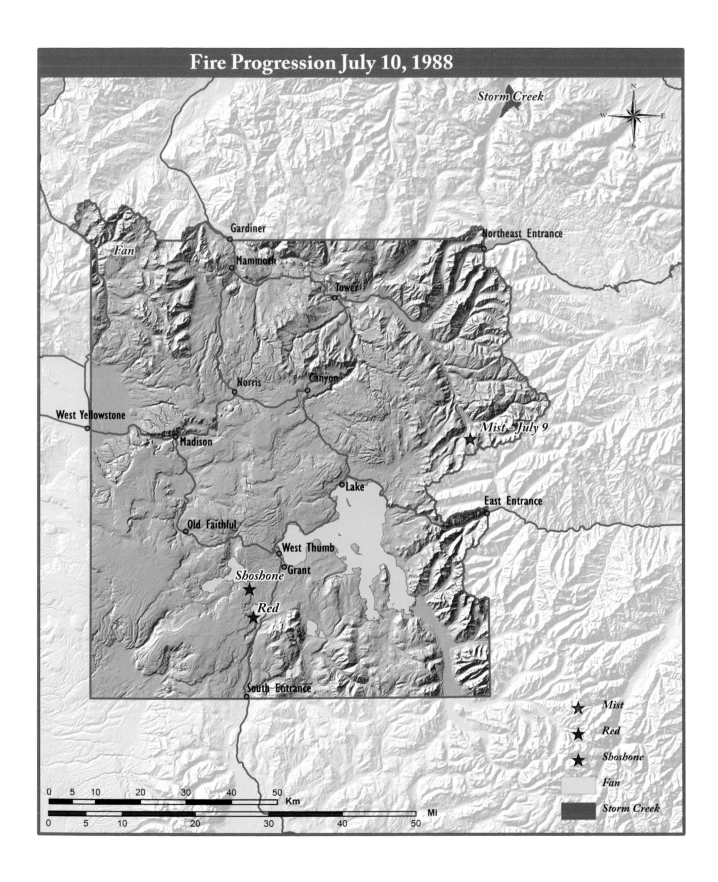

Storm Creek

Fan

Gardiner

Mammoth

Northeast Entrance

Tower

West Yellowstone

Norris

Canyon

Madison

Mist – July 9

Lake

East Entrance

Old Faithful

West Thumb

Grant

Shoshone

Red

South Entrance

★ *Mist*

★ *Red*

★ *Shoshone*

  Fan

  Storm Creek

0	5	10	20	30	40	50 Km
0	5	10	20	30	40	50 Mi

July 10, 1988

THE SIGNIFICANT development on this map is the start of the Mist Fire. It started with a lightning strike on July 9, and it is depicted here with a star near the eastern border of Yellowstone National Park, near the headwaters of the Lamar River. The fire received its name from Mist Creek, a stream descending from Mist Creek Pass; the pass, in turn, leads from upper Lamar to Pelican Valley. The whole area was a favored haunt of grizzly bears in 1988, as it still is today.

The Mist Fire was the first of at least seven fires that started in the upper Lamar country in early to mid-summer of 1988. The other fires in this incendiary shotgun blast included the Clover, the Lovely, the Raven, the Shallow, the Fern, and the Sour. As with almost all wildfires, their names were derived from prominent geographic features near their points of origin. All these fires eventually burned together and become known as the Clover-Mist Fire, although for a time fire managers attempted to maintain a sense of identity for each of the individual fires by linking their names together with hyphens. That soon became too cumbersome, however, and the name was shortened to Clover-Mist. The gigantic fire ultimately expanded to become one of the two largest fires in the region in 1988, encompassing an area of approximately 400,000 acres by the time it stopped growing in mid-September. Much of that burned acreage was outside the eastern boundary of Yellowstone National Park, where for an extended period of time the fire threatened the towns of Cooke City and Silver Gate, Montana, near the park's Northeast Entrance. Later in the fire season it also menaced private property to the east of those communities, including portions of the Sunlight Basin and Crandall Creek areas, and it actually did burn some structures, vehicles, and other property in those districts.

One of my personal memories from this time in the early summer of 1988 happened at Mammoth Hot Springs. Every spring or early summer, law enforcement rangers are required to attend a weeklong training course to refresh their knowledge of the law, as well as review techniques for enforcing it. In Yellowstone, the training usually is held at Mammoth Hot Springs, the location of park headquarters. That was the case in the summer of 1988, and for a week I had to journey from my summer home at Madison to the daily training sessions at Mammoth.

Mammoth is low in elevation relative to most of the rest of Yellowstone, so it is almost always milder in the winter and hotter in the summer. Even given that fact, however, it was unusually hot during our training at Mammoth, and because of the extreme heat nearly everyone complained even more than usual about having to sit in a classroom. I remember conversing with Les Inafuku, a friend of mine who had an even longer history in Yellowstone than I did. Les was a longtime Yellowstone ranger of the old school, a man who loved the park deeply and who was endlessly fascinated by what he saw here, and a man for whom I had tremendous respect. He and I agreed that the heat we were experiencing was off the charts, and I remember both of us using the term "greenhouse effect" in our conversations. At that time Les and I had about twenty-five years of experience in Yellowstone between us, and neither one of us had ever seen heat like we were seeing during that year's law enforcement training. And the heat was unrelenting, with us day after day.

It was also in early July that I got a chance to get a close look at the Fan Fire, the one which had so captivated my attention when I drove back from Bechler on July 1, and saw its smoke column rising from the northwestern corner of Yellowstone. Not only did I get the chance to get a close-up look at the Fan, but I also got to do it on National Park Service time as an assigned work duty. The assignment that took me to the vicinity of the Fan was to count pine cones on two different study plots of whitebark pine trees in the area of Fawn Pass, in the Gallatin Mountain Range south of Electric Peak.

Whitebark pine trees produce cones filled with highly nutritious seeds that feed a host of animals, most notably grizzly bears. Like most other mast-producing trees, however, whitebarks have evolved to produce cones on an irregular basis. If the trees produced a bumper crop of nuts every year, the interpretation of this phenomenon goes, seed-eaters would reproduce up to a level where they would consume all the seeds produced every year and there would be no seeds left over to germinate the next generation of whitebark pines. Pine nuts, as they are often called, ripen in the fall of the year and are high in calories and fat, so they are especially important to grizzly bears during the time they are trying to fatten up in preparation for winter hibernation.

Whitebark pines grow at high elevations, so in autumns of good mast production, grizzly bears spend most of their time in high, remote areas and conflicts with human beings are rare. Conversely, in years with poor cone production, grizzlies tend to spend a lot more time in lower elevations, where they are much more likely to come in contact with humans, resulting in problems for both people and bears. Because of all this, it behooves bear managers in Yellowstone and elsewhere to keep track of whitebark cone production.

Toward the end of keeping track of whitebark pine cone production, a number of study transects were established in the region in 1980. Researchers and managers count the cones on each of ten trees in each transect every summer, at a time when the cones are large enough to spot but before they are mature enough to be eaten by seed scavengers. The scheduling of the survey is also designed to give park managers time to prepare for whatever bear management eventualities the cone count might indicate to be in the offing for the coming fall.

In early July of 1988, Dan Reinhart of the Interagency Grizzly Bear Study Team (IGBST) and I were dispatched to count the cones on two study transects on Fawn Pass. I

The crown of a whitebark pine in a year of good cone production, with several of its rich cones visible in frame. © Jeff Henry/Roche Jaune Pictures, Inc.

guess both the National Park Service, for whom I worked, and the IGBST wanted to participate in the cone counting effort, and Dan and I were the two selected to do the work on the Fawn Pass transects. The Fawn Pass outing was an overnight affair, involving a stay for Dan and me in the Fawn Pass Patrol Cabin. Dan was a good choice for the assignment, as he was a long-term employee of the bear study who was devoted to and very good at his job. He also was and is an all-around fine human being.

In keeping with the impoverished nature of bear food sources in 1988, Dan and I found virtually no cones on the transect whitebark pines, but we did get a close-up look at the Fan Fire when we hiked out to the Fawn Pass trailhead on Highway 191. Overall, we had a great trip—great country, got bluff charged twice by the same grizzly bear along Fawn Creek, saw lots of other wildlife—but the big takeaway for both of us was the impressive fire behavior we saw from our close-up view of the Fan—especially when we considered how early we were in the fire season.

The other four fires that would grow to become major elements in the summer of fire are shown on this map, but had not expanded or moved much since the previous map, that of July 5.

Fire Progression July 12, 1988

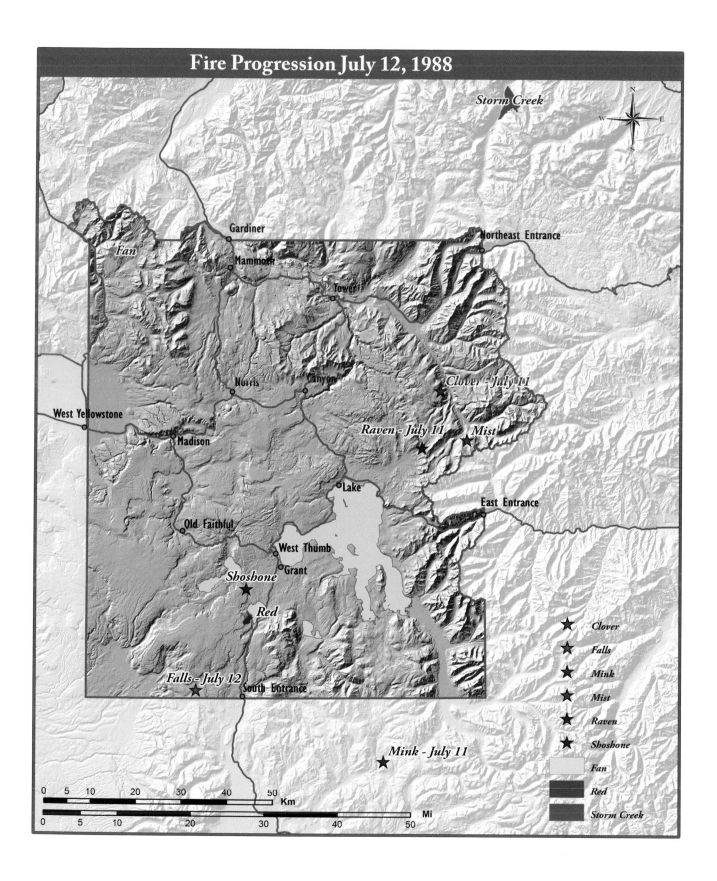

Storm Creek

Fan

Gardiner
Mammoth
Tower
Northeast Entrance

Norris
Canyon
Clover - July 11
Raven - July 11
Mist

West Yellowstone
Madison
Lake
East Entrance

Old Faithful
West Thumb
Grant
Shoshone
Red

Falls - July 12
South Entrance

Mink - July 11

★ Clover
★ Falls
★ Mink
★ Mist
★ Raven
★ Shoshone
Fan
Red
Storm Creek

0 5 10   20   30   40   50
Km
0 5 10   20   30   40   50
Mi

July 12, 1988

THE JULY 12 map shows the start of four new fires—the Mink, the Falls, the Clover, and the Raven. The Raven and Clover Fires would soon be incorporated into the huge Clover-Mist; the stars showing their starting points are in the eastern part of Yellowstone, north of the park's East Entrance Road.

The Mink Fire started on July 11 in Wyoming's Bridger-Teton National Forest, south of the southeastern corner of Yellowstone National Park. Blown along by prevailing southwesterly winds and somewhat directed by topography, the Mink eventually burned into the upper Yellowstone River Valley and then into the Thorofare region in the southeastern section of the park. For a time the park portion of the fire, in fact, would be called the Thorofare Fire.

The Falls Fire began on July 12 about 8 miles west of Yellowstone's South Entrance. Again, it was a fire that primarily followed the course of the prevailing winds and moved to the northeast. Later in the summer the leading edge of the Falls Fire would run into country already burned by the Red and Shoshone Fires, which of course stopped its progress in that direction. The Falls Fire was also responsible for one of the first political confrontations of the season, when officials in Idaho's Targhee National Forest, which neighbors Yellowstone National Park in that sector, informed park officials that they did not want the fire to cross into their jurisdiction. Forest Service insistence that the Falls Fire not be allowed to burn onto national forest land was a factor in Yellowstone's decision to begin fighting most fires on July 14, 1988; the Falls Fire was on the list of fires to be suppressed from that point forward.

About two weeks before the start of the Falls Fire, I had been assigned to work with fellow ranger Mike Ross to cut fallen logs out of a hiking trail that leads from the south boundary of Yellowstone up and onto the park's Pitchstone Plateau. The area traversed by that trail was within the perimeter of the area burned by the Falls Fire, and once again I was hit by the irony of a fire burning in a place that so recently had appeared lush and green, as it had looked when Mike and I were there doing the trail clearing work.

The Falls Fire was named for the nearby Falls River, which in turn is one of the older place names in Yellowstone. Originally called the Falling Fork by the famed mountain men of the early nineteenth century, the name was in use sometime before 1839. In that year trapper Osborne Russell, who kept a well-written journal that is one of the best sources of information from the fur trapping era, described the stream as "the middle branch of Henry's fork [of the Snake River] which is called by hunters 'The falling fork' from the numerous Cascades it forms while meandering thro. the forest." The name was later shortened to its present form by one of the official exploration parties that journeyed through Yellowstone in the 1870s. The Falls River is well named—there are indeed a number of beautiful waterfalls along its course.

Fire Progression July 14, 1988

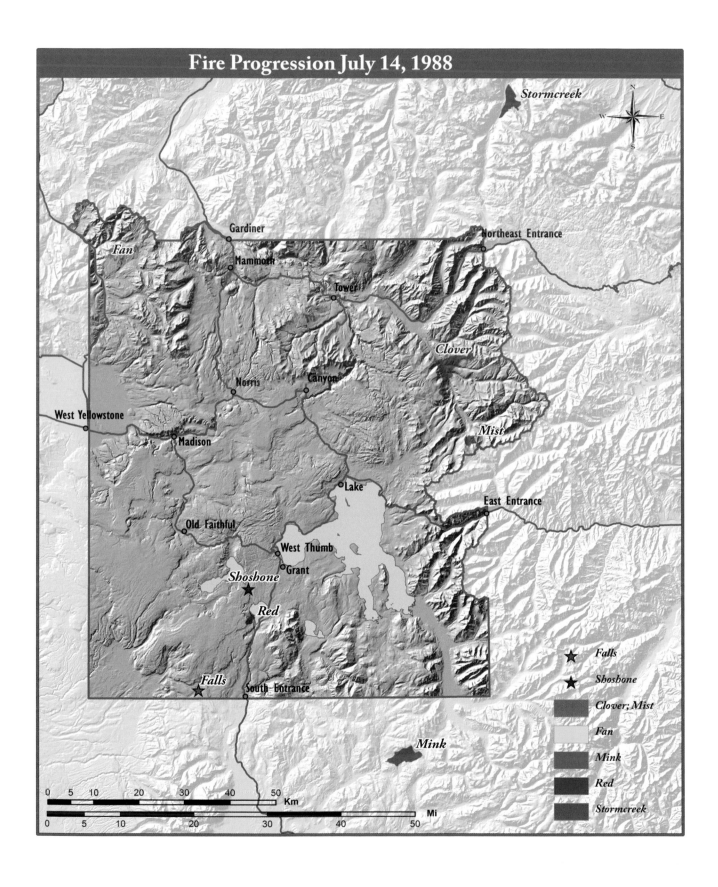

July 14, 1988

THE MOST impressive development on this map is the rapid growth of the Clover-Mist Fire on the west side of the upper Lamar River. After consuming only 200–300 acres on the first couple days of their existence, the two fires flared to over 7,000 acres during prime burning conditions on the 14th. The explosive growth was a major factor in the decision Yellowstone National Park managers made on the evening of the 14th to begin fighting most fires in the park, a move that was to be followed by another decision on the 21st to begin fighting all fires.

The dramatic growth on the 14th of the Clover-Mist had presidential implications. Vice President George H. W. Bush, who recently had been nominated as the Republican candidate for president in advance of the 1988 election, had secretly been scheduled to take a horseback trip to the very area where the Clover-Mist was now raging. Bush was also planning to do some fly-fishing on his Yellowstone vacation, during which the park not only planned to put him up in a backcountry patrol cabin but also intended to furnish him with an escort of park service brass. After the big blowup of the 14th, however, the park thought it prudent to cancel the vice president's trip.

Another upshot of the Clover-Mist's blowup on the 14th was that it occasioned yet another thrilling episode in the dramatic life of Yellowstone's then-chief ranger Dan Sholly. Sholly was a Vietnam veteran with a glass eye (a result of a war wound) and a forceful personality, a man about whom almost no one had a neutral opinion. Both his supporters and his critics usually called him "Danbo," a takeoff on Sylvester Stallone's character "Rambo." Sholly was on a helicopter flight to scout the upper Lamar country in preparation for the vice president's visit when the fire down below exploded.

Collecting two members of a crew (and leaving behind another member of the crew, Jane Lopez, because the helicopter couldn't carry everyone) who were doing maintenance work on trails Bush was scheduled to ride, Sholly had his helicopter pilot ferry him and the others to the Calfee Creek Patrol Cabin, which was unguarded and in imminent danger from the rapidly advancing flames. Sholly and the two trail maintenance workers, who actually worked for Yellowstone's helitack crew and whose names were Kristen Cowan and John Dunfee, immediately began work clearing combustibles away from the immediate area of the cabin, and were left on their own when their helicopter pilot Curt Wainwright, also a Vietnam vet, discerned what was coming and evacuated both himself and his flying machine. Before he left, Wainwright at least twice offered to fly the other three out of harm's way, too, but Sholly refused the offer in the interest of saving the patrol cabin.

Sholly, Dunfee, and Cowan did manage to save the cabin, and they also managed to save themselves by taking refuge in a nearby meadow while the fire torched through the surrounding forest. To do so, they were obliged to deploy their individual fire shelters, which are miniature, foil-like tents designed to reflect heat. The shelters are indispensable accessories firefighters always carry and often refer to jokingly as "shake-and-bakes." Trouble was, the three people had only two fire shelters between them, so Sholly and Cowan had to share a shelter designed for only one occupant. Sholly's decision to stay and fight the fire around the Calfee Creek Patrol Cabin when there weren't enough fire shelters to go around was controversial at the time, and remained so for a long time thereafter.

Positioned as it was, upwind from Cooke City, Montana, as well as from Yellowstone's eastern boundary that it shared with Wyoming's Shoshone National Forest, the Clover-Mist necessitated communication with park officials and officials of the United States Forest Service. When asked whether they would allow the fire to cross into their jurisdiction, supervisors in the Shoshone Forest initially agreed to accept it in the portions of the forest that were designated wilderness. They reversed that decision on July 21, however, which coincidentally was the same day that Yellowstone decided to fight all fires within the park.

After work on the late afternoon of the 14th, I remember taking a recreational hike from my summer home at Madison Junction with Dave Mattson and Gerry Green, two friends from the Grizzly Bear Study Team with whom I worked every spring. My friends and I hiked only a short distance, but the walk took us up a hill that was high enough to afford a view to the east across the plateaus of central Yellowstone. Despite the fact that the Clover-Mist was in the vicinity of 40 straight line miles away, literally on the other side of the park, the smoke column and pyrocumulus cloud put up by the fire were dominating.

From 40 miles away, we were awed. As we sat on that hilltop and considered the view, the term *firestorm* was spoken for the first time that summer, at least spoken for the first time in my presence. I remember the three of us spent time debating precisely what constituted a firestorm, but we all agreed that whatever the exact

One of the mushroom shaped pyrocumulus clouds that the huge Clover-Mist Fire put up through the course of the summer of 1988.
© Jeff Henry/Roche Jaune Pictures, Inc.

definition might be, the Clover-Mist must have gotten into some prime fuel and burned spectacularly hot that day. In all, the column and cloud we could see was on an order of magnitude larger than the display put on by the Fan Fire that had so awed me less than two weeks earlier. That was a pattern that was to repeat itself many times over the course of the summer of 1988. Every time I saw something like the huge smoke cloud from the Clover-Mist on the 14th, my astonishment was such that I would think that I had seen the ultimate fire show that Mother Nature could put forth, but then within a few days I would witness something that was even more extraordinary. In this I was not alone—I think everyone who was involved experienced the same progression, from being merely amazed in the early days of the fires to being rendered all but speechless by what happened later in the season.

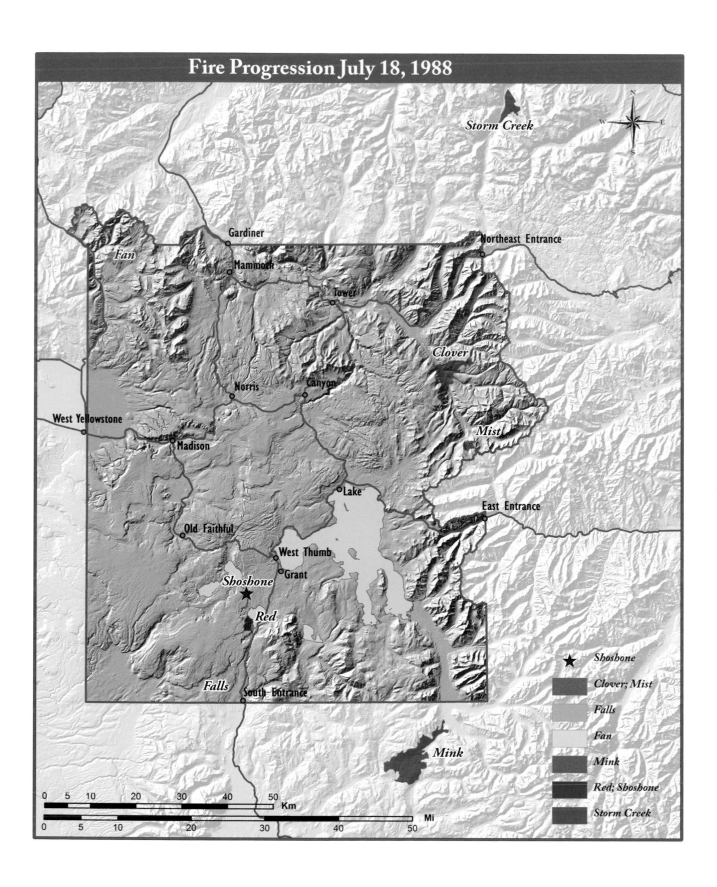

Fire Progression July 18, 1988

Storm Creek

N
W E
S

Gardiner
Fan
Mammoth
Tower
Northeast Entrance
Clover
Norris
Canyon
Mist
West Yellowstone
Madison
Lake
East Entrance
Old Faithful
West Thumb
Grant
Shoshone
Red
Falls
South Entrance
Mink

★ Shoshone
Clover; Mist
Falls
Fan
Mink
Red; Shoshone
Storm Creek

0 5 10 20 30 40 50 Km
0 5 10 20 30 40 50 Mi

July 18, 1988

THINKING BACK on the summer of 1988 in Yellowstone, most people who were involved probably remember it as an uninterrupted blitzkrieg of fire, with advancing spearheads of flame breaching or outflanking inadequate firelines, and massive walls of flame bearing down on developed areas being almost daily occurrences. I would guess that the general public who followed the story in the news media has the same memory. In reality, however, there were periods of relative quiet interspersed with the fires' spectacular outbursts.

This map of July 18, 1988 reflects one of those fairly quiet interludes. Since the Clover and Mist Fires had blown up on the 14th, the Falls Fire near the south boundary was the only fire within the park to show any discernible growth, and even that growth was slight. The Mink Fire south of the Thorofare area of Yellowstone was an exception during this particular period of quiescence; the map clearly shows the beginning of the fire's inexorable downwind march in front of prevailing southwesterly winds.

During this admittedly short time of sitzkrieg it was possible for park residents to forget about the fires for a time and to go back to a more business-as-usual regimen. I remember spraying herbicide on exotic vegetation in the Fountain Flats area during mid-July, and I remember how breathtakingly beautiful the early summer greenery was in the area where I was working and everywhere else in the park, too, for that matter. I couldn't help but be moved by how strikingly green the landscape was, when I knew how abnormally dry the underlying condition of the range to be.

Another memory I have from that time is clearing the Mary Mountain Trail from the Firehole River Valley to the Mary Mountain Patrol Cabin, which is about halfway across the trail's course from the Firehole to the trailhead on the other side, near the mouth of Alum Creek in Hayden Valley. Bonnie Gafney, a friend and coworker of mine, had recently ridden that trail on horseback, and she had told me

An adult bull elk ruminating amidst early summer greenery on Fountain Flats, just a few weeks before the North Fork Fire burned the pine-covered hills in the background. © Jeff Henry/ Roche Jaune Pictures, Inc.

that there were only about a dozen fairly small logs across the trail. My justification for taking the overnight trip to the Mary Mountain Cabin was to cut those logs out of the way before the hiking season got into full swing. Considering that there were just a few logs to be cut, I opted to take a Pulaski to do the work rather than carry a chainsaw. I would use the ax side of the Pulaski, which has a hoe-like blade on its opposing side and which is the most basic of wildland firefighting tools, to cut the logs. This, instead of toting the heavier chainsaw along with its oil and gas and other necessary accessories, and I also wouldn't have to put up with the noise and effluents from the noxious machine.

Well, apparently a big wind storm had blown through the area sometime after Bonnie's horse ride and before my trail cutting venture, because I found a total of ninety-seven downed trees in the 10 miles between the trailhead on the Grand Loop Road near its crossing of Nez Perce Creek and Mary Lake. Except for a few, large, Engelmann spruce logs, which were in the neighborhood of two to three feet in diameter, I cut all the logs with the Pulaski, and wound up with a collection of bloody blisters on my hands for my troubles.

Still, as I sat on the porch of the Mary Mountain Cabin that evening and listened to the usual chatter of rangers and other employees on the park radio, I was sure I had a better deal than most of my coworkers. Yes, I had a few blisters, but my coworkers were dealing with unpleasantries like arguments over campsites in the campgrounds and traffic jams on park roads, while I was sitting in the shade of a romantic, backcountry cabin and overlooking the placid surface of Mary Lake. A plum assignment for me, no doubt, but along the trail to and from Mary Lake I couldn't help but notice how low

Old Faithful Geyser erupting at sunset in late June of 1988 in abnormally hot and dry conditions. © Jeff Henry/Roche Jaune Pictures, Inc.

Nez Perce Creek and its tributary streams were, as well as how the surrounding forest was so dry that that shed needles and cones on the ground were brittle underfoot.

During this time I also remember being free many evenings, after my day's work rangering for the National Park Service, to drive from my summer home at Madison to the Old Faithful area to shoot sunset photos of a particular composition of Old Faithful Geyser that I had long pursued and which is possible only around the time of the summer solstice. I did manage to capture several of the sunset eruptions of the famous geyser in the circumstances that I desired, but I also remember how hot the weather was, even late in the evening when the sun was setting. Even more ominously, the temperature on the thermometer of my Park Service residence at Madison still read over 80 degrees almost every evening when I returned home, which was usually well after sunset by the time I had driven back from Old Faithful.

In my earlier years in the park it had been rare to see a temperature of 80 degrees or more at any time of day, even in the middle of the day in the middle of the summer, and here it was still over 80 degrees after the sun was well down and darkness had commenced—and that's the way it was evening after evening. Yellowstone was drying out even further, and at a rapid rate.

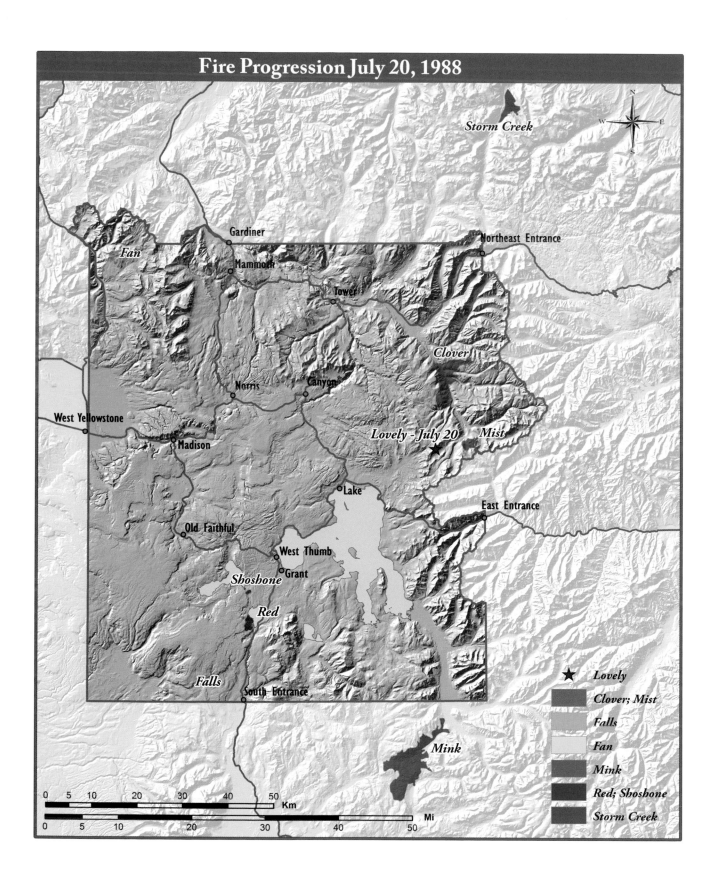

Fire Progression July 20, 1988

Storm Creek

Fan

Gardiner

Mammoth

Tower

Northeast Entrance

Clover

Norris

Canyon

Mist

West Yellowstone

Lovely - July 20

Madison

Lake

East Entrance

Old Faithful

West Thumb

Grant

Shoshone

Red

Falls

South Entrance

Mink

★ Lovely

Clover; Mist

Falls

Fan

Mink

Red; Shoshone

Storm Creek

0 5 10   20   30   40   50
                                        Km

0 5 10   20   30   40   50
                                              Mi

July 20, 1988

ON THIS MAP it is evident that most of the existing fires were beginning to grow. Most of the growth was on the northeast sides of their perimeters, where prevailing winds continually blew the heads of the fires into fresh fuel. Additionally, the Clover and Mist Fires show growth that was topographically directed by the steep terrain where they were burning.

The Lovely Fire actually started by lightning on this day. It was one of several individual fires that started in the area and that ultimately were incorporated into the massive Clover-Mist.

Most notably, the Red and Shoshone Fires were beginning to come to life. At this time the Shoshone Fire in particular posed a clear and growing danger to Grant Village, which was situated directly downwind from the fire.

Grant Village was the newest developed location in Yellowstone. Construction of the complex started in the 1960s, and was carried on in increments thereafter. As a new development, it lacked the romance and history of older properties in the park, and since it had been built in an area that had been pristine up until the time of development, it was widely disliked by environmentalists. One rationale for building Grant Village was to replace the development at Fishing Bridge, which developing research had shown was situated in an area of prime habitat for grizzly bears. Environmentalists' repugnance for Grant Village further intensified when still newer research revealed that the latter development was in important bear habitat, too, in the form of a number of cutthroat trout spawning streams that flowed through the area and fed into Yellowstone Lake.

The development at Grant Village, considered by many to be both architecturally and environmentally out of place. 1987 National Park Service photo by Jim Peaco.

And it was not just the location of the development that led to its disfavor with park purists. There was nothing appealing about the architecture of the buildings in the new development, nothing derived from or in any way reflective of the park setting in which they had been built. Personally, the buildings at Grant Village had always reminded me of hasty dormitory construction on college campuses put up during the 1960s and 1970s, when baby boomers were reaching their university years and when institutions of higher learning belatedly woke up to the fact that their burgeoning enrollments were outpacing their available housing.

There were Yellowstone aficionados in 1988 who held secret, and in some cases openly expressed, hopes that the Shoshone Fire would wipe Grant Village from the Yellowstone slate. Those people nearly got their wish. When the fire began to close in on the Grant in late July of 1988, the complex was woefully unprepared for its arrival.

Fire Progression July 22, 1988

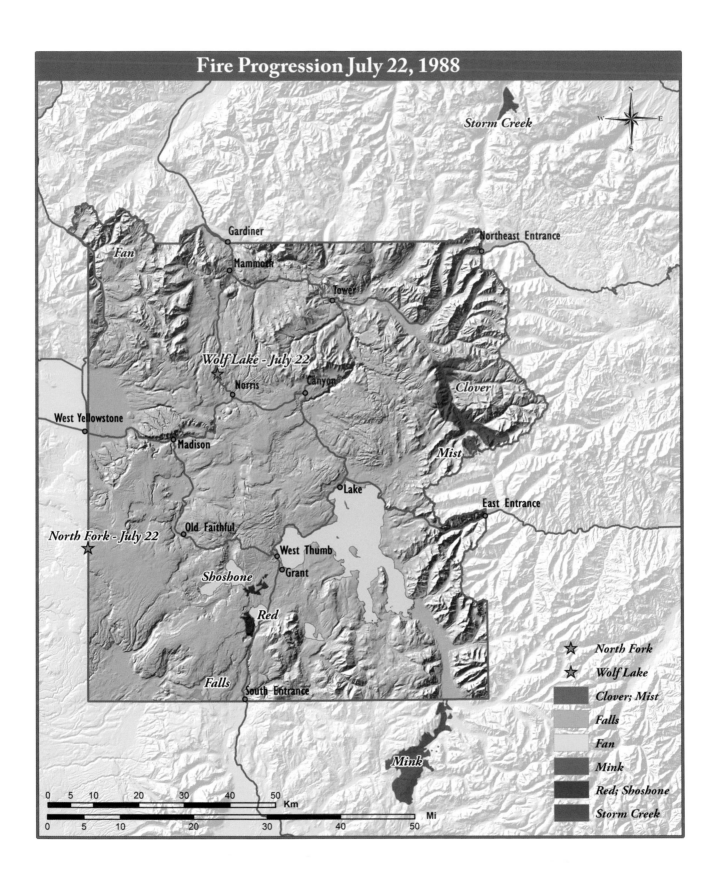

Storm Creek

Fan

Gardiner

Northeast Entrance

Mammoth

Tower

Wolf Lake - July 22

Norris

Canyon

Clover

West Yellowstone

Madison

Mist

Lake

East Entrance

North Fork - July 22

Old Faithful

West Thumb

Grant

Shoshone

Red

Falls

South Entrance

Mink

☆ North Fork
☆ Wolf Lake
Clover; Mist
Falls
Fan
Mink
Red; Shoshone
Storm Creek

0 5 10   20   30   40   50   Km
0 5 10   20   30   40   50 Mi

THIS JULY 22 map shows the continued growth of the Shoshone Fire in the direction of Grant Village. It also shows the rapid growth of the Clover-Mist in the northeastern quadrant of the park. The latter fire appears as a malignant growth along the head of Lamar River. Notice that the Clover and Mist Fires had almost burned together by this point. The other fires depicted on the map had not changed much since the map of July 20, with the exception of the Mink Fire, which by this date had burned down the Yellowstone River Valley right to the south boundary of Yellowstone National Park.

The most ominous notation on this map is the star along Yellowstone's western boundary, south of the town of West Yellowstone, Montana, that shows the start of the North Fork Fire. This great fire got its start from a woodcutter's carelessly discarded cigarette in Idaho's Targhee National Forest, just a couple hundred yards west of the forest's boundary with the park. From the very beginning, it was apparent that this was a fire that was going to go places and do things, and indeed it did. It was destined to become the largest of all the Yellowstone area's individual fires during 1988's summer of fire—it would burn over an area of more than 531,000 acres by the time November snows finally snuffed it out. The North Fork would also directly threaten seven developed locations within the park, as well as the Montana towns of West Yellowstone and Gardiner. It burned miles of electrical power lines, leaving various locations in the park either dependent on local generators or, in some cases, without any electricity at all for long stretches. Thousands of people fought the fire, with the support of large numbers of fire engines, helicopters, airplanes and other equipment. The monetary cost of the North Fork Fire ran into the tens of millions of 1988 dollars, but until the night of September 10–11, when a light fall of snow and rain dampened the fire's voracity, it couldn't be stopped. From its beginning, all through the rest of July, all of August, and the first third of September, the great North Fork Fire gathered ever more momentum, to the point where even in the towns of Bozeman and Livingston, which earlier in the summer had seemed comfortably distant from the Yellowstone fires, residents justifiably began to fear that they and their communities were in jeopardy.

For me personally, there was irony in the starting point of the North Fork Fire. In one of the many ways that my fate was intertwined with the great fires of 1988, in connection with a park service duty just three weeks before the fire ignited, I had been at almost the exact spot where it started. I had been assigned to put up a trail register at the west end of the Summit Lake Trail, which was located on the boundary between the Targhee National Forest and Yellowstone National Park about 14 straight-line miles west southwest of Old Faithful. Trailhead registers are fairly elaborate affairs that house a tablet with a writing implement, where hikers are asked to sign in before they begin their trip.

To access the trailhead I had to drive my park service pickup truck through southeastern Idaho, and then turn east in Island Park and travel to the boundary of the national park. My route took me through many miles of the Targhee Forest, almost all of which had been heavily, heavily logged by 1988. The seemingly endless clearcuts I drove through were networked together with a dense web of dirt roads. Only thin bands of original forest had been left between the vast cutover areas, and while I was driving I noticed that the forest service had brought in an enormous piece of equipment outfitted with a huge, wickedly toothed blade. The tracked machine was being used to gouge additional access roads through the slash and stumps of the clearcuts to the remaining ribbons of standing timber.

Large numbers of firewood cutters with chainsaws were swarming into the remnant bits of forest to cut down standing dead lodgepole pines, most of which probably had been killed by bark beetles, and piling the wood into the backs of their pickup trucks. There were so many woodcutters, I figured that they couldn't all have come from the immediate Island Park area, that some of them must have come from bigger towns to the south, such as Idaho Falls or Rexburg—maybe even as far away as Pocatello.

I was amazed at the intensity of use and development in the forest, which for me culminated in a road that had been gouged right along the linear boundary between the Targhee and Yellowstone. Appropriately named the Park Line Road, the track was absolutely right on the boundary—you could literally spit out the window of a vehicle and hit Yellowstone Park. I finally made it to the trailhead, where I put up the heavy trail register box and then left. The firewood cutters were still busy along my return route, and it was a woodcutter similar to the ones I saw on July 1 who started the North Fork with a cigarette butt just twenty-one days later.

A clearcut as seen on July 1, 1988, in Idaho's Targhee National Forest, with the edge of the cut extending right to the boundary of Yellowstone National Park. The North Fork Fire started only a few hundred yards from where this photo was taken, three weeks later in the same summer. © Jeff Henry/Roche Jaune Pictures, Inc.

On July 21, as the Shoshone Fire manifested a growing threat, Yellowstone National Park called in a Type I fire management team to oversee the protection of Grant Village. Type I fire management teams are the most qualified fire management specialists, usually called to the highest priority fires on the national scene. The Type I team brought in to defend Grant Village was headed by Dave Poncin, Sr. Poncin was a natural fit for the Yellowstone assignment. His career in the National Forest Service had stationed him with the Gallatin National Forest in Gardiner, Montana, for a time in the 1970s, so he knew Yellowstone and many of the people who worked there. Fifty-one years old in 1988, Poncin's home at the time was in Grangeville, Idaho, where he worked as Assistant Forest Supervisor in the Nez Perce National Forest.

Dave was and is a genial, easygoing man, but he was appalled by the lack of fire-preparedness he found when he arrived at Grant Village. Shortly after his arrival, Dave drove around the Grant area to scout things for himself. He found that after "it was constructed no effort had been made to clean up and remove the construction [trash] . . . . Roofing was cedar shakes [which are] extremely flammable when hit by falling embers . . . . My first reaction was we had . . . building[s] constructed in the middle of a clearcut with untreated slash. It was a very indefensible situation." As Dave noted, not only did thick forest grow right up to the edge of the area's buildings, there were still piles of woody debris left from the time when the land was cleared for successive rounds of construction in the 1960s, 1970s, and 1980s, leaving what looked like the leftovers from a clearcut to Poncin's forester eyes.

After surveying the Grant area, Dave had a meeting with the other members of his management team, a group of ten who had been together as a Type I team for eight years. The group realized that they had few firefighting resources on hand, so their first order of business was to order 200 firefighters, a caterer, some structural fire engines, helicopters, and other support resources. When all of the firefighters and support personnel assembled over the next few days in a fire camp at nearby West Thumb, they totaled 300–400 people.

When the initial planning meeting with his overhead team was over, Dave went down to the edge of Yellowstone Lake to reconnoiter for a helicopter landing zone. By three in the afternoon ash was falling out of the sky and onto the beach where Poncin stood. Though it couldn't be seen from where he was, by then the fire was only 3 miles away, upwind to the southwest. Peculiar winds sucked and sighed around the Incident Commander—winds that his experience told him meant the fire had arisen and was drawing air into itself as it made an afternoon run. Poncin knew there wasn't much time to get his crews to the scene and put them to work.

My personal involvement with the Shoshone Fire and Grant Village also began on July 22, when powers at park headquarters in Mammoth called me and asked me to travel to Grant and photograph the fire and firefighting efforts for the park archives. I had been shooting pictures professionally for a number of years, and I had accumulated a fair assemblage of professional quality equipment by the summer of 1988. My reputation as a photographer was known to park managers, and that's why I was selected for the photo documentation work.

It was a dream assignment, and I have always been grateful for the opportunity. My position allowed me to go to wherever I thought the hottest spot was going to be each day through the whole summer of 1988. Even more fortunate for me, the authorities at Mammoth also told me that I could carry two cameras while photographing the fires, so that I could use the extra camera to shoot some frames of the action for my own collection. I spent five consecutive days shooting photos of Grant Village as Dave Poncin's firefighters prepared for the Shoshone Fire's arrival, and then of course shot a lot more frames after the fire burned up to the edge of the complex.

Observing and photographing the initial preparations at Grant Village on the 22nd made for an exciting afternoon, but in retrospect the most memorable event of the day happened on my drive back home to Madison Junction. That evening,

Smoke plume from the North Fork Fire at sunset on the first day of the fire's existence, shot from the mouth of Nez Perce Creek on July 22, 1988. The rounded rise under the sunset-colored smoke column is the easternmost of the Twin Buttes. © Jeff Henry/Roche Jaune Pictures, Inc.

as I was driving north across Fountain Flats, off to the southwest I could see the first plumes of smoke rising from the North Fork Fire; I even took a few shots of the plumes in sunset light. Of course I knew the direction of the prevailing winds in Yellowstone, and I also was familiar with the country that lay downwind from the plumes I was seeing. That part of the park was nearly continuous forest, most of it old growth with a lot of dead, dry wood, both on the ground and in the form of standing dead trees. As soon as I saw it, I was pretty sure the North Fork would soon make it to where I was standing, and probably beyond.

Fire Progression July 24, 1988

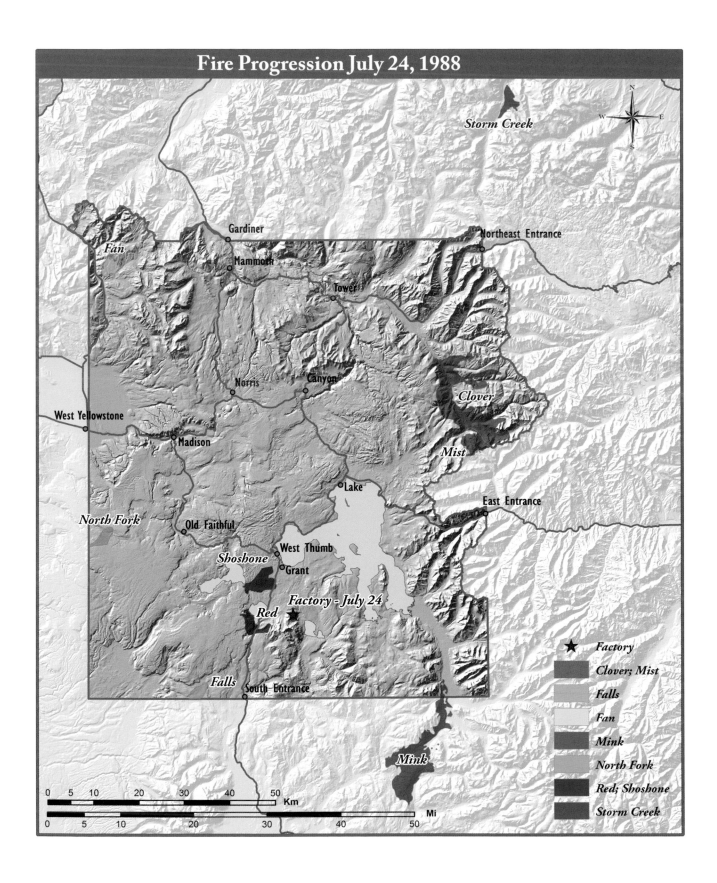

Storm Creek

Fan

Gardiner

Mammoth

Tower

Northeast Entrance

Norris

Canyon

Clover

West Yellowstone

Mist

Madison

Lake

East Entrance

North Fork

Old Faithful

West Thumb

Shoshone

Grant

Factory - July 24

Red

Falls

South Entrance

Mink

★ Factory

Clover; Mist

Falls

Fan

Mink

North Fork

Red; Shoshone

Storm Creek

0 5 10   20   30   40   50
                                    Km

0 5 10   20   30   40   50
                                        Mi

July 24, 1988

THIS JULY 24 map shows that the Storm Creek and Fan Fires were comparatively stagnant between July 22 and July 24. The Mink Fire had crossed the park boundary in the Thorofare area, and the Falls Fire showed some growth as well. The Clover and the Mist Fires had grown together by this time, and the map illustrates the inexorable spread of the combined fires.

The straight line delineating the southern edge of the Falls Fire reflects how fire crews had cut a fire break to contain the fire along the park line. The crews working there were fortunate that they had the predominant winds in their favor; it would have been next to impossible, if not absolutely impossible, to stop the leading edge of the fire in front of the prevailing southwesterly winds.

To the north of the Falls Fire, for instance, both the Red and Shoshone Fires show significant growth, most of it on their north and east edges. In spite of work by fire crews, both fires had crossed the South Entrance Road, which amounted to a preexisting firebreak in itself, but one which both fires easily jumped.

A star to the east of the Red Fire, near the northwest shore of Heart Lake, marks the beginning of the Factory Fire, which itself may have been started as a spot fire from a firebrand thrown out by the Red. It was named for nearby Factory Hill, which in turn was named by official explorers in the late 1800s because they thought that geothermal steam columns in the area resembled smoke rising from a nineteenth-century factory. The Factory Fire was soon overtaken by the Red Fire's eastward charge, and fire managers incorporated it into the Snake River Complex of fires.

The Factory Fire is indicative of just how many different fires started in Yellowstone in 1988, and may have grown into large conflagrations in their own right if they hadn't been overtaken and encompassed by still larger fires. Even if the Red Fire had never overtaken the Factory, a lot of the country the Red burned might still

Firefighter removing "ladder fuels" by trimming lower branches of conifers in advance of Shoshone Fire, near Grant Village in late July of 1988. © Jeff Henry/Roche Jaune Pictures, Inc.

have gone up in smoke because the Factory would have been free to run through unburned fuel in its own incarnation.

At Grant Village during this time fire crews continued their fevered work to prepare the complex for the arrival of the Shoshone Fire. Much of their work consisted of what is known as fuel reduction, which means they were removing combustibles from the vicinity of structures. As some of the accompanying photographs show, a lot of fuel reduction involves trimming limbs from the lower reaches of trees. These lower limbs act as what firefighters appropriately call "ladder fuels," which conduct fire from the ground, where all fires start, up and into the tree tops. Once the heat from a ground fire has climbed ladder fuels to the top of a tree, it can ignite the foliage there and burn just that one tree in a phenomenon known as "torching." If the torching of the one tree produces enough heat to ignite an adjacent tree or trees, the fire becomes a "crown fire," and then if the crown fire begins to move through the tops of a number of trees it becomes known as a "running crown fire." This is the most dangerous sort of fire, as it moves rapidly and tends to throw sparks and embers ahead of itself. It behooved the firefighters at Grant, as it does any firefighters in similar situations, to do everything they could to prevent the oncoming fire from running up into the trees before it arrived at the complex.

A slurry bomber dropping fire retardant between Grant Village development and advancing Shoshone Fire, near South Entrance road in late July of 1988. 1988 National Park Service photo by Jeff Henry

In addition to fuel reduction work in the Grant Village area, which included removing piles of building debris and forest slash left over from the development's original construction, Incident Commander Dave Poncin, Sr., was instituting a general strategy to stop the Shoshone Fire along the South Entrance Road. The strategy involved fuel reduction along the west side of the road, and using slurry bombers to lay a fire retardant line to the west of the strip where fuels had been reduced. The plan was then to start backfires to the west of the retardant line when the main fire front approached. The hope at that point would be for the updraft of the main fire to draw the backfires inward, effectively burning out fuel in front of the main fire's advance. This is a classic wildland firefighting strategy.

The other major development at Grant Village was that all park visitors and nonessential employees had been evacuated on July 23. Grant Village would be reopened after this first fire emergency passed, only to be evacuated again when the fire threat returned on August 20. A number of Grant employees enjoyed their distinction of having been evacuated twice that summer.

The most dramatic occurrence on this map is the implacable growth of the North Fork Fire just outside Yellowstone's west boundary, in Idaho's Targhee National Forest. Despite being fought aggressively almost as soon as it started, the fire exploded from its start as a smoldering cigarette butt to a fire that grew, according to various estimates, to cover an area of 300 to 500 acres during the first afternoon of its existence.

A team of smokejumpers was called to the North Fork almost immediately, in midafternoon of the 22nd. Smokejumpers are at the very pinnacle of the wildland

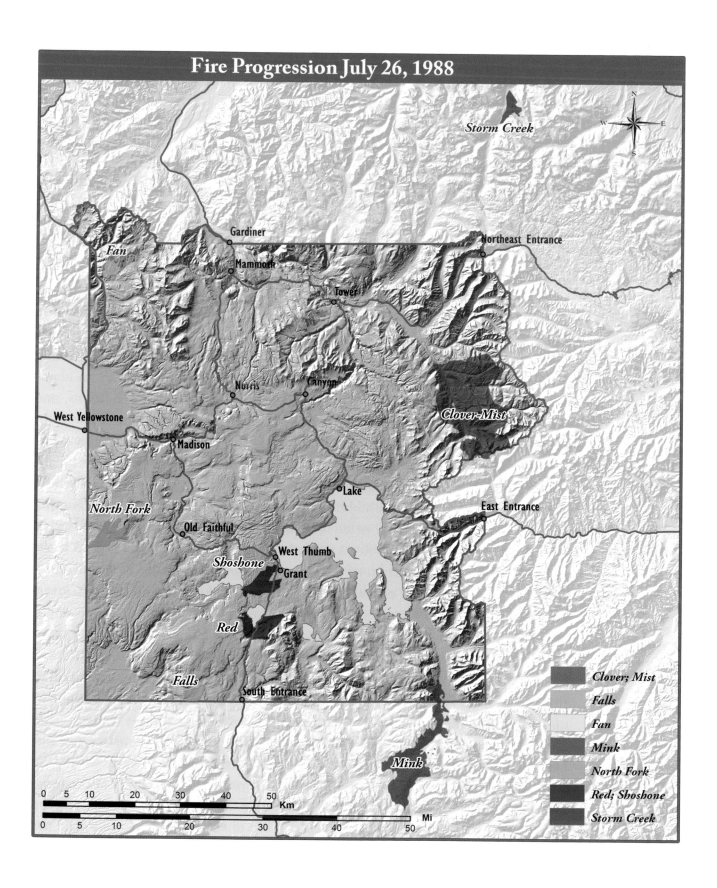

Fire Progression July 26, 1988

Storm Creek

Fan
Gardiner
Mammoth
Tower
Northeast Entrance

Norris
Canyon
Clover-Mist

West Yellowstone
Madison

Lake
East Entrance

North Fork
Old Faithful

West Thumb
Shoshone
Grant

Red

Falls
South Entrance

Mink

	Clover; Mist
	Falls
	Fan
	Mink
	North Fork
	Red; Shoshone
	Storm Creek

| 0 | 5 | 10 | 20 | 30 | 40 | 50 | Km |
| 0 | 5 | 10 | | 20 | | 30 | 40 | 50 | Mi |

July 26, 1988

THE MOST graphic development on this map is the quickening growth of the Clover-Mist Fire. One source shows that the Clover-Mist gobbled its way through 26,085 acres of the mountainous country around the head of Lamar River in the two days since the previous map, that of July 24.

At this time in the summer of 1988 the air over Yellowstone, except in the immediate areas around the growing fires, was generally clear and long views across the park were still possible. This would change later in the summer when fires were larger and more widespread, and the ambient level of smoke had increased. By then the smoke was so pervasive that long distance views were usually occluded. In late July, however, those of us around the park could see the awesome displays put on by the Clover-Mist on an almost daily basis. Visible even from great distances, the Clover-Mist's smoke columns and pyrocumulus clouds were stunning. They rose tens of thousands of feet into the air, and the brilliantly white thunderheads atop the smoke columns had a crenelated, knobby appearance, which actually was indicative of billowing heat within the clouds but which visually resembled enormous heads of cauliflower in the sky. As the afternoon burning period waned and sunset light came on, those massive thunderheads turned varying shades of red.

The North Fork Fire also grew noticeably during this same time. Situated as it was to the west of Old Faithful, officially it was seen as an immediate threat to that complex. In response to the initial danger, the National Park Service assembled a large force of firefighters and equipment, all of which staged in one of Old Faithful's large parking lots. Secretary of the Interior Donald P. Hodel flew in to make an appearance at Old Faithful in what even some in the NPS privately admitted was orchestrated as a grandstand play to impress congressional delegations and the

The Shoshone Fire arriving at Grant Junction on the afternoon of July 26, 1988. © Jeff Henry/
Roche Jaune Pictures, Inc.

general public with the sincerity of Yellowstone's firefighting efforts. As one Yellowstone official would later say, "We had thousands of firefighters on hand and all this
equipment. We had to show people we were doing *something*."

The Clover-Mist and the North Fork Fires may have shown the most growth in
terms of acreage between July 24 and July 26, but the biggest story at the time was at
Grant Village. As this map shows, both the Red Fire and the Shoshone Fire by this
time had jumped across Yellowstone's South Entrance Road. The Shoshone Fire in
particular was closing rapidly on Grant. Indeed, the leading edge of the Shoshone
had split into two prongs, both of which had crossed the South Entrance Road and
were advancing to the northeast. The map clearly shows how the two fiery forks were
reminiscent of a classic military pincers movement intended to envelop an enemy.

Wildfires usually follow a daily pattern of lying relatively quiet at night, when
air temperatures are lower and relative humidities tend to be higher, and then rising
up and burning more actively from early to midafternoon until early evening. That is
what the Shoshone Fire did on July 26. A strong southwesterly wind came up in the

early afternoon that day, as happens on most summer afternoons in Yellowstone, and the Shoshone soon picked up momentum and blew up into the forest canopy, where it became a running crown fire bearing down on Grant Village. Incident Commander Dave Poncin, Sr., the man in charge of protecting Grant Village, quickly realized that his plan to stop the fire on the South Entrance Road was not going to work. By midafternoon the wind was blowing embers across the road and landing them in the immediate area of the Grant Village development. Poncin then switched to his Plan B, where he had some of his crews begin burnout operations around the edges of area roads, parking lots, and in the vicinity of structures. He had other crews stand by to put out spot fires that started around area buildings when burning brands fell out of the sky, and the Incident Commander also had structural fire engines placed strategically around the complex. As Poncin would later write in his diary, with justifiable pride, "This strategy worked and by early evening the facilities at Grant Village had been saved. There were no structures lost at Grant Village."

One of my strongest personal memories of the action at Grant Village was at the local fuel station. At that time fuel stations in the park were operated by Yellowstone Park Service Stations, which in turn was co-owned by Hamilton Stores, Inc. The latter company was a pioneering institution that ran general stores in Yellowstone from 1915 through 2002. Patrick and Terry Povah, two members of the family who owned Hamilton Stores, were present at the Grant gas station when the fire arrived. The two brothers were there to protect their property, and as an extra hand they had brought along a long-term Hamilton Stores employee, Tom Diette.

The Povah brothers had furnished their own fire truck and were spraying water into the nearby forest, but the fire nonetheless advanced to some large propane tanks that were enclosed within a chain-link fence behind the station. By the time the fire arrived Pat and I were alone at the station, as Tom and Terry had gone off on another assignment. Fortunately, someone unknown to us called in a retardant drop right on top of our position at the gas station, and sure enough a big slurry bomber swooped in and dropped a load of the red-colored slime. We both ran for cover under the canopy that covered the gas islands, but some of the mist from the retardant did hit us—I still have a camera bag stained with the red spatters from that day (as well as burn scars from falling embers). The drop did save the propane tanks and the surrounding structures—at least they didn't burn or explode, as seemed possible before the drop. After the retardant had settled and the immediate crisis had eased, I couldn't help making comparisons between what had happened at the Grant gas station and a desperate battlefield situation in which a unit about to be overrun by an enemy calls for artillery or aerial bombardment on their own position.

Another memory I have of the Shoshone Fire arriving at Grant Village took place at the Grant Ranger Station. A couple of aluminum canoes had been stashed outside the building; Grant rangers used them to patrol backcountry portions of Yellowstone Lake. The canoes were the subject of any number of jokes by firefighters

Patrick Povah of Hamilton Stores, Inc., hosing fire in forest next to Grant Village service station, July 26, 1988. © Jeff Henry/Roche Jaune Pictures, Inc.

working around the ranger station, most of which had to do with how there would be fistfights over the craft if the Shoshone Fire got out of hand and "things really went to hell." If things really had gone south that day it would have been a long portage for the winners of the fistfights to haul the canoes down to the shore of Yellowstone Lake, as the Grant Ranger Station is several hundred yards from the lake.

Each night when I drove home to Madison Junction from Grant Village I could see smoke plumes from the North Fork Fire as I drove down the Firehole Valley north of Old Faithful. The North Fork was growing rapidly from day to day and even then, early in its development, it seemed likely that it would soon command most of Yellowstone's attention.

Fire Progression July 28, 1988

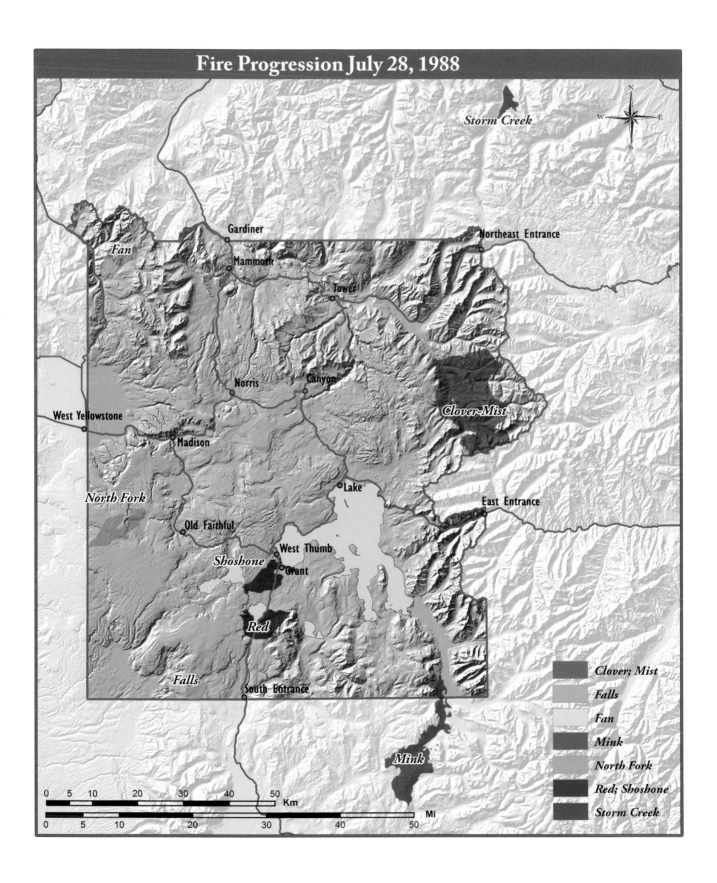

Storm Creek

Gardiner

Northeast Entrance

Fan

Mammoth

Tower

Norris

Canyon

Clover-Mist

West Yellowstone

Madison

North Fork

Lake

East Entrance

Old Faithful

West Thumb

Shoshone

Grant

Red

Falls

South Entrance

Mink

Clover; Mist

Falls

Fan

Mink

North Fork

Red; Shoshone

Storm Creek

0 5 10   20   30   40   50   Km

0   5   10   20   30   40   50   Mi

July 28, 1988

THIS MAP from July 28 shows how the Shoshone Fire had passed Grant Village and had run off to the east, along the south shore of the West Thumb of Yellowstone Lake. Unusually, the Clover-Mist and most of the other fires in the park had not covered much new ground since the map of July 26. The perimeters of the fires mostly show slight growth around the flanks of each fire, as though each were consolidating its earlier gains and merely catching its breath before making its next big move. Most notable, perhaps, was how the head of the North Fork Fire had split. On the west side of Yellowstone, it resembles a side view of a human right hand with the index finger pointing toward the northeast, as though the fire were pointing in the direction it intended to go, and perhaps mocking any attempts that humans might make to stop it.

By late July the Yellowstone fires had achieved enough prominence on the national scene that President Ronald Reagan dispatched Secretary of the Interior Donald Hodel to Yellowstone to evaluate the fire situation in the park and to speak to the public in the government's behalf. Amidst an impressive fleet of firefighting equipment staged in the parking lot between the historic Old Faithful Inn and the Old Faithful Ranger Station, Hodel gave a press conference on July 27. He spoke about the ecological benefits of the fires burning in Yellowstone, how they were burning out accumulated forest debris and in the long run would clear the way for new growth that many animals in the park would find beneficial. He also spoke about how the National Park Service, with the assistance of several other government agencies the park service had brought in to help, was now doing all it could to fight the fires. The duality of his message, that on the one hand fires were beneficial,

Impressive smoke column and cumulus cloud from Shoshone Fire on the south side of the West Thumb of Yellowstone Lake, as seen from West Thumb Geyser Basin, late July 1988. © Jeff Henry/Roche Jaune Pictures, Inc.

but on the other hand the government was trying to put out these beneficial phenomena, did much to confuse the issue, both for the public and their representative politicians.

The massive assemblage of firefighters and firefighting equipment that the Park Service had put together at Old Faithful to serve as a backdrop for Secretary Hodel's appearance was primarily a demonstration intended to impress the media and the public. At the time the North Fork Fire was several miles away from Old Faithful, out on the Madison Plateau, and there was no fire of any kind to be fought in the immediate area of the complex where the firefighting resources had been staged.

Moreover, the North Fork was actually situated due west of the complex, and most anyone familiar with Yellowstone's prevailing southwesterly winds would have reasonably predicted that the North Fork would burn off to the northeast and probably never get to Old Faithful. I know that was my personal interpretation at the time. No one then could have predicted the erratic movements most of the park's fires would manifest later in the season—movements that included an anomalous southward spread of the North Fork in late August and early September that would put it in position to burn with storm-like intensity through the Old Faithful area

Secretary of the Interior Donald P. Hodel speaking at press conference in front of Old Faithful Ranger Station, late July 1988. © Jeff Henry/Roche Jaune Pictures, Inc.

on September 7. But in late July the fire trucks were parked in long neat rows in the parking lots at Old Faithful, and firefighters in clean uniforms were so bored that many of them were playing hacky sack in front of their idle vehicles. As Chief Ranger Dan Sholly told a friend of mine while they were on a reconnaissance flight in Sholly's helicopter, "If you haven't figured it out yet, this is a political fire. You're here so we can say we are actively managing all the fires in the park."

I attended and photographed Hodel's press conference at Old Faithful, and I also took some shots of the staged firefighting equipment and the men and women who were on standby with their trappings. I also took note of the large fire camp that had been set up in an open area near the NPS maintenance yard at Old Faithful. Part of the fire camp had taken over the employee softball field. At about the same time another fire camp was set up in an old road maintenance area along the Firehole River about 12 miles north of Old Faithful, on the east side of the Grand Loop Road across from the Firehole River picnic area.

There is a sad sidebar story concerning the Old Faithful fire camp. Wildfires were a nationwide problem in 1988, a year of record drought, and consequently firefighting crews were hard to come by. Other sources of labor were tapped to make up for the shortage of regular fire crews, and in the case of Yellowstone in the early stretches of the fire season, that meant bringing in groups of young people in the Student Conservation Association, SCA for short. It also meant bringing in crews of prisoners, including one such crew from a prison in Utah. Unfortunately, the

Firefighters on standby in parking lot playing hacky sack to pass the time, with trucks and other equipment parked in background, at Old Faithful in late July 1988. © Jeff Henry/Roche Jaune Pictures, Inc.

prison crews and the crews of young SCAs were camped together in close proximity in the Old Faithful camp, and one of the prisoners raped a young SCA girl. As a ranger I was privy to some of the details of the sexual attack, and I remember having dark thoughts toward the perpetrator of the crime. Ranger Dub Kennedy, who also was stationed at Madison Junction at the time and who was one of my closest coworkers, somewhat eased my anger when he pointed out to me how the guilty prisoner would probably face harsh retribution from his fellows, who no doubt would be enraged by the fact that his crime was the reason they were all being sent back to the Utah prison, rather than continuing to have a chance to work outside for a while in Yellowstone.

With or without crime, fire camps are odd establishments. In some ways a fire camp is similar to a traveling circus in the way it can appear overnight in a vacant spot of land on the outskirts of town, and is similarly composed of a collection of tents, canvas canopies, and hastily constructed shanties built of 2x4s and plywood. Usually some trailers are hauled in, too, trailers for food catering, showers, and office space for fire managers. Portable, plastic toilets are brought in and arranged in long,

Ranger Carl Schreier pausing to look at the Old Faithful fire camp, late July 1988. © Jeff Henry/ Roche Jaune Pictures, Inc.

straight rows. Naturally, some level of smokiness usually pervades a fire camp. There is a constant drone of generators, and the dirt underfoot is soon ground into a fine powder by the tramping of so many heavy boots in a confined area. Many strangers are brought together in the closed environment. Everyone, even administrators who rarely go anywhere near a fireline, is clad in green pants and yellow shirts. The outfit is the uniform clothing of all wildland firefighters, and the clothing is permeated with the chemically sweet smell of a fire retardant. There is always activity in a fire camp, with crews and machinery coming and going at all hours and the repetitive *thwok thwok thwok* of helicopters close by, but in some portion of the camp there are always other people trying to catch a bit of sleep, even in the heat and bright light of midday. A fire camp is also rigidly hierarchical, with a command structure bearing a close resemblance to a military paradigm. For other long-term Yellowstone employees and me, it was strange to see fire camps suddenly appear in places we knew well, places that usually were clean and cool and pretty and quiet, and where one was more likely to see an elk or a grizzly than to see marching strings of Nomex-clad men and women carrying Pulaskis and chainsaws.

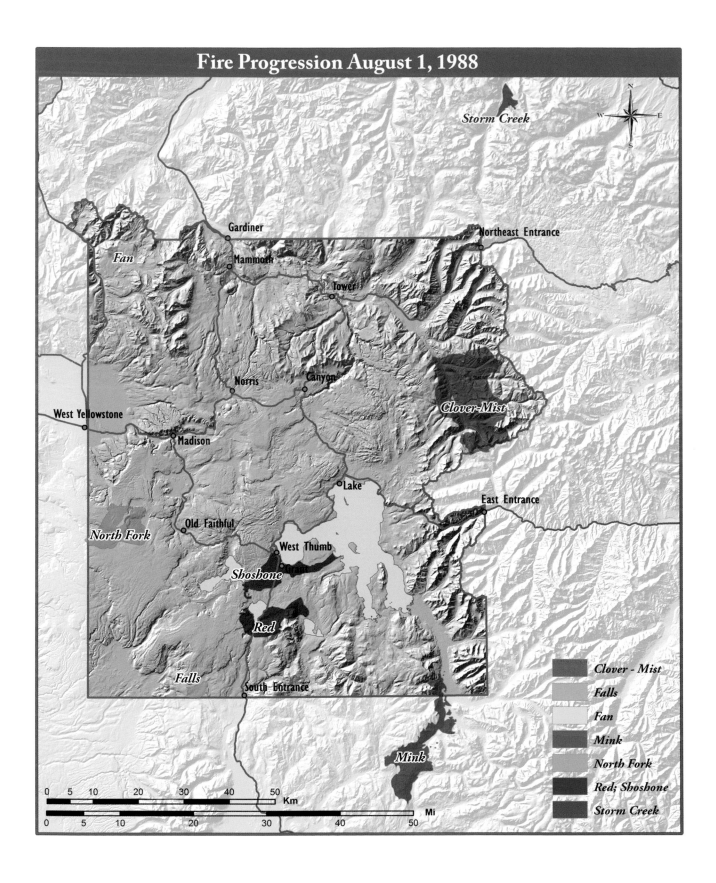

Fire Progression August 1, 1988

Storm Creek

Fan

Gardiner

Northeast Entrance

Mammoth

Tower

Norris

Canyon

Clover-Mist

West Yellowstone

Madison

Lake

East Entrance

Old Faithful

North Fork

West Thumb

Shoshone

Grant

Red

Falls

South Entrance

Mink

	Clover - Mist
	Falls
	Fan
	Mink
	North Fork
	Red; Shoshone
	Storm Creek

0 5 10   20   30   40   50   Km

0 5   10   20   30   40   50 Mi

August 1, 1988

THIS MAP shows only modest growth on the North Fork, the Clover-Mist, the Mink, and the Falls Fires. The Storm Creek Fire also continued to smolder, although its smoldering was in reality a ticking time bomb that would explode later in the month.

Both the Red and the Shoshone Fires, on the other hand, show evidence of major northeastward runs that they had made on July 30, and especially on the 31st. The Shoshone Fire had burned an arcing path all the way to the western shore of Yellowstone Lake at Wolf Bay, while the Red had made it as far as the north shore of Heart Lake, in the vicinity of the park service's Heart Lake Patrol Cabin.

Perhaps most significantly, at least at this point in the summer of fire, the Fan Fire burned well over 11,000 acres on July 31. That figure was in contrast to the total of about 3,000 acres that the Fan had burned since it started back in June. The explosive growth of the Fan on July 31 was cause for concern, as the movement of the fire was predictably downwind and as such posed a mounting threat to the town of Gardiner, Montana. A look at the accompanying map shows how the movement of the Fan put it on a bull's-eye course with the gateway community at Yellowstone's North Entrance. The fire also threatened the property of an unusual New Age religious cult known as the Church Universal and Triumphant, a group whose members called themselves the "Keepers of the Flame."

The Church had arrived in the Yellowstone area back in 1981, when they purchased a 12,000 acre ranch along the north boundary of the park from the extravagant capitalist Malcolm Forbes, of *Forbes Magazine* fame. The Church renamed their holding the Royal Teton Ranch, and soon moved a large number of their members to the site from their previous headquarters in California. They also built many new structures on the property, including a number of bomb shelters, seen by the group as essential for surviving an apocalypse that was close at hand. The Royal Teton Ranch was and still is located just west of Gardiner, which in August of 1988 meant that it was between the town and the Fan Fire.

The peculiar cult was led by a woman named Elizabeth Clare Prophet, who, among other unique attributes, claimed to be able to communicate with a number of what she called "ascended masters." Some ascended masters were names most in the general public would recognize, such as King Arthur or Saint Germain, while others were quite a bit more obscure. These ascended masters could speak to the living through the voice of Prophet, whom devoted followers affectionately called "Guru Ma."

Another hallmark of the sect was a ritual of collective prayer, wherein a group in unison would rapidly recite the same mantra over and over in a singsong chant. The penchant for group intonation served the cult well when Guru Ma determined that the best way to fight the fire threatening their property was to assemble a large body of her followers and have them chant the flames into submission. A contingent of 250 gurus, as local residents were wont to call them, gathered in a meadow just outside the Yellowstone Park boundary in advance of the Fan Fire, where in harmony they rapidly and repetitively recited "Reverse the tide. Roll them back. Set all free."

The Fan Fire actually did stop at the park boundary, and of course church members and their leader credited their intonations for the success. The alpine crest of the Gallatin Mountain Range that marks the boundary in that sector, a crest that is sparsely vegetated and just plain bare rock along a lot of its course, deprived the fire of fuel across a wide swath and probably also had something to do with arresting the spread of the Fan. In all probability the collective efforts of a force of up to 1,500 firefighters assigned to the fire were also a factor in holding the Fan at the park line.

Another dramatic development at this point involved the spread of the Red Fire to the north shore of Heart Lake, about 7.5 miles southeast of Grant Village. That brought the fire to the park service's Heart Lake Patrol Cabin, occupied that summer by a friend of mine named Ann Marie Chytra. Ann Marie was a longtime devotee of Yellowstone, having started her career in the park as a waitress at the Old Faithful Inn back in the 1970s. I still remember Ann Marie roller skating around the lobby of the great building during employee parties back in those days, after the Inn had closed for the season. By 1988, Ann Marie had been working as a ranger for the National Park Service in Yellowstone for seven years, and considered herself fortunate to have been assigned to the duty at Heart Lake, which was indeed a enviable assignment in a beautiful setting. As Ann Marie herself puts it, the position at Heart Lake was "the best job I ever had," but she is quick to add that it "was a real honor to be able to work in the Old Faithful Inn." As a longtime, interested observer of Yellowstone phenomena, Ann Marie recorded many entries in the Heart Lake Patrol

A photo shot by Heart Lake ranger Ann Marie Chytra showing menacing smoke clouds rising above mountains around her duty station before the Red Fire actually arrived at Heart Lake. © Ann Marie Chytra

Cabin log book in the spring and early summer of 1988 that noted how unusually hot, dry, and dusty conditions were.

In 1988 a young man named Pat Hnilicka, who was with the Student Conservation Association (SCA for short), was stationed at Heart Lake with Ann Marie. For several days in late July, Ann Marie and Pat watched as stupendous columns of smoke from the Red, Shoshone, and other fires rose into view above the mountains and ridges surrounding Heart Lake. Without question it was just a matter of time before one or more of the fires made it to their duty station, so Ann Marie and Pat were pleased to receive a Mark III firefighting pump to use to defend the patrol cabin where they lived.

They were also grateful when a six-person fire crew from the Kootenai National Forest in western Montana showed up to assist. With the crew's help, they scratched a narrow fire line around the perimeter of the cabin and its horse barn. Trees were trimmed and other debris removed in the interest of reducing the fuel available to any fire that might make it to the immediate area of the cabin. The pump, which was capable of moving 70–80 gallons of water per minute, was set up in adjacent Heart Lake, and hoses and sprinklers were laid out. In spite of their preparations, Pat and Ann Marie were awed by the power of the fires they could see moving toward them, and daunted by the continual fire-related chatter they overheard on their park radios, so they made sure they had their canoe ready to launch into the nearby lake as a final escape option. To be sure, they had their canoe absolutely ready for hasty flight, with life jackets and paddles already loaded and the bow of the craft pointed out into the open lake.

Ann Marie remembers that when the Red Fire did arrive it moved in with astonishing rapidity, burning from Paycheck Pass, the low gap to the west through which the Heart Lake Trail passes, down to the cabin in a very short time. She further remembers the profusion of spot fires that were started around her cabin by burning brands that were flung ahead of the main fire. In the beginning there were just a few spot fires, and Ann Marie and the others were able put them out as they started, but fiery brands kept coming faster and faster, and before long they were falling in overwhelming numbers and the defenders couldn't keep up.

Fire continued to burn around the Heart Lake Cabin for several days in early August, as first one section of forest would torch and then be followed by another pocket of fuel that had not burned previously. On at least one occasion the defend- ers used a classic backburn strategy to try to stall out the main fire's advance by burn- ing out fuel in front of it. Timing is paramount with a backburn, and the defenders of the Heart Lake Cabin waited until an approaching crown fire was close enough for them to feel its nearly unbearable heat before they set their fusees to the grass of an intervening meadow. Then, in one of the great mysteries that are nearly always pres- ent with fire, the grass in the meadow didn't burn all that well from its fusee-induced torching—the close in grass wouldn't burn that well while just a short distance away burning forest was throwing up flames 200–300 feet high.

At another juncture Ann Marie and the others thought the surrounding fire was becoming too intense and that the situation was about to be lost unless they could procure the help of a helicopter with a water bucket. Those in control of air operations in the area didn't think the Heart Lake Cabin was a high enough priority to dispatch a helicopter to its rescue, so Ann Marie's request for aerial assistance was at first denied. Jerry Mernin, a very long-term Yellowstone ranger who was the 1988 district ranger in the district that included Heart Lake, then pulled strings and Ann Marie got her bucket drops. Once on scene, the helicopter stayed and contin- ued to ferry water from Heart Lake until the immediate danger had been resolved, and Ann Marie gives much credit to the pilot, as well as to the Kootenai National Forest fire crew, for the successful defense of the Heart Lake Cabin. As Ann Marie wearily noted in the cabin log at the end of one of the trying days when the issue had been in doubt, "The cabin and barn remain standing." By the end the Red Fire had blackened the surrounding forest within 40 yards of the structures Ann Marie and the others had worked so hard to protect.

In response to the intensifying crisis, in late July a number of the nation's best wildland fire experts gathered in West Yellowstone to discuss the fire situation in Yellowstone, and to try to forecast fire behavior for the rest of the season. With

The green valley of the Madison River in early summer 1988, with Mount Haynes in the background. Fire managers hoped and thought that the lush meadows of the Madison Valley, as well as the river itself, would contain the North Fork Fire on the Madison Plateau. They were wrong. © Jeff Henry/Roche Jaune Pictures, Inc.

impeccable academic credentials, the collected experts were often referred to as "Fire Gods." There was a wry mixture of respect and sarcasm implied in the nickname. On the one hand, the fire gods really had spent decades researching the nature of fire, some of the individuals involved having pioneered new techniques for unraveling the mysteries of the elemental force. On the other hand, many individuals on the ground, especially firefighters who swung hand tools to oppose real flames, saw the academics as too far removed from the soot and ash to really understand the nitty-gritty of their subject.

The assembled gods considered several factors in trying to divine what the fire future held. In recognition of how fires burn with different speeds and intensities through various species and densities of vegetation, they looked at maps outlining the patterns of forest cover types ahead of the different fires. They considered topographic features, researched fire histories from park records, and noted the locations of existing fire breaks such as wet meadows, roads and rivers. They considered fuel moistures, figures that show how much water is absorbed in organic material that can serve as fuel, which in turn indicate how readily that fuel will ignite as well as how much energy it will release if it does burn. Most of all they studied park weather records, especially with regard to precipitation and what fire gods like to call "wind events," or times when the wind blows hard.

The short version of the fire gods' conclusions at their late July/early August meeting in West Yellowstone was that the worst of the fire season was over. They were certain that it would rain in August, as weather records showed it almost always does when traces of the North American monsoon make it this far north. They further asserted that the park would probably experience only one wind event between the time of their meeting and the time when cool temperatures and autumn precipitation would bring the fire season to a final end.

Others in Yellowstone at the time weren't so sure. Without exception, people participating with the fires at ground level, or really at any level lower than the fire prognosticators' lofty lookout, recognized that the fire conditions that summer were exceptional, and that consequently, fires were already exhibiting exceptional behavior. Moreover, everyone seemed to realize that the driest portion of the fire season was still ahead, and already things were so dry that no amount of moisture the park might realistically receive before autumn would make a substantial difference.

These sentiments weren't just the grumblings of the dirty, discontented rank and file. Veteran and astute firefighters like Incident Commander Dave Poncin, the chief defender of Grant Village, noticed how much the park had further dried out during the two weeks he had spent here. So had another incident commander named Curt Bates, who had been assigned to the Clover-Mist Fire. The two incident commanders and many others had noticed strong and erratic winds around the various fires, and more generally over the whole region.

As the summer unfolded, it became apparent that some of the fires were growing so large that they were creating their own winds as they inhaled oxygen into their infernos, and as their awesome updrafting heat columns created turbulence in the atmosphere. As a park service ranger, I was summoned to a meeting with my district ranger, a friendly man named Joe Evans, along with most of the other rangers in Yellowstone's west district. Joe briefed us on what the fire gods had foretold. Specific to the west district, which included Old Faithful, Madison, and West Entrance, Joe related how the fire gods thought the North Fork Fire would remain on the remote Madison Plateau. They had based this conclusion, Joe said, on the fact that much of the forest for a distance south of Madison Junction was new growth, usually resistant to spreading forest fire. South of that young forest, further along the road toward Old Faithful, were wide expanses of meadow and barren geothermal plains, features also not likely to carry fire in the view of the soothsayers who had gathered at West Yellowstone. Along the road west of Madison Junction, it was thought the North Fork would be halted by the wide valley and riparian meadows of the Madison River, a natural fire break augmented by the pavement of the West Entrance Road itself. That is, all these described barriers would halt the North Fork even if it managed to burn up to them, which itself was not considered to be a likely scenario by the fire gods on high.

Similar barriers were present to contain the spread of other fires then burning in the park, again according to the information passed on to us from the fire gods

White Dome Geyser in eruption in Yellowstone's Lower Geyser Basin. Fire managers hoped that wide geothermal plains in the geyser basins along the Firehole River would prevent the North Fork Fire from spreading to the east from the Madison Plateau. Smoke from the North Fork is visible in the background of this photograph. © Jeff Henry/Roche Jaune Pictures, Inc.

through District Ranger Joe Evans. It was thought, for example, that the rocky crests of the Absaroka Mountain Range along Yellowstone's east boundary would keep the Clover-Mist Fire from passing out of the park in that direction. Yellowstone Lake was mentioned as another big barrier to fires burning in its vicinity.

That these features on the landscape were barriers that might have stopped wildfires under normal conditions was not arguable, but 1988 was not a normal summer. After our meeting with Joe Evans, I had a chance to have a private conversation about the matter with my friend Dub Kennedy, the veteran ranger who had grown up in Butte, Montana, and the one who had pointed out to me earlier in the spring that "pretty soon the smoke's gonna be rollin'." As we talked, it quickly became apparent that the big man with his trademark handlebar mustache was not impressed by the predictions of the fire lords. Dub succinctly expressed his view of what the rest of the summer held for us: "Now we're really gonna have fire." I believed Dub was right and that the official fire prognosticators were off target, that in spite of the high drama that had happened already that summer in Yellowstone, we really hadn't seen anything yet.

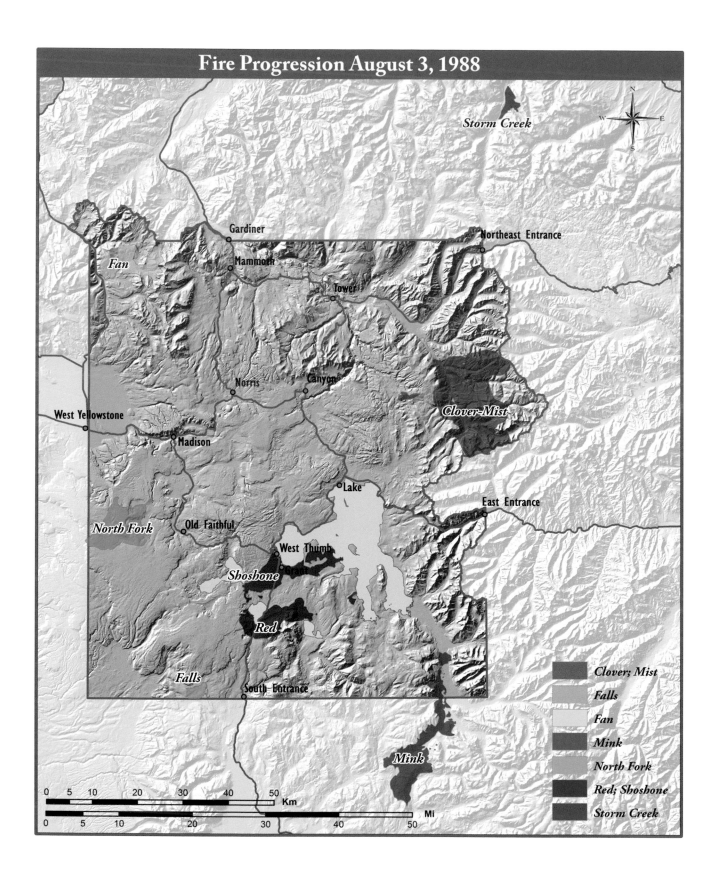

Fire Progression August 3, 1988

Storm Creek

Gardiner
Northeast Entrance
Mammoth
Fan
Tower
Norris
Canyon
Clover-Mist
West Yellowstone
Madison
East Entrance
Lake
North Fork
Old Faithful
West Thumb
Grant
Shoshone
Red
Falls
South Entrance
Mink

Clover; Mist
Falls
Fan
Mink
North Fork
Red; Shoshone
Storm Creek

| 0 | 5 | 10 | 20 | 30 | 40 | 50 | Km |
| 0 | 5 | 10 | 20 | 30 | 40 | 50 | Mi |

August 3, 1988

THIS MAP shows how the Shoshone Fire had burned another large section of land south of the West Thumb of Yellowstone Lake; the narrow swath between the two leading fingers of the Shoshone Fire is actually the outline of Delusion Lake, rather than forested land that somehow escaped the blaze. The Shoshone Fire had also spotted ahead of itself, "spotted ahead of itself" being firefighting argot for a new fire that has started out in front of the main conflagration by flaming material blown forward by strong winds. The round, pink blotch due north of Lewis Lake and just west of Yellowstone's South Entrance Road shows the location of a new spot spawned by the Shoshone Fire.

The Red Fire had grown, too, especially in the area north of Heart Lake. The map also shows a new fire on the west side of the South Arm of Yellowstone Lake. The fire is not labeled on this map, but it was called the Continental Fire, and it shows as a pink blotch on the shore of the South Arm, about midway along its west shore. The Continental escaped labeling on this map, probably because in the grand scheme of things it was only a minor player. A minor player in the sense that it did not burn that much country, it did blow up one day and nearly overrun some of Yellowstone's own firefighters in what had to be one of the closest calls of the season. The irony in the case of this near tragedy was that the Yellowstone crew had been sent out with the understanding that they were not to do much other than just be present at the fire, as part of the effort to create the appearance that all fires in the park were being attended to. But then once on scene, the leader of the group decided to use the outing as a training opportunity, and set his people to work cutting and scratching fireline, and that's when some of the crew were nearly caught in the fire's blowup. But even with the blowup that nearly caught some firefighters, the Continental never burned that many acres; its spread was limited on its downwind side by Yellowstone Lake, and in time it would be overtaken and encompassed by the Red-Shoshone Fire.

The map also shows continued growth of the Mink Fire southeast of the Southeast Arm of Yellowstone Lake. At this time the park portion of the fire was still called the Thorofare Fire because it was burning in the Thorofare region of the park. "Thorofare" is one of the older place names in Yellowstone, referring to how the legendary mountain men of the early nineteenth century used the travel corridor of the upper Yellowstone Valley so frequently and found the going there so good that they used it as a thoroughfare. In 1988 the Mink Fire found the Thorofare to be a good course to travel as it burned its way north into Yellowstone National Park.

One set of fire records shows that the North Fork Fire burned a total of 4,278 acres on August 1 and 2. The same records showed that the Clover-Mist burned almost as much, a total of 3,775 for the same two dates. Both acreages would be impressive by the standards of almost any year other than 1988, but in the context of that summer, they don't seem like much. The two huge fires were really just biding their time in preparation for the colossal blowups they would make later in August, and again in September. Growth on the other park fires at this time was also fairly marginal.

It was around this time that some of the fire crews that had been assembled to serve as a backdrop to Secretary of the Interior Donald P. Hodel's ballyhooed press conference on July 27 proved that in reality they were good for more than just show. Many of the crews went to work in the Old Faithful area, thinning fuels in the vicinity of the historic complex. At the time it seemed unlikely that the North Fork Fire would ever reach Old Faithful, as it was then burning in remote sections of the Madison Plateau to the west and was moving off to the northeast. A little more than a month later, however, the prep work that these fire crews did in early August would prove to be a godsend when the North Fork maneuvered around to where it could make a roaring run through the area.

Other crews did the same sort of work in the Madison area and around West Entrance, while still others worked more directly on the North Fork where it was burning out in the backcountry. Even then, fairly early in the fire season, on most days the North Fork was far too dangerous for crews to attempt to build firelines on the downwind side of the fire. Most of the time the fire crews built lines along the sides of the fire, work that fire managers described as "pinching its flanks." Ultimately this flank pinching would prove to be unsuccessful, as winds became increasingly erratic as the summer progressed and fires made major runs in unpredictable directions, often jumping firelines along their flanks to do so.

Many outlying camps were set up to fight fires in the park's backcountry during this time, known to firefighters as "spike camps." Conditions were rough in the spike camps, with minimal personal gear and most meals consisting of military MREs,

Fire crews thinning fuels along the Old Faithful egress road in early August of 1988. © Jeff Henry/Roche Jaune Pictures, Inc.

or Meals Ready to Eat. The plastic-pouched meals indeed were ready to eat, but for most people their novelty wears off after the first day or two, sometimes after the very first meal, and then the predominant sense is one of highly processed food that is heavily impregnated with preservatives and a plastic-contaminated taste. In spike camps even drinking water comes from a cubically shaped five gallon plastic container known as a "Cube-a-tainer," designed that way so that they will be stable when transported by helicopter, and also so that a number of them can be stacked up. No showers are possible in a spike camp, of course, and firefighting is the ultimate dirty job. Most find a few days of fighting fire and sleeping on the ground in the backcountry to be quite wearing.

In the case of Yellowstone, the normal concerns of fighting fire and of dealing with the discomforts of spike camp living were compounded by considerations unique to the park. Firefighters might find themselves near backcountry thermal areas, for example, where there was the possibility of scalding, and of course their spike camps might be invaded by bears or other animals, especially at night. A number of Yellowstone rangers were assigned to monitor the numerous spike camps, as well as the backcountry helicopter landing zones that were established to transport and supply backcountry firefighters. I did not work in any of the 1988 spike camps myself, but I remember several of my friends who were sent out on monitoring details told me many disconcerting stories about how poorly some of the spike camps were managed in terms of cleanliness in bear country. Later in the year, after

Firefighters in a spike camp on Madison Plateau, 1988. © Jeff Henry/Roche Jaune Pictures, Inc.

the fires had quieted down, I was assigned a crew to do postfire rehabilitation work in the park. Part of our work was cleaning up the aftermath of the spike camps that had been established to fight the North Fork Fire on the Madison Plateau. Judging by what I found left behind at some of those campsites, I can believe there was a lot of truth in the stories my friends told me about the lack of bear-proofing on the part of some of the firefighters, most of whom had been brought in to Yellowstone from other areas and were not familiar with the special circumstances present in the park.

Also around this time in early August, I was temporarily taken away from my photo documentation work and reassigned to work with two of the fire crews that were essentially on standby in the Old Faithful/Madison Junction area. First off, I took it upon myself to use the crews, who were from the United States Forest Service, to fireproof the Nez Perce Patrol Cabin, which is located a mile or so east of the Grand Loop Road and just north of its eponymous stream.

In my time with the National Park Service the Nez Perce Cabin was usually overlooked by most of my coworkers because it was situated just a mile or so off the road and was accessible by vehicle, and therefore lacked the appealing remoteness of a lot of the park's other patrol cabins, most of which were located far out in the backcountry. Indeed the practical usefulness of the cabin as a way station had ended long before I showed up in Yellowstone. Built in the days before oversnow vehicles had been invented, it was used as a stopover between Old Faithful and Madison for rangers on ski patrol. Then it was a useful way station even though it was just off the main road. After the advent of snowmobiles and other over-the-snow conveyances, the Nez Perce Cabin was used mostly for employee parties, especially by park service brass who wanted to show visiting VIPs a good time in a private, pastoral setting.

For my part, I spent many winters at Old Faithful, and I liked going to the cabin during that season because at night, after the snowmobiles and snowcoaches had left the park, the area around the cabin was as quiet and in a way as remote as almost any other patrol cabin, and it gave me a place to go for an overnight or two away from the busyness of the Old Faithful area. The cabin held many fond memories for me, and I wanted to do what I could to protect it from the North Fork, which I felt was pretty certain to get there before the fire season was over. Having two full crews totaling about forty people at my disposal, along with their trucks and other equipment, meant we could get a lot done in a short span of time.

We started our fire preparation work by moving stacked firewood away from the cabin. We also felled dead trees near the building, and trimmed low hanging branches from other trees nearby. Some of the firefighters raked up accumulated forest litter around the cabin, and we hauled it and a lot of the branches and firewood to a dump on an old service road near Madison Junction.

Later in the season, when the arrival of the North Fork Fire at the Nez Perce Cabin was even more imminent, I returned to the site with some of my park service coworkers to further the prep work I had started with the Forest Service crews. Bonnie Gafney and Amy Recker, who were rangers at Old Faithful, and Rick Hutchinson, a noted geologist and by far the most knowledgeable person regarding Yellowstone's geothermal features, returned with me to the cabin to staple heat-reflective fire shelters to its roof and walls. In the end the North Fork never did burn right up to the cabin, so the structure probably would have survived without our fireproofing work. But the fire did burn all around the Nez Perce neighborhood, and if we hadn't prepared the place in advance all concerned would have suffered a lot of anxiety worrying about the cabin when fire was burning in its vicinity.

With forty-odd people working on the first go-around of fireproofing the Nez Perce Cabin, we finished in pretty short order. The crews were still on standby, however, waiting for a specific firefighting assignment, and I still had them at my disposal, so I opted to use them to do some rehabilitation work on an old dump that was situated just off the Firehole Lake Drive, almost within sight of the Fountain Paint Pot area. Actually, it usually was possible to see white steam from some features in the area, such as Celestine Pool and Silex Spring, through the narrow band of trees separating the site from the thermal area.

The dump was an interesting phenomenon in the context of Yellowstone's ideological evolution, having been established (along with many others around the park) in the distant past when park values were different. It may have been

Rick Hutchinson, Bonnie Gafney, and others working to protect Nez Perce Patrol Cabin from advancing North Fork Fire, August 1988. © Jeff Henry/Roche Jaune Pictures, Inc.

originally established in the distant past, but it was used, at least for nonfood items, up until the early 1980s. I know, because for several years in the late 1970s and early 1980s I worked as a laborer on a heavy equipment crew called the "Bull Gang" for the old Yellowstone Park Company. In the course of that work I hauled many truck loads of junk, including multiple loads of free asbestos, to the site, where I simply pulled a hydraulic lever in the cab of the truck and dumped the stuff out. Then, in 1988, just six years after the last time I chucked junk in the dump, I was back at the site with firefighters on standby trying to clean up the mess I had helped make. Unfortunately, after just a couple days of dump rehab, my fire crews were called away to fight real fire in an emergency that was becoming more pressing by the day, so we really didn't get that much done. What junk we did manage to collect we hauled to another dump near Livingston, Montana, over 100 miles away from the Firehole Lake Drive.

Until now the North Fork Fire and most of the other fires had been burning in the remote backcountry and, with the exception of the Shoshone Fire at Grant Village in late July, had been visible mostly by the big smoke columns they were putting up in the distance. Now the fires were spreading ever closer to major park roads and developed locations, and soon were going to be up close and very much in our faces. They would demand the full attention of park workers, to say the least, and the time for working on resource management projects such as cleaning up old dumps was at an end for the summer of 1988.

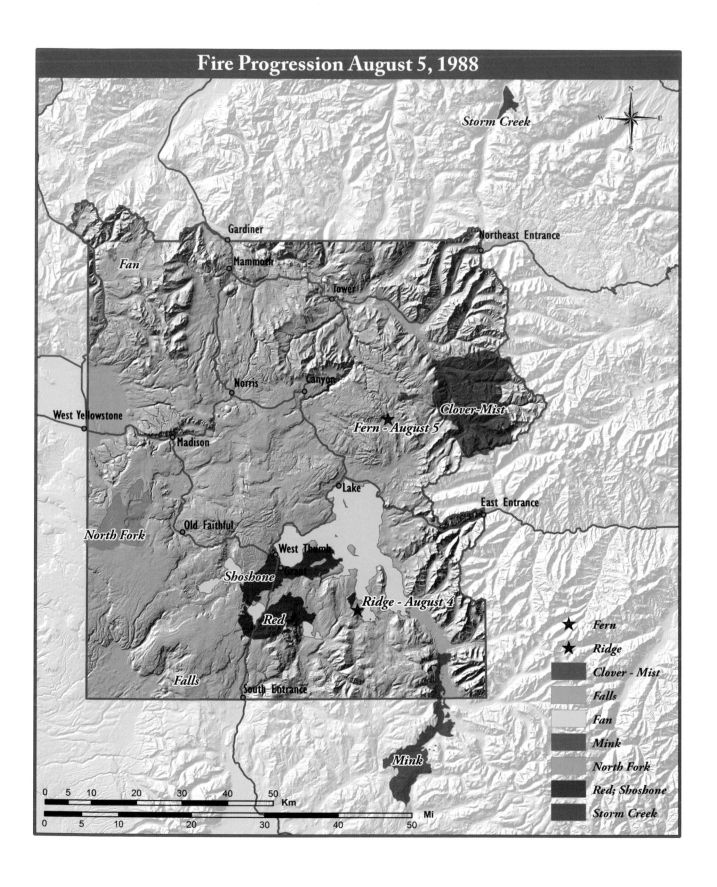

Fire Progression August 5, 1988

Storm Creek

Gardiner

Northeast Entrance

Fan

Mammoth

Tower

Norris

Canyon

Clover-Mist

West Yellowstone

Fern - August 5

Madison

Lake

East Entrance

Old Faithful

North Fork

West Thumb

Grant

Shoshone

Ridge - August 4

Red

Falls

South Entrance

Mink

★ Fern

★ Ridge

Clover - Mist

Falls

Fan

Mink

North Fork

Red; Shoshone

Storm Creek

| 0 | 5 | 10 | 20 | 30 | 40 | 50 | Km |

| 0 | 5 | 10 | 20 | 30 | 40 | 50 | Mi |

August 5, 1988

FOR A BRIEF time in early August there were a few factors that might have indicated that the fire gods' prediction that the worst of the fire season was over in Yellowstone might be true. Most of the big fires burning in the park were still out in the backcountry, with sizable space cushions still in place between them and roads and developments. A light rain fell on parts of the park on August 3, which put a temporary damper on the burns. And Grant Village had been saved, so firefighters could feel good about that success. Most of the delineations on this map reflect the fact that most of the blazes had not grown much since the previous fire map from two days earlier.

The notable exception was the North Fork Fire. Notice the large splotch of burning country to the north of the main body of the North Fork. The outlying fire was the result of a backburn gone awry. The strategy of all backburns is to burn out organic material in front of an advancing fire, to deprive it of fuel and thereby halt its spread. For obvious reasons, however, fighting fire with fire always carries a heavy risk, and in the case of the North Fork Fire many of the backfires that were intentionally started to stop the larger fire actually took off out of control and added to the conflagration. A lot of the firefighters deployed on the North Fork Fire, which at this point was burning solely on the Madison Plateau, felt that many of the backfires had been haphazardly done, and therefore it was not much of a surprise when the backburns not only didn't work but also contributed to the overall size and rate of spread of the blaze. None of this is intended as a criticism. The situation in 1988 was desperate, and firefighters had to try to do something, even if their actions were a gamble and that sometimes they lost the gamble. To repeat, fighting fire with fire is a chancy proposition that can backfire, but trying to do *something* is better than doing nothing.

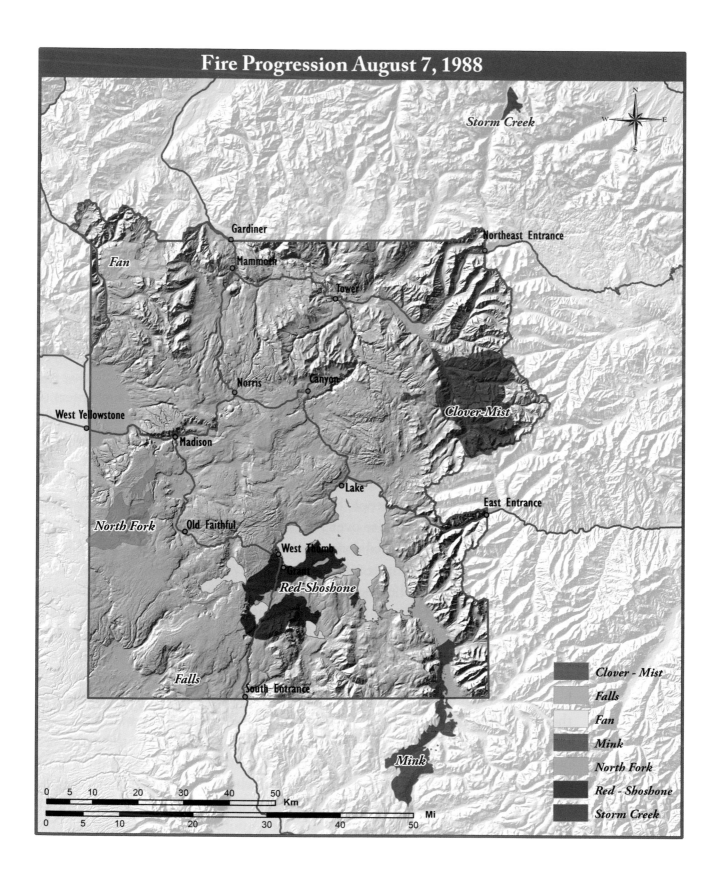

Fire Progression August 7, 1988

Storm Creek

Gardiner
Northeast Entrance
Mammoth
Fan
Tower
Norris
Canyon
Clover-Mist
West Yellowstone
Madison
Lake
East Entrance
North Fork
Old Faithful
West Thumb
Grant
Red-Shoshone
Falls
South Entrance
Mink

	Clover - Mist
	Falls
	Fan
	Mink
	North Fork
	Red - Shoshone
	Storm Creek

0 5 10 20 30 40 50 Km
0 5 10 20 30 40 50 Mi

ON THIS MAP all the major fires show discernible growth. This was especially true for the North Fork Fire. By this time it was becoming more visible from the road north of Old Faithful, and the perimeters of several pullouts at the better vantage points were cordoned off to keep tourists from overloading the parking spots and crushing adjacent vegetation with their cars. Interpretive messages that had been hastily scrawled on cardboard placards were suspended from some of the cordons, and sometimes rangers were on hand, too, trying to answer questions about the fires.

The Clover-Mist Fire was busy, too. It was about this time that it burned up to the crest of the Absaroka Range in the vicinity of Frost Lake. This small lake is situated just inside the boundary of Yellowstone National Park; the boundary in this sector follows the crest of the Absarokas. The lake was named for Ned Frost, an early-day outfitter and guide who first came to Yellowstone in 1885, when he was four years old, and then stayed in the area for the rest of his life. He was an accomplished woodsman, and prided himself on the fact that he had learned his craft from an old trapper named Billy Whitworth, who in turn had learned his outdoor skills from Jim Baker, a well-known mountain man from the frontier era. For his part, Baker had learned much of what he knew from the most eminent mountain man of all, Jim Bridger. To have that sort of direct, linear connection to the legendary Bridger was quite a distinction for Frost.

A long-term Yellowstone ranger named Mike Robinson was on backcountry patrol when the Clover-Mist burned up to Frost Lake. Mike was a special ranger with a deep regard for Yellowstone: I remember being with Mike once when he

Ranger Jason Jarrett explaining fire situation to park visitors at pullout along Grand Loop Road near the mouth of Nez Perce Creek, early August 1988. Black smoke from the North Fork Fire darkens the sky in the background. © Jeff Henry/Roche Jaune Pictures, Inc.

found a cigarette butt someone had discarded near the Lamar Ranger Station. He stooped and picked it up, and then with clenched thumb and forefinger, held it up in the air between us, where I could get a good look at it, and said indignantly "Look at this. Nobody should use Yellowstone Park for an ashtray."

As a backcountry ranger, Mike had a special love for Yellowstone's backcountry and was a man who had much in common with Ned Frost. In the course of this particular patrol, Mike found himself high on a ridge that afforded a good view of the area around Frost Lake. Night came on, a time when most wildfires typically slow down because of cooling temperatures and rising relative humidities. But as Mike was watching, the Clover-Mist did not lay down, as firefighters like to say. Instead it rampaged on into the night, putting on a spectacular display of raging flames towering over the lake and lighting up the surrounding peaks in a flickering, lurid glow. I distinctly remember Mike calling in to report what he was seeing on the park radio. Normally a man of few words, Mike called in repeatedly to describe what was happening in the view in front of him. As I listened I got the sense that Mike felt he was witnessing something so extraordinary that he was compelled to share the experience somehow with someone, and in his remoteness his only outlet was the park radio. Mike kept repeating "It's really impressive. . . . It's really impressive."

By now, the fire gods in West Yellowstone had assumed overall management of fires in the region under the auspices of something they called "Area Command." They actually began to demobilize fire crews and resources during the first few days of August. This move was, of course, in accordance with their view that the fire season in the Yellowstone area had shot its bolt and was about to wind down. In view of what happened in the park and in the surrounding region just a short time later, this move to "demob" (in the parlance of firefighters) resources now seems inconceivable, but it did actually happen.

A wind event blew through the area on August 6, however, and another one was predicted for August 10, so the demobilization move lasted only a short time before it was reversed and fresh crews and equipment were brought back into Yellowstone and neighboring jurisdictions. This stop and go pattern was further reflected in the summer of 1988 by the way Type I and Type II management teams were cycled through the park area. Over the course of the fire season a total of twenty-one such teams rotated in and out, and many then and now thought that the lack of continuity with such "overhead teams," as they are called, made the already tough challenge of managing the summer's wildfires all the more difficult. There's probably something to that assertion, especially when one considers that most of the teams worked for other land management agencies in other parts of the country and were not familiar with the terrain, people, policies and other factors present in Yellowstone.

For my part I continued shooting lots of 35mm color slides of fire and firefighting efforts during this time. As the ominous smoke columns moved ever closer, I clearly remember the sense of being present in front of a gathering storm. I was also bemused by the whirlwind of activity as the Park Service and other land management agencies scrambled to assemble and distribute firefighters and equipment.

Late one night I happened to drive through Mammoth, and looked over at the park's fire cache as I passed by. Even at that late hour there were uncountable people scurrying about in front of the depot's roll-up door, shuffling and stacking big boxes filled with tools and other supplies. Spotlights illuminated the parking lot outside the cache, where there were so many vehicles waiting to be unloaded or reloaded that gridlock had set in. So many people, so much equipment in a tight area—it was obvious that the size of the fire cache was not adequate for the demands that were being put upon it.

Meanwhile, other arms of the agencies, especially within the park service, were trying to get the park's messages out via the throngs of media who by now had gathered in Yellowstone. In a profound way 1988 was a turning point for Yellowstone in terms of the amount of public and official scrutiny it received. The park had had a high profile in the consciousness of the nation for a long time before 1988, of course, but to a great degree it was just a destination for summer vacations in a remote part of the country, an area that was far removed from major population centers and

Mountains of gear assembled to supply Yellowstone firefighting effort. © Jeff Henry/Roche Jaune Pictures, Inc.

especially isolated during its long winters. After 1988, partly as a result of the fires and also due to a number of other factors, such as improved access and communications, Yellowstone was scrutinized down to a much finer level of detail, where even seemingly insignificant management actions were often minutely examined and then challenged by people both inside and particularly outside the park.

With all the fire-related activity in the summer of 1988, so much of it mechanized activity, I couldn't help but be struck by the irony of how on the one hand I suspected that the magnitude and ferocity of these fires probably had something to with the buildup of carbon dioxide in our atmosphere, and yet our response to the situation involved massive deployments of trucks, airplanes, helicopters, generators, chainsaws, pumps—just more of the same that had contributed to the situation in the first place. Of course the contribution of carbon dioxide to the atmosphere by all the motorized equipment used in fighting all the 1988 fires in Yellowstone was infinitesimally small in a relative sense, but I saw the response as reflective of our culture's obsession with machinery and technology.

Further reflection led me to wonder how past cultures might have dealt with similar situations. I knew something about Yellowstone's fire history, how there was clear evidence that large scale fires had burned in the area many times in the past. The most recent episode of big burns had happened in the mid-1700s, and of course the fires of 1988 were not solely attributable to human-induced climate change. But I did wonder how the Indians who no doubt had been present in the area reacted to the rounds of fires that occurred in their time. I suspected, admittedly without any concrete knowledge, that most likely they simply picked up and moved out of the way when big fires bore down on them, set up new camps somewhere safe, and then wove stories to explain how and why the fires happened and what the blazes meant within the scope of their view of the world.

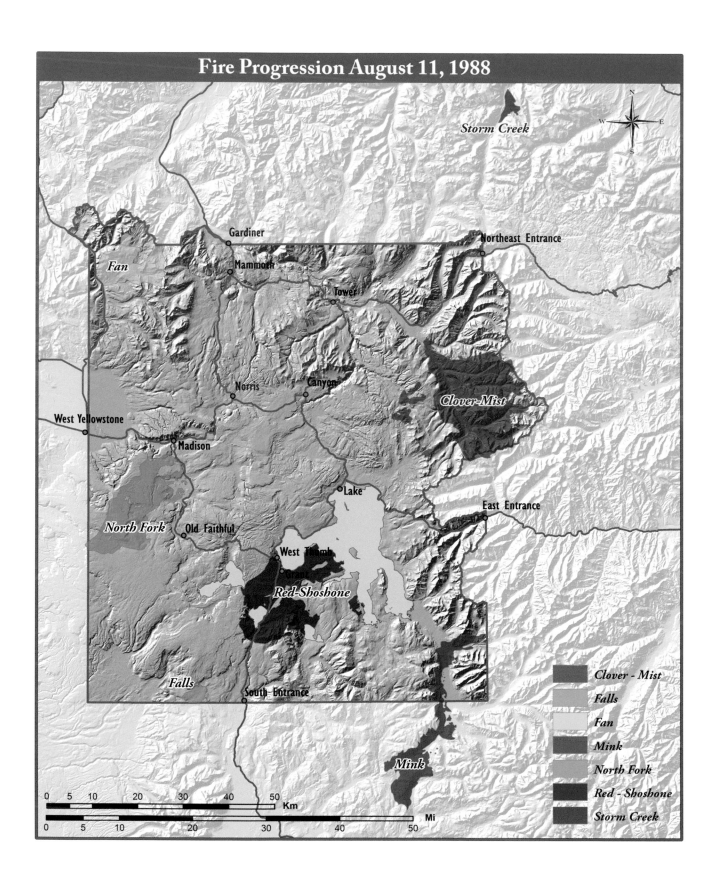

Fire Progression August 11, 1988

Storm Creek

Gardiner

Fan

Mammoth

Northeast Entrance

Tower

Norris

Canyon

Clover-Mist

West Yellowstone

Madison

Lake

East Entrance

North Fork

Old Faithful

West Thumb

Grant

Red-Shoshone

Falls

South Entrance

Mink

Clover - Mist
Falls
Fan
Mink
North Fork
Red - Shoshone
Storm Creek

0 5 10   20   30   40   50   Km

0   5   10   20   30   40   50   Mi

August 11, 1988

THE BIG WIND event that had been forecast for August 10 arrived on schedule, and actually carried over into the 11th. It was the second major wind event that had occurred in the 10 days or so since the fire prognosticators had looked into their smoky crystal ball and predicted there would be only one more such event for the entire rest of the fire season. The wind event of August 10–11 manifested itself most dramatically on the North Fork Fire as it approached the Fountain Flats area north of Old Faithful. The large and quickly growing fire was also moving ever closer to Madison Junction.

On this map the Clover-Mist Fire also has grown noticeably, and several of the ancillary fires to the west of its larger mass showed discernible growth as well, as they began to burn eastward toward what in terms of nomenclature was the parent fire. The Fan Fire in the northwestern corner of Yellowstone showed significant growth, as did the Red-Shoshone and the Continental Fires to the west of the South Arm of Yellowstone Lake. The Mink Fire in the park's Thorofare area also had made a major run up Mountain Creek, the drainage north of the Trident that feeds into the upper Yellowstone River upstream from the Southeast Arm of Yellowstone Lake. The Mink's run had taken it well up Mountain Creek, to the point where it was nearing the park's boundary with the Shoshone National Forest. Future wind events did indeed blow the fire out of the park and onto the forest.

The fast-moving Mink Fire had passed by the mouth of Thorofare Creek on the run that took it into Yellowstone on August 6. The famous Thorofare Ranger Station is situated near Thorofare Creek not far above the stream's junction with the Yellowstone River, a strategic location that puts the patrol cabin just north of the park's boundary with the Bridger-Teton National Forest. In the summer of 1988 a fine man named Dave Phillips was stationed at Thorofare. Dave was working his twenty-first season as a ranger for the park service, during which time he had served at various duty stations around Yellowstone. Living with him at Thorofare in 1988 were his wife Kathleen O'Leary and Dave's children Tyson and Linnea, who at the time were respectively thirteen and ten years old. As a backcountry ranger, Dave's job was to look after trails in the area, and especially to patrol the park's boundaries to watch for poachers. Kathleen, Linnea, and Tyson were taking advantage of the chance of a lifetime to live in one of the most remote districts in the Lower 48 states; the Thorofare Station was and is about 32 miles from the nearest road. The summer of 1988 was the fifth season the four had spent together in the Thorofare. Removed from the distractions of the more developed world while spending 24 hours a day amidst fascinating wildlife and incomparable landscapes, they thought their lives there in the southeastern corner of Yellowstone were idyllic.

One of the first signs that their idyll would be different in 1988 was when they were able to ride their mounts and lead their pack animals to Thorofare two weeks earlier than normal. The trail to the remote station crosses a number of tributary streams, such as Mountain Creek, that flow out of the Absaroka Mountains to the east and into the Yellowstone Lake and River to the west. The Absarokas around the heads of these streams are the highest peaks in Yellowstone, so normally the runoff in that district doesn't crest until the first or second week of July, and sometimes later than that. When runoff is high in the tributary streams, some of which are quite large, fording while en route to Thorofare is difficult to impossible. In 1988, however, the runoff peaked early and never amounted to that much anyway, so Dave, Kathleen, Linnea, and Tyson were able to pack into Thorofare in late June. On his very first trip into Thorofare in June, Dave made an entry in the station's logbook noting how dusty the trails were for so early in the season.

Even before the family packed in to the Thorofare Station, they were aware that some fires already had started in other parts of the park, such as the Fan Fire in the Yellowstone's northwest corner on June 25 and the Shoshone Fire near Shoshone Lake on June 23. Then on July 11 the Mink Fire flared to life south of the park boundary, and soon thereafter the Thorofare residents began to smell smoke. Even more disruptive of the normal peace and quiet, a helicopter flew in to their location on July 17, loaded with a pump, hoses, sprinklers, and other firefighting equipment to be deployed in defense of the Thorofare cabin and horse barn should any fire arrive there. And then on July 22 they were able to see flames from the cabin itself as the Mink Fire burned to the tops of high ridges to the south. From there the fire burned north along the opposite side of the Yellowstone Valley from the Thorofare Cabin, before crossing the river and making its run up Mountain Creek. With this latter move, it crossed the trail that leads from Thorofare to most of the rest of Yellowstone Park. Forest fires leave many toppled trees in their wake, and with all the burned logs the Mink Fire left across the trail to the north, Dave Phillips and his family were even more isolated than usual.

Fire filled the days of early- to mid-August for Dave and his wife and children. With help from Kathleen and Linnea and Tyson, Dave set up the sprinkler system to wet down the Thorofare cabin and barn. He followed behind the Mink Fire as it burned through the upper Yellowstone Valley to cut fallen logs out of trails, not only because that was his job but also to keep escape routes open for himself and his family in case they had to evacuate. Once when things became especially threatening he actually did send Kathleen and his children, along with nine horses, out to the Trail Creek Patrol Cabin at the end of the Southeast Arm of Yellowstone Lake. The fire hadn't reached there yet and besides, the lake itself offered a watery refuge of last resort. In mid August came the time when Linnea and Tyson had to leave Yellowstone anyway, to make a scheduled reunion with their mother. Watching his children leave must have stirred more mixed emotions for Dave than usual, as he undoubtedly was sad to see them go, but also relieved to get them away from the raging fires and choking smoke.

After the children left Dave and Kathleen returned to the Thorofare Station, where they remained until the 24th. By that time they had witnessed a series of fiery events that were nothing short of extraordinary, especially on August 20 when approximately 160,000 acres burned in the Yellowstone area on a day that has been known ever since as Black Saturday. In common with many other observers of other Yellowstone fires in 1988, Dave and Kathleen were struck by the way the Mink Fire kept burning day after day in the immediate vicinity of their summer home. It seemed to the couple that the fire was so intense that it should have consumed all the fuel in the surrounding area in a short time, and then moved on and left them in a burned out safety zone. But that wasn't the case. As the Red Fire had done around Ann Marie Chytra's Heart Lake Patrol Cabin a few days earlier, the Mink kept incinerating first one pocket of previously unburned fuel and then another, keeping up an almost continuous siege of the couple who were now feeling more marooned than ever.

August 24 was the date when Kathleen and Dave had to leave Yellowstone to meet the obligations of the life they led in the winter in California. Finding a way out of Thorofare through all the various fires burning at the time was a challenge, however. Instead of the long but straightforward trip on the Thorofare Trail to the Nine Mile trailhead near Lake Butte on Yellowstone's East Entrance Road, the couple had to wend a convoluted route to the west, a route that took them through many miles of burned out forest. The route also took them through a lot of forest that was still burning, and even in forest that was still green the couple never could be sure how far away the next pocket of flame might be. With many adventures and several near brushes with flames, the couple finally made it to Ann Marie Chytra's post at Heart Lake, where they laid over for a time, and then ultimately made it out to the Heart Lake trailhead on the South Entrance Road.

For my part, on August 10 I left my summer home at Madison Junction to go to my more permanent home in Gardiner, Montana. I had to take care of some of

The enormous smoke cloud put up by the North Fork Fire on August 11, 1988, with Terrace Spring near Madison Junction in the foreground. © Jeff Henry/ Roche Jaune Pictures, Inc.

the normal business of life—things like collecting my mail and paying bills. I spent the night in Gardiner, and then early the next morning drove the 40 miles back to Madison. The wind came up early in the day, becoming quite strong before I made it back to Madison. By the time I reached Norris Junction, 14 miles northeast of Madison, I could see the most tremendous smoke column and pyrocumulus cloud I had ever seen, greater than anything I had seen so far in the summer of 1988. I could tell that the column was emanating from the North Fork Fire, somewhere around the head of Sentinel Creek to the west of the Lower Geyser Basin.

I took a few photos of the astonishing column and cloud from Terrace Spring, a large geothermal outlet just north of the Madison government area, and then hurried to my park service mobile home in the residential area and quickly changed into my fire garb. Then I drove my park service pickup truck south to Fountain Flats, where I found a large helicopter base set up on the Fountain Freight Road, also known as the Fountain Flats Drive.

Sign indicating entrance to emergency helicopter base set up on Fountain Flats Drive during fire emergency on August 11, 1988. © Jeff Henry/Roche Jaune Pictures, Inc.

The base had actually been set up a few days earlier—I had seen it and even had shot a few snaps of it already—but now it was bustling with more activity than ever. Helicopters were coming and going, as were fuel trucks and other support vehicles. Large numbers of ground support people were also spread along the road, and all the people and equipment were trying to make do with the inefficient linear arrangement to avoid impacting the natural meadows adjacent to the road. Helicopters were flying in and out, and their racket combined with that of the support machinery to create an appalling din. The helicopters were coming and going primarily to shuttle firefighters to the fire, which was indeed burning in upper Sentinel Creek, to the west of Sentinel Meadows.

The fire's atmospheric expression was breathtaking. A dark, angry spiral rose from ground level upward into that huge column, which was capped by the gigantic cumulus cloud. The cloud was crenelated and startlingly white compared to the dirty smoke below. The whirling smoke column rose upward, but it wasn't exactly vertical. Instead it leaned toward the northeast, heeled over by powerful southwesterly winds blowing aloft. In its entirety, the colossal creation bespoke of an awesome release of energy down below.

As for the fire itself, most of the time it was hidden by all the smoke that was blowing out in front of the flames. Once in a while, though, the vagaries of the wind would be such that the curtain of smoke in front of the fire would part. The partings usually would last for just a few seconds before the curtain closed in again, but in those few seconds I could see lashing flames such as I had never seen before. They towered far above the trees they were burning. Most of the trees out there were mature lodgepole pines, probably 100–110 feet tall. Using that figure as a reference, I could see that the flames were around 200–300 feet high.

More impressive than just the flame height, however, was the way a whole wall of forest was burning as a unit. Earlier in the summer, when fires were burning at places like Grant Village in late July, I had seen individual trees torch, and sometimes a whole stand of trees flare off at once, but now the flames on the other side of Sentinel Meadows had formed themselves into a long line and were steadily advancing on a broad front. The oncoming flames resembled a grass fire in the way they had established themselves in the linear arrangement, but instead of burning in a line across blades of grass that were just a few inches high, this fire was burning mature conifers that were over one hundred feet tall.

I moved away from the helicopter-landing zone to get away from the hubbub there and to try to gain different views of the fire off to the west. The wind was so strong that I was still deafened, even though I had moved away from much of the mechanical noise. For a time there was so much smoke I couldn't see the fire at all, and it was sometimes so smoky I couldn't even see the big smoke column and cloud overhead.

During this interlude, my mind drifted back in time and out to Sentinel Meadows, and I thought of the things I had seen and done there over my years in Yellowstone. There was the time in the spring of 1986 when I was in the big meadow searching for winterkilled elk and bison while working on the spring carcass survey for the Inter-agency Grizzly Bear Study Team. While scanning the area with my binoculars from a vantage point on the south side of the meadow I spotted a female grizzly with two cubs stalking some elk that were out of sight but upwind from their position. As I watched, the mother bear was trying to sneak up on the elk, and for a little while the cubs would go along with the program, being quiet and careful, following their mother's example. But then cubhood would take over and the two cubs would wrestle, after which they would resume the stealthy mode, only to fall to wrestling again a short time later. Not surprisingly, the elk detected the approaching bears before the female was in position to strike, and they ran off. I was impressed by what a challenge it must be for a mother bear to manage her cubs and to provide for them at the same time.

I thought also of the old bathhouse that was situated near an amazing hot spring called the Queens Laundry. The spring was large and colorful and lethally hot, while the bathhouse had been made of logs by park superintendent Philetus Norris in the early 1880s. The structure had never been completed and what there was of it was now in a state of disrepair, with the remaining logs stacked only a few feet high, but I had often sat inside the walls to get out of the wind while I ate lunch or took a break.

Emergency helicopter base set up on Grand Loop Road at Mary Mountain trailhead by Nez Perce Creek, with the visually overwhelming smoke cloud from the North Fork Fire in the background on August 11, 1988. © Jeff Henry/Roche Jaune Pictures, Inc.

I also remembered many autumns when I had made the short hike out to Sentinel Meadows to listen to the bugling of rutting elk, and how in the late summer the water of the Firehole River often became too warm for trout and many fish swam up Sentinel Creek to take advantage of the cooler water there. Always surprising, to see so many large trout in such a small stream, but Sentinel Creek not only had cooler water, but also was deceptively deep for such a narrow bed, and it also had overhanging banks that trout found appealing. All these thoughts and more, and now the North Fork Fire was rampaging in the field of my memories, and I had to wonder how much things would be different after the ash settled and the smoke cleared.

The North Fork was advancing quickly, however, and soon cut off my nostalgia. From my vantage near the present-day barricade on the Fountain Flats Drive, the fire appeared to have split into two prongs, one burning northeastward along the face of the ridge north of Sentinel Creek, while the other was burning in the same direction but south of my location, on a course that was taking it toward Midway Geyser Basin and the stretch of forest along the Grand Loop Road between Midway and the entrance to the Firehole Lake Drive.

The managers of the helibase along the Fountain Flats Drive realized they were being bracketed by fire and quickly decided to evacuate their location. They moved their operations to the Grand Loop Road on Fountain Flats, centering their new base on the Mary Mountain trailhead by the Porcupine Hills. The road between Madison and Old Faithful by this time had been closed to public travel, so other than firefighters there was no traffic to contend with at the new base. The helicopters and their support crews, however, still had to deal with the awkwardness of

Tall flames erupting from stand of lodgepole pines near Pocket Basin on the west side of Fountain Flat, afternoon of August 11, 1988. © Jeff Henry/Roche Jaune Pictures, Inc.

having everything arranged in a long narrow line along a highway—something like working on the deck of an aircraft carrier, I suppose, but an aircraft carrier without multiple decks and elevators. And the helicopters and their support crews still had to deal with the same violent wind that had been blowing at their previous base. I moved over to the Grand Loop Road near the Mary Mountain trailhead as well.

The wind continued to blow, if anything even more fiercely than before. For a better view I climbed a short distance up the westernmost of the Porcupine Hills, the eminence just above the trailhead. From there I could see that the advancing fire had no trouble jumping the Fountain Flats Drive in many sectors. It also jumped the Firehole River just on the other side of Fountain Flats from me, where it commenced burning in a thermal area named Pocket Basin, another place that held a lot of memories for me.

I was impressed by how the fire not only jumped the Fountain Flats Drive and the Firehole River, but how it also easily crossed the rather broad geothermal plains around Pocket Basin and other thermal areas. The geothermal expanses were mostly barren silica deposits, without much vegetation to fuel or to carry a fire, but the North Fork seemed to have fiery fingers that reached out and found and ignited the sparse pockets of vegetation that were there. On the northeast side of Pocket Basin, a couple of small hills stood above the geyserite plains and therefore were fairly heavily timbered. The timber there exploded into tall flames that burned intensely until they had consumed all the foliage on the trees.

Now it seemed likely that the fire would continue its spread toward the Grand Loop Road and might cut off the firefighters and their equipment staged along the road at Fountain Flats. I remember the dire directive that came over the park radio as though I heard it a lot more recently than twenty-five years ago. A voice I didn't recognize, so probably a voice belonging to one of the professional firefighters brought in to help Yellowstone deal with the fire emergency, came on and said, "Evacuate north or evacuate south, whichever way you can go. Just go somewhere and get out of the way." In front of me the collection of helicopters, trucks, and firefighters quickly disintegrated as everyone abandoned Fountain Flats to the oncoming fire. Later a pilot who was present that day would tell me that in all his years of flying helicopters to fight fires he had never been forced to abandon a base, and then on August 11, 1988, the implacable North Fork Fire had made him do that very thing two times within the space of a couple of hours.

I decided to stay behind, at least for a while. I did not see the fire as imminently dangerous, at least not for someone who was not in charge of looking after equipment and not part of an unwieldy crew. And besides, it was my job to photographically document the fires and I thought I was in a good place to shoot some special pictures. On top of that, I felt I knew the area much better than the imported firefighters, and was confident that no matter what happened I could think of a safe place to go and would have the ability to get there in time.

In a short while I was all alone on Fountain Flats. It was a unique experience, to be alone on the Grand Loop Road in mid-August, a time when usually the road is jammed with summer traffic, and also to be alone in a place where just a few minutes before there had been so many firefighters and so much firefighting equipment. The wind continued to buffet my ears, but in a way the scene now seemed quiet, what with everyone else gone.

After I watched the fire for a while, it became apparent that the grass and forbs on Fountain Flats were too moist to carry the fire. I wasn't that surprised, as I knew the underlying meadow to be quite wet in places, with many seeping springs across its expanse. Much more surprising, however, was how the fire burning in the forest both north and south of Fountain Flats also stalled out, even with a lot of fresh fuel still ahead of it and the hard wind still blowing behind it. I'm sure the scientific explanation of what happened is that evening was coming on and temperatures were falling and humidities were rising. This meant that combustion was not as hot as it had been earlier in the day, insufficient energy was being released to ignite new fuel in front of the flames, and the fire consequently was slowing or even halting in its spread.

From another point of view, because of this and other similar experiences in the summer of 1988, I found it easy to understand how people of earlier times developed images of fire as a conscious organism, as a dragon or as some other embodiment, with capricious moods and unpredictable actions. Even with all of our sophisticated instruments and scientific acumen, fire frequently surprised us in 1988, as it still does today. As August of 1988 moved along, a great many more surprises were going to be rolled out in front of Yellowstone observers.

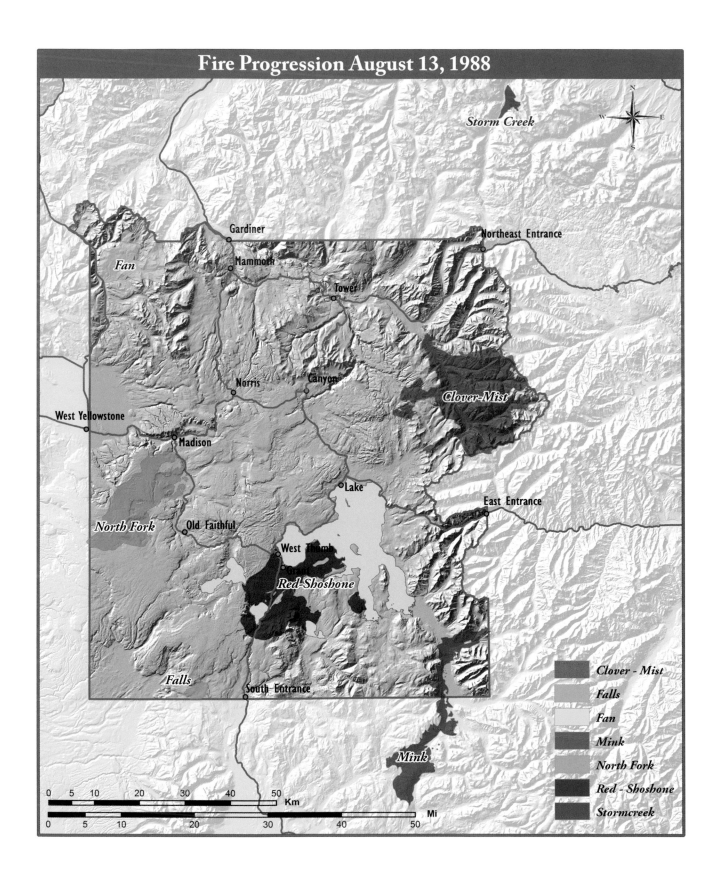

Fire Progression August 13, 1988

Storm Creek

Gardiner

Mammoth

Fan

Tower

Northeast Entrance

Norris

Canyon

Clover-Mist

West Yellowstone

Madison

Lake

East Entrance

North Fork

Old Faithful

West Thumb

Grant

Red-Shoshone

Falls

South Entrance

Mink

| Km |
| 0 5 10   20   30   40   50 |
| Mi |
| 0   5   10   20   30   40   50 |

Clover - Mist

Falls

Fan

Mink

North Fork

Red - Shoshone

Stormcreek

August 13, 1988

THE AUGUST 13 map reflects more of the capricious and unpredictable nature of fire. After burning almost 16,000 acres on the 10th and the 11th, for instance, the North Fork Fire burned exactly zero on the 12th. By way of contrast, the Clover-Mist burned nearly 4,000 acres on the 12th, while the Snake River fires burned nearly 2,000—this, even though essentially the same weather conditions must have been present at all the various fires in Yellowstone on the 12th. The increased acreages burned by the Clover-Mist and the Snake River Complex Fires can be seen as enlarged coverage on the accompanying map. Of particular note is how the satellite fires to the west of the Clover-Mist had burned into the mass of the larger fire.

August 13 brought moderate fire growth, as the North Fork and Clover-Mist each burned about 2,600 acres. That actually amounted to a light burning day in the context of 1988. But to put things in perspective, 2,600 acres equates to about 4 *square miles* of country burned by each of Yellowstone's two largest fires. The fires in the southern part of the park also chipped in by charring about 900 acres on the 13th.

On just about a daily basis through the summer of 1988, park headquarters in Mammoth distributed a situation report, complete with a map showing the present extent of the various fires, to park service employees in Yellowstone. Reports from this time, after the North Fork's big run on August 11, relate that fire crews on the east flank of the fire were "mopping up and burning out" in front of the fire. A break in the weather allowed firefighters to work in close proximity to the North Fork; on many days it would have been suicidal to move in close, especially out in front on the downwind side of the blaze.

Firefighter on watch at Grand Loop Road crossing of Nez Perce Creek, in a successful effort to keep the North Fork Fire from crossing the road toward the east on the afternoon of August 11, 1988. © Jeff Henry/Roche Jaune Pictures, Inc.

The wording "mopping up" is interesting, as the term usually refers to putting out residual hot spots inside a fireline after the main fire has been contained. As events on August 15 would show, the North Fork was far from contained. Perhaps the writer of the daily situation report was motivated by wishful thinking, or perhaps was still influenced by the fire gods' prediction that the North Fork would not be able to cross the roads, rivers, and other fire breaks surrounding the Madison Plateau. I wasn't there, but I strongly suspect that no firefighters were working literally "out in front" of the volatile North Fork on this day. I know I would not have wanted any part of such duty myself.

On the 12th and 13th I couldn't stay away from the country west of Fountain Flats that the North Fork had burned on August 10 and 11. Actually, I had driven the full length of the Fountain Freight Road on the evening of the 11th, just after the fire had passed through the area and left smoking snags and blackened deadfall in its wake, and found that the Freight Road was burned along almost its entire length. I wanted to see the area that had burned so spectacularly earlier in the day; I suppose it was somewhat akin to a morbid desire to walk around a battlefield after the battle is over. But I also was fascinated by the eerie aftermath of fire, which of

YELLOWSTONE FIRES
August 14, 1988, 8:00 a.m.

North Entrance
Northeast Entrance
Mammoth Hot Springs
Tower-Roosevelt

Fan Fire

Clover-Mist Fire

Norris
Canyon

West Entrance
Madison

Lovely Fire
Fishing Bridge
Lake
East Entrance

Bridge Bay

Old Faithful
West Thumb

Cub Fire
Yellowstone Lake

North Fork Fire
Shoshone Lake
Grant Village

Lewis Lake

Continental-Ridge Fire

Red-Shoshone Fire
Heart Lake

Falls Fire

Mink Creek Fire

South Entrance

NATIONAL PARK SERVICE

FOREST SERVICE US DEPARTMENT OF AGRICULTURE

To date, 50 fires in Yellowstone have burned over 240,000 acres. All but the North Fork Fire started from lightning. Note: Only about half of vegetation has burned within most fire perimeters. All new fires are being attacked when small. Large fires are being kept from visitor facilities and from leaving the park. The sizes and shapes of the fires are <u>estimates</u>.

Clover-Mist Fire: 94,724 acres. Mist Fire started July 9. Clover started July 11. They joined on July 22. Shallow Fire started July 31. Fern Fire started August 5. These two fires joined Clover-Mist August 13. Contained outside the park. 80 fire fighters patrolling for hot spots.

Continental-Ridge Fire: 2,442 acres. Found July 29. Being monitored.

Cub Fire: 25 acres. 80 fire fighters have contained this fire in a fire line.

Falls Fire: 2,971 acres. Started July 12. Crews patrolling 'hwest flank.

Fire: 20,370 acres. Started June 25. 1021 fire fighters on it. Little activity yesterday. 70% contained. Crews mopping up.

Lovely Fire: 555 acres. Started July 11. Being monitored.

Mink Creek Fire: 12,278 acres in Yellowstone. Started July 11 outside the park in Teton Wilderness.

North Fork Fire: 52,960 acres. Started July 22 by human. Crews working on west flank to keep in park. Mopping up and burning out on east flank, near Madison-Old Faithful Road. Expect delays today. Firehole Canyon Drive and Fountain Flats Road both closed.

Red-Shoshone Fire: 55,000 acres. Red Fire started July 1. Shoshone Fire started June 23. Joined August 10. Crews mopping up along park roads and developments.

There are several other small fires in the park that are either being monitored or are now contained.

This is an example of the situation maps that were put out by the National Park Service for the elucidation of its employees on an almost daily basis during the summer of 1988. National Park Service

Smoldering aftermath of the North Fork Fire in August of 1988. © Jeff Henry/Roche Jaune Pictures, Inc.

course I had seen before in other times and places, but never on such a scale and never in an area so familiar to me. Among other things, I was taken by the mystery of how certain clumps of trees, in some cases just a single tree, had somehow escaped the conflagration and were still green within a sea of scorched forest.

Bizarre burned patterns on the ground also caught my eye. In some places where fallen logs had been crisscrossed, the "x" pattern was revealed by the different colors of ash left behind after the deadfall had burned completely away, leaving only ghost images of downed logs that were. Other logs that had been crossed on the ground had burned completely in two at the point of their crossing, while their extremities beyond the "x" were still present, blackened and still smoldering. In some places the

Patterns of burned logs on the ground after passage of the North Fork Fire in August of 1988. © Jeff Henry/Roche Jaune Pictures, Inc.

ash underfoot was unbelievably light and fluffy, and my feet sank in to my ankles or deeper as I walked around the spooky snags. Grotesque, charred stumps still smoldered in their closed interiors. Some glowed so hot inside that looking into them was like looking inside a burning woodstove.

The wind blew through the tops of the burned pines, now denuded of their foliage, making haunting sounds like wind blowing through a deciduous forest after the leaves have been stripped in autumn. It was a much different sound than the Yellowstone wind normally makes when it sighs through pine needles. Once in a while a zephyr would blow through the dead trees at ground level and kick up some of the loose ash, sometimes in the form of a miniature tornado that would go spinning off into nothingness. Still smoldering fuel sent up ethereal little columns of smoke, while the sun shone with a lurid light through the general smokiness above.

There were subtle cracklings as small pockets of fuel that had somehow escaped the main conflagration ignited and burned. In the distance I could hear the sounds of trees falling as their roots finally burned away from the heat that took a while to penetrate down through the ground to the trees' anchor points. Rocks on the ground were now exposed because overlying vegetation had been burned away. Some of the rocks had shattered from the intense heat, and in some places I found the bones of

A young cow elk exploring the changed landscape of its home range in the wake of the North Fork Fire, near Madison in August 1988. © Jeff Henry/Roche Jaune Pictures, Inc.

animals that had died sometime in the natural course of things before the fire; those bones were charred and shattered, too. I suppose there were other bones that had incinerated completely and were no longer there for me to see. With an eye for patterns, I was struck by the contrast of verticality and horizontality between fallen logs on the ground and the snags that were still upright. Vertical or horizontal, almost all of the logs were black. Other trees had literally been yanked out of the ground by their roots by the tremendous updrafting of heat during the height of the fire. They looked like they had been pulled out of the ground by some Bunyanesque gardener pulling weeds from his garden.

Spending time in these radically altered landscapes stirred further memories for me, as watching the fire burn in the same areas had done a couple of days before. In the many springs I had spent in the area, for instance, I had often seen male ruffed grouse drumming, or beating their chests with their wings, along the Fountain Freight Road between Goose and Feather Lakes and Midway Geyser Basin. For some reason, a reason I never came close to figuring out, the area must have held a special appeal for ruffed grouse, because I saw a lot more of them there than I did anywhere else in Yellowstone. I wondered how the grouse had fared when the fire came through, and where the males of the species would go now to beat their chests in the annual proclamation of their masculinity.

A very smoky sunset after a big burning day by the North Fork Fire, over the Twin Buttes west of the Lower Geyser Basin in August of 1988. © Jeff Henry/Roche Jaune Pictures, Inc.

Each time I returned to the Fountain Freight Road from my contemplative wanderings through the blackened forest to the west, the strip of unburned greenery along the edge of the Firehole River below the road caught my eye. Upriver I could see signal steam columns billowing from the Midway Geyser Basin, along with a host of waterfowl along the river. Usually there were also some elk in sight somewhere in the scene, too, either unconcernedly grazing on the vegetation that was still present, or wading and splashing in the river, as elk always seem so fond of doing. It seemed to me that the big fires might be more disruptive to Yellowstone's two-legged inhabitants than to its four-legged and feathered ones.

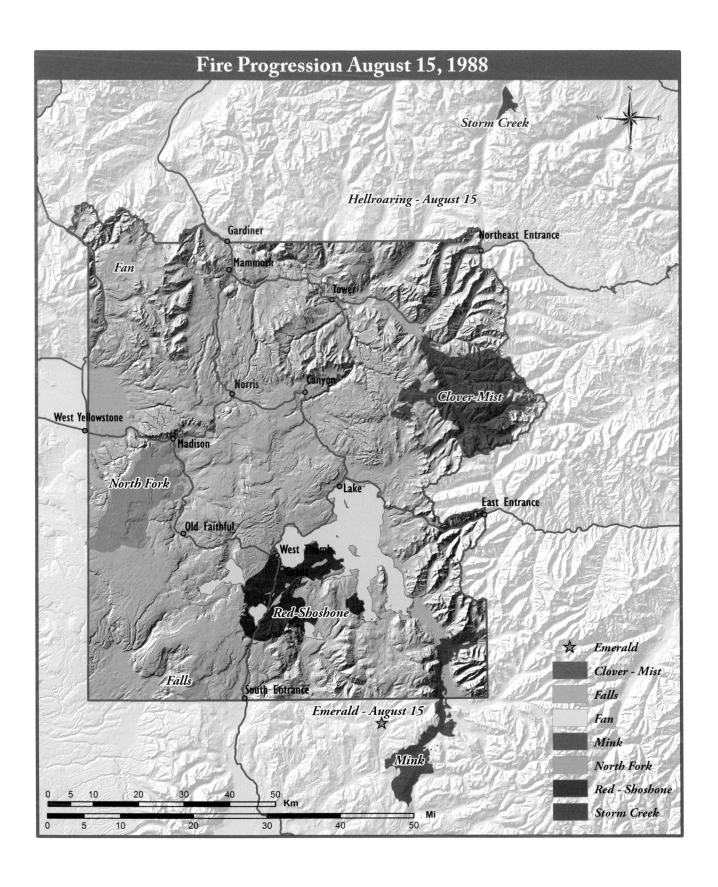

Fire Progression August 15, 1988

Storm Creek

Hellroaring - August 15

Gardiner

Mammoth

Fan

Tower

Northeast Entrance

Norris

Canyon

Clover-Mist

West Yellowstone

Madison

North Fork

Lake

East Entrance

Old Faithful

West Thumb

Grant

Red-Shoshone

Falls

South Entrance

Emerald - August 15

Mink

☆ Emerald

Clover - Mist

Falls

Fan

Mink

North Fork

Red - Shoshone

Storm Creek

0 5 10   20   30   40   50 Km

0   5   10   20   30   40   50 Mi

August 15, 1988

AUGUST 15 was a spectacular, standout day in Yellowstone's summer of fire, with most of the spectacle focused on the North Fork Fire. While the other major fires in the park burned a collective total of only about 1,800 acres on the 15th, the North Fork alone burned almost 10,000. But the acreage figure by itself in no way communicates the level of drama the park's biggest fire engendered that day. It was on the 15th that the North Fork exploded off the Madison Plateau and crossed not only the Firehole River to the east, but also the Madison River to the north. In doing so, it exceeded in one day the spread the collected fire gods had predicted it would make over the course of the whole rest of the summer when they had met and made their forecasts a couple of weeks earlier.

First thing in the morning on the 15th, the winds were deceptively calm at Madison Junction. A good friend of mine named Rick Bennett, who in 1988 was the Madison Subdistrict Ranger, made a helicopter flight over the North Fork Fire early in the day. Rick found the fire still on the Madison Plateau, but not far from the Firehole Canyon to the east and from the Madison River Valley on the north. When Rick flew, the wind was still calm and the North Fork still quiet under a lingering blanket of cool night air. Rick also saw that the whole plateau was covered with thick smoke that had settled in during the usual nighttime inversion.

Shortly after Rick returned to Madison, however, the winds began to pick up and it became evident that the North Fork had arisen from its nighttime torpor. By late morning the fire had "built up a head," as the firefighters say, meaning that it had organized itself into a burning cell that was being pushed along by the wind. In

Ranger Rick Bennett trying to deal with the emergency situation caused by the North Fork Fire in August of 1988. © Jeff Henry/Roche Jaune Pictures, Inc.

fact, it had built up a number of heads that were simultaneously moving outward toward the boundaries of the Madison Plateau. Rick collected several others of the park service community at Madison, including rangers Bob Duff, Les Brunton, Bonita Garrett, Dub Kennedy, and Kim West, and with one old fire engine, the group moved west to the vicinity of Seven Mile Bridge, where they had been instructed to keep the North Fork from crossing the Madison River corridor and moving to the north. In retrospect it seems ludicrous—and those involved would fully agree—that such a small crew with one old fire truck were sent out to stop a juggernaut such as was moving in their direction, but more later about this group and their experiences on the 15th.

Incident Commander Dave Poncin, Sr., who had orchestrated the defense of Yellowstone's Grant Village development in late July, returned with his Type I overhead team to take charge of the North Fork on August 11, just in time to see the fire make the big run it made that day. Almost immediately, Dave accurately assessed that the North Fork's northeastward spread would soon bring the fire to both the Madison and the Firehole Rivers. At first, however, Dave thought that the fire could

Ranger Les Brunton watching a huge Columbia helicopter haul water from the Madison River to dump on the North Fork Fire burning around Mount Haynes in the background.
© Jeff Henry/Roche Jaune Pictures, Inc.

be stopped at those natural barriers. To augment the chances of stopping the fire along the Firehole Canyon, the Incident Commander had ordered a burnout on the west side of the Firehole late on the afternoon of the 14th, this to broaden the existing firebreak already in place in the form of the Firehole River itself, as well as the Grand Loop Road paralleling the river on its east side. In keeping with the exceptional fire conditions extant that summer, and quoting from Poncin's diary, it was not surprising that "the burn out was very hot, we brought crews back on duty to hold the line [meaning the park's Grand Loop Road], chase spot fires and mop them up. These crews worked until 2200." At the time Dave thought the burnout had been successful, but the next day the North Fork would be so fierce that it would

Incident Commander
Dave Poncin, Sr.
at briefing in the
Madison Fire Camp
in August of 1988.
© Jeff Henry/Roche
Jaune Pictures, Inc.

leapfrog not only the burned-out sectors, but also the Firehole River and the park highway as it burned up the Gibbon River and points north.

Along with Rick Bennett and everyone else in the Madison area, Dave Poncin noticed that the winds picked up around 10:30 in the morning, and wrote that a short time later "the relative humidity was down to 7%, the winds at eye level were 40 mph, and the temperature [was] at 80 degrees." Even before that morning, actually as soon as he assumed command of the North Fork, Dave had discerned that the portion of the Madison Plateau near Madison Junction had a southwest-to-northeast orientation, portentously in line with the area's prevailing winds. This compass orientation and the ominous weather factors combined with abnormally low fuel moistures to produce a fire show the likes of which no one present had ever seen.

One of the first places the show presented itself was at Seven Mile Bridge, where the small park service contingent from Madison had been positioned with their old truck, an engine that dated back to the 1940s. "You could see it coming," Rick Bennett said later in an interview, "not the actual flames themselves but in the reflected orange glow off the smoke above the fire." The little crew could also hear the fire's deafening roar as it neared the rims on the south side of the Madison Valley. When it finally did appear at the top of the cliffs the fire "was the sight of a lifetime," and Rick "couldn't believe it had that kind of power." Shortly after it appeared on the rim of the Madison Plateau, the fire rolled down the cliff face, an avalanche of sparks and embers cascading down to the valley below.

Les Brunton, another member of the crew with the old truck, had hurriedly packed his personal items in his car earlier in the day and then parked the car in what he thought was a safe zone near the Madison Museum, the same parking lot where the Madison Warming Hut is located in winter. Now he, too, was awed as the North Fork roared over the tops of the cliffs in front of him at Seven Mile Bridge. Fantastic tongues of flame blew out horizontally from the lip of the Madison Plateau. Trees burned off at their bases, and the flaming logs careened down the face of the precipice. Fire whirls and swirls flew through the air for great distances out and away from the burning forest at the lip of the plateau, but the most astonishing thing of all for Les was a tornado of fire that twisted across the flat by the Madison River and picked up "a downed log ten inches in diameter and five or six feet long and sucked it up out of sight into the sky."

Rick Bennett said that "embers rained from the sky," and started spot fires all around. For a time the crew managed to keep up with the spot fires, and stomped or otherwise put them out before they could spread. But the firebrands kept coming faster and faster, and soon the crew couldn't keep up. One of the spot fires escaped and began burning up the steep slope on the north side of the West Entrance Road behind the crew, and they decided it was time to give up their post or run the risk of being surrounded and cut off from escape routes. They evacuated back to Madison.

The first thing Les Brunton saw when he returned to Madison was a flaming forest just one hundred yards from the parking lot where he had parked his car packed with his personal belongings. That fire must have started from a flying firebrand, or perhaps from a backfire gone bad. Les had thought the parking lot was the safest spot in the Madison area, certainly safer than the housing area from which he had evacuated his things earlier in the day, but now it appeared that was not the case. And then looking up from the parking lot, which was located next to the Madison Campground on the valley bottom, Les and the others saw the same sort of spectacular pyrotechnic display they had seen a little while earlier on the cliffs above Seven Mile Bridge. At Madison the fire was tumbling down the rocky face of National Park Mountain, as well as from Three Brothers Mountain a short distance to the west.

Dave Poncin saw it too. "It was awesome. Fingers of flame were rolling down the bluffs and I saw the wind lift the fire up, lofting it up, sending great banners of flame flashing out from the smoke. I'd never seen anything quite like it: the fire was blowing out horizontally, right off the cliff face. It was a spectacular sight. The very heavens seemed afire." And this was from a man who had spent a career fighting fire, starting as a smokejumper and working his way up to incident commander. Indeed, Dave would later write in his diary that conditions on August 15 combined to create an "event one could only watch, and a fire one could only chase." The Incident Commander added further that the situation "was a day to observe human actions under duress," and that "we had everything from panic to cool professionalism as our wildland firefighters witnessed fire behavior they had not experienced before." Dave also noted that he was proud of his profession.

For the time being the proud firefighters could only get out of the way, but they did manage to protect the Madison Campground and the Madison residential area. Rick Bennett, Les Brunton, and the others pulled back to the Madison housing area as a last refuge, where they and others parked their fire trucks in a circumference to protect the structures inside the ring. Rick remembers it as looking like "covered wagons in a wagon train circled for the night." Even so, Rick still "can't believe that Madison didn't burn." Profuse spraying of water from the circled fire wagons, along with the fuel reduction work that had been done beforehand, did save the housing area. According to a tally compiled by the Incident Commander Dave Poncin himself, the only structural losses incurred on the 15th at Madison were a roof on a stream flow gauging station, the insulation on a water storage tank, some guard rails on the Firehole Canyon Drive, and two power poles on a secondary power line.

"Secondary line" is the term power company linemen use to refer to the distribution wires leading from a main transmission line to a residential area, in this case the Madison housing and maintenance area. Indeed, only two utility poles were lost to the North Fork Fire along this short segment of line within the local Madison area, but elsewhere the main line seems to have taken a much bigger hit.

Not surprisingly, many of Yellowstone's roads follow stream drainages, and also not surprisingly most of the park's power lines parallel the roads. Fires also tend to burn along valleys, especially in the upstream direction, and that is what the North Fork Fire did after it crossed the Madison to Old Faithful Road in the area of the Firehole Canyon on August 15. In this case, the North Fork burned up the valley of the Gibbon River, which is also aligned with prevailing southwesterly winds, almost as far as Gibbon Falls. On the way it pretty much destroyed the main power transmission line in that sector.

In 1988 Jack Altimus was part of a crew of good guys who worked in Yellowstone for Montana Power, the company that supplied electricity to the park at the time. I know they were good guys, because I worked with Montana Power's crew in the park myself for a couple of months in the autumn of 1985, after my summer season for the park had ended. Jack related that "hundreds of poles burned off and fell over," leaving their wires on the ground and severing power transmission to Madison and Old Faithful. Jack further related that the intense heat of the fire annealed the wires themselves, to the point where the old wire couldn't be reused even after the burned-off poles had been replaced. Annealing the wires left them with too much stretch to be drawn tightly enough between poles ever again, so in addition to hauling in and erecting hundreds of replacement poles, Montana Power also had to bring in miles of new wire and string that up, too.

A Montana Power Company work truck and associated employees working to fireproof one of their power lines during the fire emergency in summer 1988. © Jeff Henry/Roche Jaune Pictures, Inc.

And that wasn't all. Montana Power's fire-related problems actually had begun nearly a month earlier, when the Shoshone Fire was burning around Grant Village. Poles had burned and power service had been interrupted there, too, and some of the Montana Power linemen had nearly been trapped by fire while they were working to protect the Grant Village substation. Jack Altimus and others who were working at the substation "heard the fire coming, and got out just in time." Their escape was aided by water bucket drops from a huge Columbia helicopter, which dropped water directly on the besieged linemen. The Columbia helicopters carried 1,000 gallon buckets, and even though the buckets were never filled to capacity (because of the machines' reduced lift caused by Yellowstone's high, thin air), they still dumped a lot of water with each shot. Tor Pederson, another lineman with Montana Power, remembers that there was so much water with each drop that "it hit with a lot of force." Tor himself was in some trees, which broke the impact of the drops, but he remembers that some of his coworkers were knocked off balance, and all the men got "thoroughly wet." The substation was saved, but because of burned down lines the power company was forced to switch over to generator power at Grant, and the antiquated nature of the generator they used was such that at least one of the power workers had to babysit the machine twenty-four hours a day.

The North Fork Fire had also destroyed a great deal of line previously, on the big run it made on August 11, when several miles of line had burned in the area of Fairy Meadows and Sentinel Meadows. The park's fires grew larger as the summer went on, and the growth consumed ever more miles of power lines in a problem that grew larger right along with the size of the fires. And work continued at a fevered pace for the Montana Power crews even after the fires themselves cooled down in the middle of September, as it took a long time to replace the line burned down when the fires were raging. Tor Pederson remembered that "30–35 miles of the 92 miles of main line in the park were taken out" during the course of the summer of 1988.

In a twist of personal irony, the North Fork burned some handiwork my coworker Dub Kennedy and I had constructed just a few weeks before. In 1988 the swimming hole in the Firehole River Canyon just south of Madison Junction was very popular, as it still is today. Over the years visitors walking from the Firehole Canyon Drive down to the swimming hole had beaten down a braided network of trails. It was a situation that offended the sensitivities of the park service, which desired to have pedestrian traffic limited to a few officially delineated pathways.

There were also a large number of dead lodgepole pines around the access trails. Mountain pine beetles had killed the trees, as they had so many other pines in the Yellowstone area in the years leading up to 1988. The trees around the Firehole swimming area may have become weakened and therefore predisposed to beetle-kill because of foot trampling and soil compaction around their bases. In any event, Dub Kennedy and I were dispatched to rectify the situation by cutting down the dead trees in such a manner as to block the undesirable footpaths. They sent me because of my ability to use a chainsaw to drop trees in specific alignments, while Dub contributed his tremendous physical strength to the project. He was fifty-one years old in 1988, but the ranger with the flaring handlebar mustache was also a former star football player at the University of Montana who had been drafted by the Philadelphia Eagles, only to have a potential pro career short-circuited by injury. Dub was still phenomenally strong, at least as strong as I was at sixteen years his junior, and between the two of us we repositioned by hand the logs that didn't fall exactly right. The result was well-crisscrossed barriers on the trails the park service wanted blocked, but our piled up logs constituted an ideal fuel/oxygen mix when the North Fork Fire burned past the Firehole swimming area on August 15, so our obstructions burned completely and the trails to the swimming hole were left wide open once again, albeit in a very charred condition. Afterward, Dub Kennedy shook his head and said, "that must have been a hot [expletive deleted]."

I am embarrassed to admit that I was not present at Madison on August 15. I was away on another assignment and missed one of the most impressive displays of the summer, even though it literally happened right in the front yard of my temporary summer home at Madison. It was the biggest strategic mistake of the summer for

Ranger Dub Kennedy in the summer of 1988. © Jeff Henry/Roche Jaune Pictures, Inc.

me, and consequently I have no photographs of the North Fork Fire tumbling over the cliffs at the edge of the Madison Plateau above the Madison River. As far as I have been able to determine, no one else shot any photos or video that day either, so there is no visual record of the event. It was a regrettable oversight, to say the least.

As an aside, it frequently occurred to me through the fire events of 1988 that those involved in documentation, such as myself, often got short shrift at the fire scenes. In the heat of the moment, within the context of a given day on the fire front, that might have been understandable. But it further occurred to me that after the given day had passed, the documentation work immediately became more important than anything else that was done that day. Whether successful or not, the effort put into directly fighting the fires on a given day was passing, while the results of the documentation efforts will hopefully be with posterity for a very long time to come.

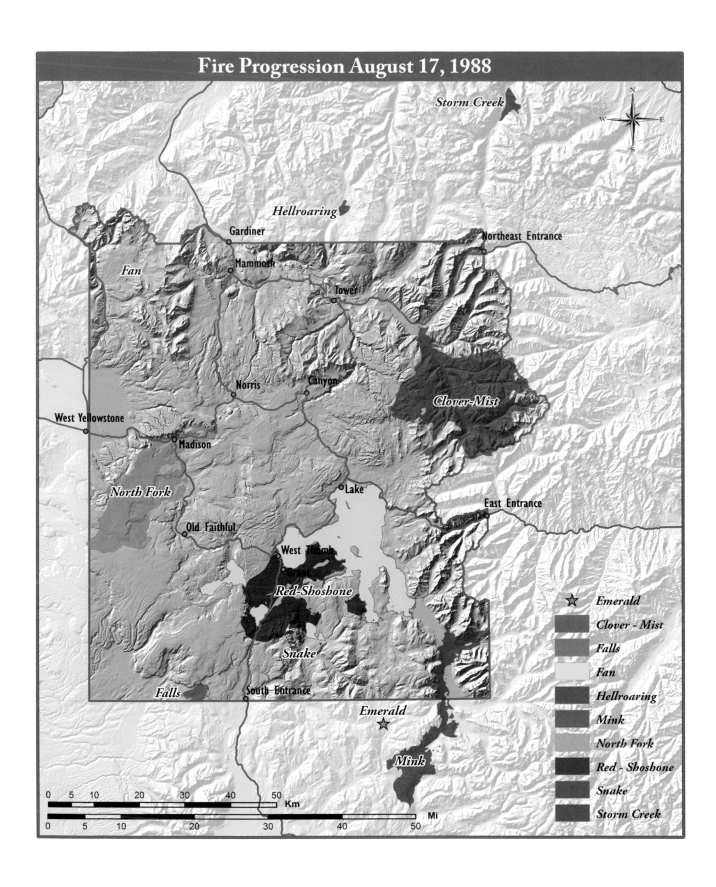

Fire Progression August 17, 1988

Storm Creek

Hellroaring

Gardiner

Northeast Entrance

Mammoth

Fan

Tower

Norris

Canyon

Clover-Mist

West Yellowstone

Madison

North Fork

Lake

East Entrance

Old Faithful

West Thumb

Grant

Red-Shoshone

Snake

Falls

South Entrance

Emerald

Mink

☆	Emerald
	Clover - Mist
	Falls
	Fan
	Hellroaring
	Mink
	North Fork
	Red - Shoshone
	Snake
	Storm Creek

0 5 10   20   30   40   50
Km

0 5 10   20   30   40   50
Mi

August 17, 1988

THE GROWTH the North Fork Fire made on the 15th and the 16th is evident on this map for August 17, 1988. Note that the portion of the North Fork that crossed Yellowstone's West Entrance Road just west of Madison Junction had not expanded much. That probably was because the steep south-facing slopes above the north side of the Madison River are too hot and dry to support much vegetation, and consequently fuels there were too sparse to readily carry the fire, even though the upslopes are steep and in line with prevailing winds. The fairly narrow head of the North Fork that ran up the Gibbon River on the 15th, on the other hand, does show discernible growth. Moreover, by the 17th that leading finger had split into two prongs that had looped back into each other on the steep slopes on the north side of Secret Valley. In fact, the North Fork Fire didn't burn that much acreage, at least in a relative sense, on the 16th and 17th, with one set of fire records showing a total of only about 8,000 acres combined for the two days. From a perspective after the fact, however, the North Fork was figuratively just marshaling its strength in preparation for its next surge.

In contrast to the North Fork, the Clover-Mist Fire did have a big burning day on the 16th, expanding over 19,000 acres in just that one burning period. The fire kept pushing hard on the boundary along the east side of Yellowstone National Park, threatening to move out of the park and into the Shoshone National Forest. This was an eventuality the Park Service in Yellowstone was trying hard to prevent.

There was a widespread perception in 1988 that the National Park Service in Yellowstone could have prevented much of the fire damage that occurred that summer if the fires had been attacked and contained early in the season, before they had a chance to grow into the uncontrollable monsters they became later on.

That perception was especially strong in the gateway communities around Yellowstone, where residents and business owners made frequent statements like, "This is bureaucratic arson." Sardonic jokes were common, too, such as, "How do you keep your living room from burning in a house fire?" with the punch line being "Start a backfire in your kitchen."

First, there is no way to know exactly how the summer of 1988 might have unfolded differently if park management had tried to suppress all fires from their outset. As the erudite CBS News commentator Eric Sevareid once observed, history never reveals its alternatives. But in my opinion there is only limited merit to the perception that park managers could have done much differently to prevent the great firestorms of the summer of 1988. The Fan Fire would be one exception. That fire did smolder for the better part of a week before it exploded and took off, and I believe it would have been possible to corral the fire during its smoldering period. The Red Fire and the Shoshone Fire also could possibly have been contained before they grew large. And the Storm Creek is another fire that smoldered for an especially long time before it flared up and began to move, so it is believable that it, too, could have been contained before it came to life.

On the other hand, the Falls Fire was fought pretty much right off the bat, and it burned away from containment efforts until it moved into areas previously burned by the Red and Shoshone Fires, where it stopped because it no longer had any unburned fuel in front of it. The Mink Fire, too, was fought very soon after it started in the Bridger-Teton Wilderness, and it still moved off to the north and west, until it ran into country burned out by fires of the Snake River Complex to the north, while the portion of the fire that moved to the east continued burning until the weather changed in the fall.

The Clover-Mist Fire, in the park's northeastern quadrant, was an amalgamation of several different fires that started independently. It was allowed to burn without containment efforts for a period of ten days after it started on July 11, during which time it burned a total of a little less than 13,000 acres. After July 21, when Yellowstone officially switched strategies to a full fire-suppression mode, the Clover-Mist went on to burn somewhere around 385,000 more acres. Given the number of different starts that burned together to form the Clover-Mist, and the steep and inaccessible nature of the country where the various component fires began, it is doubtful that any effort could have been made that would have successfully contained the great fire to any significant degree.

In addition to the profusion of fire starts and the remoteness of their locations two other factors must be considered here. The first, of course, would be the unprecedented fire conditions that existed in 1988, and the second would be the nationwide nature of the drought that summer. Not only were fuels in the Yellowstone area dry and ready to burn early in the summer, with a long burning season still ahead, but many other fires burning elsewhere in the United States put exceptional demands on national firefighting resources. In making any request for firefighters or equipment in controlling its early summer fires, Yellowstone would have had to compete with other jurisdictions who were dealing with their own fires and also in need of resources.

As far as the Hellroaring Fire was concerned, it started in the Gallatin National Forest on August 15. Human-caused, it started well after all jurisdictions in the Yellowstone area had switched to full suppression mode. In spite of all efforts to fight it, the Hellroaring burned fiercely until nature cooled it off with a light fall of snow and rain on the night of September 10–11.

Which leaves the great North Fork Fire, started with one single cigarette discarded by a woodcutter in the Targhee National Forest outside Yellowstone's west boundary. As a human-caused fire, it was fought from the beginning. The response included a considerable force of people and equipment that arrived at the fire in an admirably quick response time on the very first afternoon of its existence. And through the course of the rest of the summer, more firefighters and equipment were assigned to the North Fork than to any other of the park's fires. All this, and still it couldn't be challenged until it was arrested by the same weather change that dampened all the other fires in the region in mid-September. It was, after all, "a fire one could only chase."

Here is a final point regarding the assertion that Yellowstone's managers were just a bunch of nature-loving Pollyannas who let nascent fires burn out of control until they threatened all sorts of life and property both inside and outside the park. In the case of the fires that might possibly have been contained in their early stages, such as the Fan Fire, the country they burned would very likely have been overtaken and consumed by other of the area's positively uncontrollable fires, even if the smaller fires themselves had been contained before spreading. That was definitely the case with the Fan Fire, as a finger of the North Fork Fire arrived in its locale in September, and probably would have burned most of the area burned by the Fan had the smaller fire not already done so. And the Falls Fire would probably have consumed some of the country burned by the Red and Shoshone, as the Mink Fire would have, had the Red and Shoshone Fires not beaten it to the punch. Finally, there is no doubt that the Hellroaring Fire would have burned much of the country burned by the Storm Creek, even if the latter fire had been corralled during the time that it was only smoldering and vulnerable to containment.

Regrettably I missed the North Fork's big run off the Madison Plateau and up the Gibbon River on the 15th, but I did manage to spend a lot of time combing through the aftermath of that run on the 16th and 17th. I had the same experiences walking around the burned out, eerie landscapes I had had in the country burned by the North Fork on its run of August 11, but this time I astonishingly found a garter snake in the blackened area that had somehow survived the holocaust of the day before. Snakes of any species are rather rare in most of Yellowstone, so seeing one any time outside of the strip of low elevation country around Gardiner and Mammoth is something of an event. But to see one in the ash of a very hot fire that had burned through the area just the day before was a marvel. How did the snake survive? Where had it gone when the forest all around had utterly torched? Did it take

A garter snake in the ash of the North Fork Fire, along the Gibbon River on August 16, 1988, the day after this particular area burned very hot. © Jeff Henry/Roche Jaune Pictures, Inc.

refuge in the Gibbon River when the fire came through, or in a bog, or in a burrow deep enough to be underneath the lethal heat? However the snake had managed to escape, it had come through apparently unscathed—at least I couldn't see a mark on it, and its movements and demeanor seemed normal.

Another amazing thing I saw at this time was a large black bear that had killed a smaller black bear right at Gibbon Falls. I missed the actual take down, but I did arrive at the scene just after the kill, and there I talked to two friends of mine, Steve and Marilyn French, who had witnessed the kill just minutes before. Steve and Marilyn spent a great many summers filming and photographing Yellowstone bears back in those days, and because of their dedication they quite often found themselves in the right place at the right time, as they had that day at Gibbon Falls.

As the Frenches, a few others, and I watched the larger bear dragged the carcass of the dead bear up the very steep and jagged scree slope on the other side of Gibbon Falls. I think the predatory bear was trying to move the carcass a little farther away from the watching humans, but at any rate those of us watching found it very interesting that the first body part the cannibalistic bear ate was the tongue of the dead bear. He (and I do think it was a male) reached in the mouth of the dead bear, bit off the tongue and then chewed it down. It was a primeval, surreal scene, to see a black bear munching down a member of his own species against a backdrop of a blackened trees still smoking from the passage of a huge forest fire just a day or two before.

Steve, Marilyn, and I all agreed what we were watching was unusual, although not unheard of, behavior, but we didn't necessarily think that the predatory event had to do with the fires *per se*. In fact, even though 1988 was a very poor food year

A predatory black bear dragging the carcass of a smaller black bear he had just killed up a steep scree slope by Gibbon Falls, amidst smoke from the North Fork Fire, August 1988. © Jeff Henry/Roche Jaune Pictures, Inc.

for bears, there were surprisingly few bear management incidents that summer and fall, and as far as could be determined there wasn't much alteration of bear behavior on account of the fires. Apparently most bears had the sense and ability to get out of the way, for the fires directly killed only four or five black bears, all of which died near Cooke City, Montana. The Mink Fire injured another black bear near Hawk's Rest just outside the southeastern corner of Yellowstone National park. Two radio collared grizzly bears disappeared during the holocausts, but one of those turned up several years later, and the other was never confirmed to have been killed. Its collar may simply have quit working coincidentally with the fires.

That bear behavior did not discernibly change because of the fires wasn't just my opinion. Kerry Gunther, who started working in Yellowstone in 1983 and has been in overall charge of bear management in the park since 1989, and Mark Haroldson, who has worked for the Interagency Grizzly Bear Study Team since 1984, concurred with the same opinion. Both are former coworkers of mine, and men I trust and respect. All of us agree that perhaps one of the reasons that few bear-human conflicts occurred in the autumn of 1988, a year of particularly poor food production for bears, was because the bears might have found enough carrion from fire-killed animals to carry them through the fall season. In a relative sense, not many of Yellowstone's famous animals were killed by the flames, but park employees found several hundred fire kills, and there undoubtedly must have been more that the postfire carcass surveyors never spotted.

Fire Progression August 19, 1988

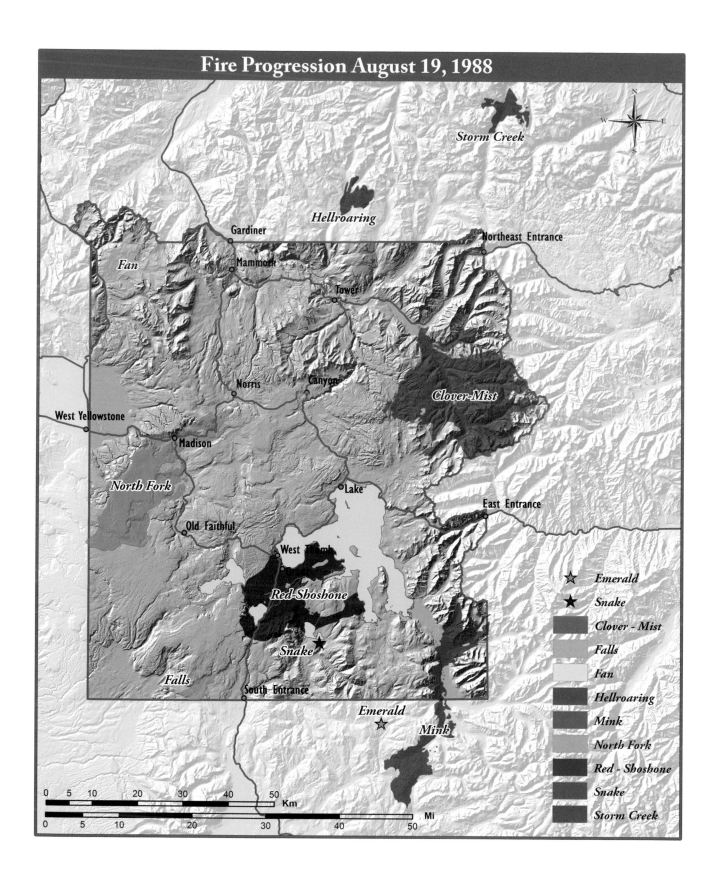

August 19, 1988

THIS AUGUST 19 map shows the rapid growth of the Hellroaring Fire, along Hellroaring Creek in the Absaroka-Beartooth Wilderness north of Yellowstone National Park. The human-caused fire started on August 15, so it was fought from its onset. In spite of all efforts to stop it, the fire burned almost 1,200 acres on the day it started, then more than 2,000 the next day, almost 5,000 more the next, and then really got serious on the 19th, when it burned another 20,000 acres in one day. As with most of the fires in Yellowstone in 1988, the Hellroaring had times when it made anomalous runs against the prevailing wind, and wound up burning south into the park on August 27. Ultimately it merged with the North Fork Fire just north of Tower Junction in the great crescendo the Yellowstone fires made during the first week of September.

Also on this date, the Storm Creek Fire rose from more than two months of somnolence and began to expand. Its growth is readily noticeable north of Yellowstone's Northeast Entrance. Growth on the Mink Fire in the park's Thorofare country is evident as well. And another new fire also started on this date just west of the Mink. It was the Emerald Fire, but it was a comparative nonevent in the overall scene in 1988. The Emerald almost certainly would have burned a lot more country than it did, had not the Mink Fire already burned out much of the fuel downwind from the Emerald's staring point.

The huge Clover-Mist Fire continued to probe up the drainages that feed into the Lamar River from the east. Most of those drainages are in line with the prevailing wind, so in many cases the fire burned very hot and fast up those streams. Originally it was hoped that the rocky divide of the Absaroka Range that marks the boundary in that area would stop the fire from moving out of the park, but as the summer progressed and fires became more intense, it became apparent that the

Grass fire burning in Gibbon Meadows near the Artist Paintpot trailhead, August 18, 1988. © Jeff Henry/ Roche Jaune Pictures, Inc.

barren crests above timberline would not pose an adequate barrier. The Clover-Mist by this time had also moved downriver on the Lamar to the river's junction with Soda Butte Creek. That positioned it perfectly to make a downwind and up-drainage run at Silver Gate and Cooke City, Montana, a possibility that greatly worried the residents of those tourist towns and park managers alike. The head of the Clover-Mist can be seen on this map just south of Yellowstone's Northeast Entrance Road and just west of the massif depicting Mount Norris.

Burning along the roads on Yellowstone's west side, the North Fork Fire continued to be the most visible of all the park fires to the average visitor. On August 16 and 17 it carried on its march up the Gibbon River past Beryl Spring and into Gibbon Meadows. The Gibbon River was named for Colonel John Gibbon, a veteran of both the Civil War and the Indian wars, and also a player in the early history of Yellowstone National Park. In 1872 Gibbon spent several days in an unsuccessful attempt to travel up the Gibbon River from Madison, probably making it no farther than Gibbon Falls. In August of 1988 the North Fork Fire didn't have nearly as much difficulty finding its way up the river as Colonel Gibbon had 116 years earlier. By August 19 the fire had made it all the way to Gibbon Meadows and had also climbed Paintpot Hill and Gibbon Hill on the east side of the Grand Loop Road. Burning over 7,000 acres on the 19th, the fire left itself poised on the edge of the Norris Geyser Basin by the morning of August 20. By the evening of the 20th it would be apparent just how loaded that word "poised" could be.

I spent a lot of time on August 18 and 19 in the area of Gibbon Meadows and Elk Park, at first waiting for the North Fork Fire to show up there, and then actually watching it arrive. I shot a lot of photos, as I always did in those days, including some of elk bedding and feeding in those meadows, apparently without concern, as large flames flared as a backdrop in the forests just behind them. I also watched as the grass and forbs in portions of Gibbon Meadows burned, in one spot taking out the boardwalk to the Artist Paintpot area. Once again, it was affecting to watch familiar places being transformed so radically right in front of my eyes.

One of many film crews attracted to Yellowstone by fire during the summer of 1988, in Gibbon Meadows, August 18, 1988. © Jeff Henry/Roche Jaune Pictures, Inc.

More and more news media were showing up in Yellowstone, as the fires assumed a larger profile in the national spotlight. I encountered a lot of news people, especially film crews, in the area around Gibbon Meadows and Elk Park during this time. I found myself a little irritated with many of the crews, impatient as they were to hurry in and capture the dramatic or the unusual and then hurry away again. They had no willingness to watch and wait, no time to contemplate the situation in order to gain an authentic feel for what was really going on.

While in Gibbon Meadows during the afternoon burning period on August 19, I ran into park geologist Rick Hutchinson and his wife Jennifer Whipple. Jennifer was and is an exceptional botanist, while Rick was a walking encyclopedia regarding Yellowstone's geothermal wonders. In early March of 1997 Rick unfortunately was killed in an avalanche near Heart Lake, a tragic blow for Jennifer and others who knew him personally, as well as an incalculable loss to Yellowstone National Park. On the 19th, Rick and Jennifer had an anemometer with them to gauge the wind speed in Gibbon Meadows. The whirligig on the wind gauge was spinning so fast it was blurred in the photo. But it wasn't necessary to look at the anemometer to know that the wind was blowing like mad, and even stronger winds were forecast for the next day, Saturday, August 20, 1988.

Yellowstone geologist Rick Hutchinson gauging wind speed with an anemometer in Gibbon Meadows on a very windy day, August 19, 1988. © Jeff Henry/ Roche Jaune Pictures, Inc.

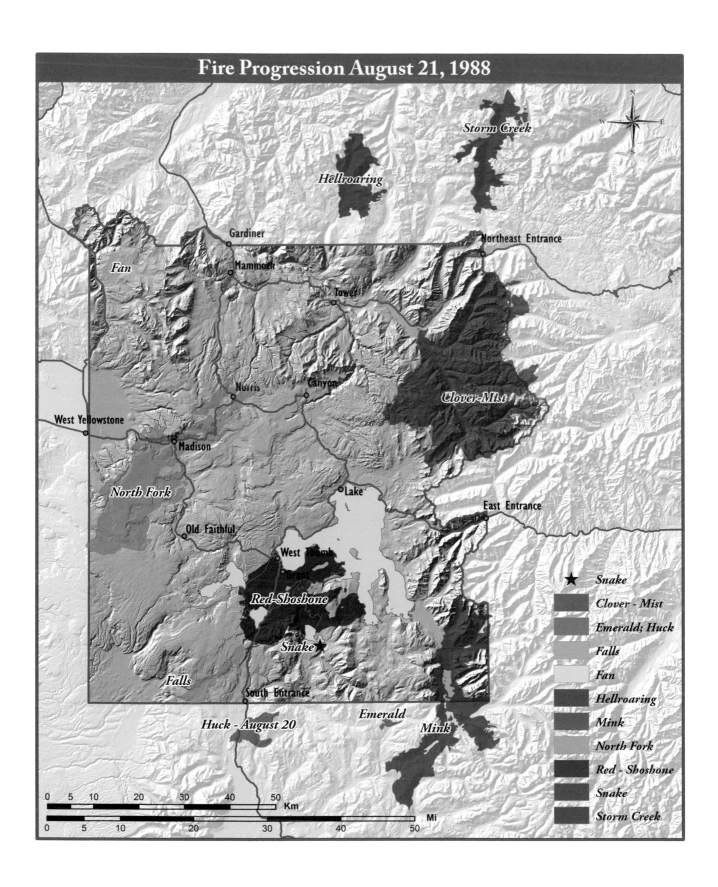

Fire Progression August 21, 1988

Storm Creek

Hellroaring

Gardiner

Northeast Entrance

Fan

Mammoth

Tower

Clover-Mist

Norris

Canyon

West Yellowstone

Madison

East Entrance

North Fork

Lake

Old Faithful

West Thumb

Grant

Red-Shoshone

Snake ★

Falls

South Entrance

Emerald

Huck - August 20

Mink

	Km
0 5 10 20 30 40 50	
0 5 10 20 30 40 50	Mi

★ Snake

Clover - Mist

Emerald; Huck

Falls

Fan

Hellroaring

Mink

North Fork

Red - Shoshone

Snake

Storm Creek

August 21, 1988

THIS WAS the day after the famous Black Saturday in Yellowstone's summer of fire, a name and an event known to even casual students of Yellowstone history. Approximately 160,000 acres burned in and around the park on just this one day. To put that figure in perspective, since the Fan Fire kicked up on July 1 as the first fire in the Yellowstone area to do so that summer, all the fires in the area collectively had burned a little over 370,000 acres—so just that one burning period increased the total burned acreage by more than 40 percent. Many noticed with a strong sense of irony that Black Saturday occurred on the exact anniversary—August 20—of the Big Blowup in 1910, which burned vast portions of northern Idaho and western Montana, annihilating several towns and killing quite a number of people along its way, and which coincidentally also was a Saturday. It is probably fair to say that no one saw fire like the Big Blowup of 1910 until there were comparable flaming displays during the summer of 1988 in Yellowstone.

This map, based on information collected on August 21, reflects the explosive growth displayed by all the major fires other than the Fan Fire, which by that time had been mostly contained and on the 20th moved only slightly to the south as it backed against the wind. The massive Clover-Mist Fire, which burned an incredible 87 square miles that day, accounted for more than one third of all the acreage burned on Black Saturday. By day's end, the perimeter of the Clover-Mist would encompass a total area of about 175,000 acres. The map also shows the start of yet another fire, this one named the Huck Fire, which exploded when a tree fell into a power line just outside Yellowstone's south boundary along the John D. Rockefeller Parkway between Yellowstone and Grand Teton National Parks. The Huck Fire, too, put on an unbelievable and dangerous spectacle as it burned across almost 10 miles of forest

Intense flames of the North Fork Fire. © Jeff Henry/Roche Jaune Pictures, Inc.

near the Snake River by Yellowstone's south boundary and claimed nearly 8,000 acres during the first few hours of its existence. The Huck Fire also posed an immediate threat to the Park Service development at Yellowstone's South Entrance and an even more dire threat to Flagg Ranch, a large tourist development about 2 miles south of the park's entrance. But more later on the dramatic events surrounding Flagg Ranch and the Huck Fire on August 20.

Very early in the morning it was apparent that August 20 was going to be a big burning day. The weather forecast called for a "red flag" warning, the most dreaded forecast possible, and as one firefighter later wrote in his diary, "the weatherman was cruelly accurate." A red flag warning forecasts critical burning conditions based on factors of drought, low humidities, high temperatures, and most of all the threat of strong winds. A red flag warning was more than appropriate for Yellowstone on August 20, 1988.

It didn't cool off that much the night before, and humidities hadn't gone up much during the night, either. That was one of the unusual characteristics of the summer of 1988—the air at night usually not only cools but also becomes more humid as temperatures fall, in a phenomenon firefighters like to call "humidity recovery." But many nights that summer provided little or no humidity recovery, and consequently there were many nights when fires continued to burn with undiminished intensity well after darkness had set in, in some cases virtually all night long.

That was the case on the night of August 19–20. There was little to no lull in the wind, either. I arose very early in the morning at Madison that day, and already the wind was blowing hard—no morning calm that morning. Everything was smoked in, to the point that it never got as light as you would expect it to get on a midsummer day. The smoke blew past with a palpable presence on one's face, like walking through a thick fog, but a fog without moisture. Lurid colors showed in the morning smoke—a mixture, I suppose, of sunrise colors filtering through from above and the glow of flames reflected from ground level. The weird light, the hard wind, and the dense smoke all combined to make a surreal scene, one heavily expectant with the sense of things to come.

Early in the morning I drove from Madison Junction to Norris, where I expected hot action later in the day. During the summer of 1988 I spent much more time with the North Fork Fire than I did with any of the park's other fires. After all, the North Fork was literally right outside the front door of my seasonal home at Madison, and it was also the most visible of Yellowstone's fires from park roads. I didn't have to arrange for helicopter or plane flights to access the fire, as I had to do with other of the park's more remote fires. Another factor was the way the North Fork had a penchant for attacking the park's developed areas. Photos of flames in proximity to Yellowstone's icons were a given for built-in drama.

At Norris I found even more of the strong wind and macabre, smoky light; everything was intensified ahead of the fire's flaming front. Firefighters and equipment wisely had been positioned around Norris Junction to protect structures near the Norris Geyser Basin, and also in the Park Service housing and utility area. Very soon after I arrived at Norris it became obvious that the fire to the south was picking up steam to make a major run, even though it was still earlier in the day than what would usually be considered the burning period. The fire was not visible, but I could hear it coming as its uncountable millions of snapping and popping sounds combined with the wind to make a deafening roar. It occurred to me that, in a way, the sound of the fire and the sound of the wind were just manifestations of the same thing, so it seemed fitting that you couldn't precisely distinguish just how much of the roar was caused by the fire and just how much was due to the wind itself.

Horizontal rivers of smoke began to pour out of the fire as it blew toward us. I looked back down the road I had just driven from Madison, and intense flames were already flaring in the forest along both sides of the corridor. The smoke and fire made a sort of tunnel above the pavement, with air in the tunnel so searingly hot that it glowed orange. The effect was like looking into the orifice of a gigantic boiler and being appalled by the intensity of the heat within.

I left the crossroads at Norris and moved over to the geyser basin. With firefighters striving to protect the Norris Museum and other structures, I thought the

A firefighter spraying water onto the advancing flames of the North Fork Fire, in front of the museum at Norris on Black Saturday, August 20, 1988. © Jeff Henry/Roche Jaune Pictures, Inc.

chances for good photos were better there. I also thought that if things really got out of hand, the barren geothermal expanses of the geyser basins would offer a refuge from the flames.

Sure enough, firefighters were hosing down the Norris Museum, and also spraying water into the surrounding forest to slow down the fire's approach. I also found Larry Mayer and Bob Ekey of *The Billings Gazette* in the area of the geyser basin. Larry was the longtime lead photographer of the *Gazette*, while Bob was a reporter the same newspaper had assigned to cover the Yellowstone area. I knew and liked both men, and also knew that they did outstanding work. In fact the coverage of the Yellowstone fires provided by Larry Mayer, Bob Ekey, and others of the *Gazette* would later be considered for a Pulitzer Prize. Isolated by the fire as we all were, the two men attached themselves to me for much of the rest of the day.

Together we watched the unstoppable fire blow into the geyser basin south of the museum. It was as though the very air itself was on fire—isolated bits of fuel on the geyserite plains, things like a geothermally killed bush or an upturned stump, just widely separated bits and pieces of organic matter—and would burst into spontaneous combustion. A heavier stand of lodgepole timber stood near the historic museum, and when the fire reached there it quickly climbed into the tree tops and proceeded as a classic crown fire. A firefighter with a large hose and nozzle made a stand at the rail fence in front of the museum, and knocked the fire down with a surprisingly small amount of water. The museum and all the other structures at Norris were saved.

My friend Mike Bader was also present in the area of the Norris Museum. Mike was a ranger at Canyon that summer and had been assigned to the Norris area that day. Mike joined two newspapermen and me. All of us shot a lot of photos of each other and of the fire, and without ever saying anything specific, we also looked out for one another. It was an informal arrangement that worked well—no one in our group had anything approaching a close call that day.

Pockets of flame burning isolated bits of organic matter in the Norris Geyser Basin on Black Saturday, August 20, 1988. Conditions were so dry and the wind so strong that blowing sparks and embers were able to find and ignite separated pockets of fuel. © Jeff Henry/Roche Jaune Pictures, Inc.

Later in the day, after the main fire front had passed on to the north and east of Norris, Mike and I were assigned to escort a Wells Fargo armored car through the recently burned stretch of roadway to the south, on the truck's route to Old Faithful. Yes, in spite of the fire emergency Yellowstone's retail outlets were still open and their revenues had to be collected by the armored car and trucked out of the park. It seemed that the armored car had been stopped for some time at one or another of the various roadblocks in the park, waiting for fires to clear and for at least limited travel to resume. Now the driver and the guard had made it as far as Norris, where they were stopped once again.

Somehow powers higher up the chain of command in the park service bureaucracy selected Mike Bader and me to escort the armored car through the fire zone south of Norris, the same stretch of road I had seen glowing with heat a few hours before. Mike and I smirked at each other, both of us amused by the park service's arrogant belief that anyone who donned the green and gray immediately became more capable than anyone who wasn't wearing the uniform. Mike was also a bit resentful of the way the park was making a special effort to accommodate commercial activities. The commercial aspect didn't bother me much—I mostly thought that the Wells Fargo driver was probably just as capable of driving through the fire zone without Mike and me looking over his shoulder as he would have been without us riding along in his truck, the park service's exclusionary sentiment to the contrary. Judging by the smirk on Mike's face, I think he felt the same way.

As Mike Bader and I and many others can testify, the North Fork Fire erupted spectacularly around the Norris Geyser Basin on August 20, but the biggest show of Black Saturday took place in Yellowstone's northeastern quadrant. In that district the Hellroaring and Storm Creek Fires made big runs on Black Saturday, but the

principal performer was the huge Clover-Mist, which by itself burned nearly 56,000 acres on just that one day.

The northeastern part of Yellowstone, the area including Lamar River and the spectacular Absaroka Mountain Range, was one of the quietest sections of the park. This was especially true in the days before wolves were reintroduced to the ecosystem in 1995 and 1996, after which visitation in the Lamar area greatly increased with an influx of avid wolf watchers. In 1988 the area was still lightly visited by Yellowstone tourists and, other than Roosevelt Lodge near Tower Junction, there were no large developed locations with lodges or hotels. As a result, rangers working in the district didn't have as many of the problems attendant with large numbers of visitors and employees as had occupied most of the time of rangers elsewhere in Yellowstone. Instead rangers in the northeast focused more on the backcountry, and spent a great deal of time doing classic ranger work in front of breathtaking backdrops. Backcountry patrol on horseback in the summer and ski patrol on cross country skis in the winter were more the order of business for rangers in the northeast.

Rangers who were in many ways throwbacks to an earlier era worked in the northeast, with the roster including Joe Fowler, Randy King, Richard Jones, Brian Helms, Dan Krapf, Mike Robinson, and others. With few developed locations in their sector, these rangers placed much of their focus on protecting their backcountry cabins during the 1988 fires.

The first cabin threatened by the Clover-Mist was, of course, the one at Calfee Creek, where Chief Ranger Dan Sholly and some members of Yellowstone's Fire Cache saved the cabin with a last minute effort. But they were burned over in the process, surviving the Clover-Mist's fury by huddling in their fire shelters.

After the close call experienced by Sholly and the helitack people at Calfee Creek, Joe Fowler and his rangers more proactively defended their other patrol cabins. They followed the classic formula of first removing as much fuel as possible from the immediate vicinity of the structures—moving firewood away from the cabins,

A pair of images painted by artist and park ranger Dan Krapf of his impressions of the fires of 1988. © Dan Krapf

felling dead trees, trimming low hanging limbs from other standing trees, things like that. They also installed pumps with hoses and sprinklers by their cabins, taking advantage of the fact that almost all backcountry cabins were not surprisingly located near reliable sources of water. In most cases, a ranger or rangers would stay at a cabin until just before the fire arrived, start the pumps and sprinklers spraying on the cabin, and then get away from the area as soon thereafter as possible.

Many great anecdotes came out of their efforts: stories about how pumps were ruined by the intense heat of the fires, how hoses were burned into segments, and the like. But in all cases their efforts succeeded, as all cabins in their area were saved. The same couldn't be said for patrol cabins elsewhere in the park, where in the rush and confusion surrounding the fast-changing fire emergencies, some cabins were forgotten and left unprotected. For example, the Sportsman Lake Cabin near Electric Peak was one such cabin that was overlooked, and it burned to the ground; and the cabin at Cougar Creek near the park's west boundary lost its outhouse.

Action started early on August 20 in the park's northeast, as it did everywhere in Yellowstone on Black Saturday. By 9:00 a.m. the Hellroaring Fire had put up a smoke column some estimated to be 30,000 feet high. An enormous pyrocumulus cloud of course capped the column, as the Hellroaring burned 20,000 acres in the one burning period. This fire moved predominantly in a northeasterly direction, in accordance with the area's prevailing winds. Its movement on August 20 took it mostly away from Yellowstone National Park, as it burned into the upper reaches of the Hellroaring Creek drainage north of the park. Burning out the Hellroaring country as it did, the Hellroaring Fire greatly altered the appearance of one of the most popular big-game hunting districts in the entire Yellowstone region.

On the second day of its resurgence after two months of dormancy, the Storm Creek burned more than 23,500 acres. Somehow this fire's predominant movement was to the *south*, even though it was situated in a parallel stream drainage less than 20 miles east of Hellroaring. Even the most veteran of firefighters were stumped by this phenomenon. One explanation that was suggested for the Storm Creek's anomalous southward movement was that the enormous updraft created by the Clover-Mist Fire to the south was drawing the Storm Creek in toward itself. Whatever the cause, the Storm Creek's southward movement brought it closer to the park's Northeast Entrance, and to the small towns of Silver Gate and Cooke City just outside the gate. Not only was the Storm Creek geographically closer, but the head of the fire was also moving to a position more in line with the normal southwesterly winds, winds that very believably could take the fire right to those vulnerable communities.

The Storm Creek wasn't the only fire menacing Silver Gate and Cooke City. The runs the Clover-Mist made on Black Saturday carried it many miles to the north and east, leaving it much closer to the timbered tourist towns. The huge fire had also spilled out of the park and onto national forest land to the east, a development fire managers had been fearing for weeks. Another finger of the Clover-Mist Fire had made it as far as the eastern slopes of Mount Norris, putting it near the junction of Lamar River and Soda Butte Creek. From there the fire was positioned downwind from the Northeast Entrance and the two Montana tourist towns, and it also was in a position to funnel up Soda Butte Creek itself, the valley of which becomes progressively narrower and steeper toward its upper reaches closer to the towns. The steep and narrow aspect of the upper canyon, it was feared, could act as a nozzle and direct the fire with blow torch intensity at all the developments around and outside Yellowstone's Northeast Entrance.

Another finger of the Clover-Mist Fire had roared with unimaginable speed and fury up Cache Creek, the next drainage to the south of Soda Butte Creek. Cache Creek suffered an almost total burnout, and the fire behavior there served as an example of what could happen if the Clover-Mist made a similar run up Soda Butte Creek. As it was, the run up Cache Creek had carried the fire all the way up to the crest of the Absaroka Range on the park line, where it threatened to cross out of the park via Republic Pass. If the fire managed to escape containment efforts at the top of the pass and continued on to the northeast, it would have more or less a straight shot at Cooke City, down the valley of Republic Creek.

To the south of Republic Creek, the fire actually did pass out of Yellowstone on the 20th, as a long finger of flame raced down the valley of Pilot Creek, just south of the iconic landmarks of Pilot and Index Peaks along the valley of the upper Clark's Fork of the Yellowstone River. And two other masses of fire escaped from Yellowstone to the south of Republic Pass on Black Saturday. One was centered around the upper reaches of the North Fork of Crandall Creek, and the other, south of that around Indian Peak in the North Absaroka Wilderness of the Shoshone National Forest. Both of these latter bodies of fire quickly established themselves to be a considerable size after they crossed the rocky divide marking the boundary between Yellowstone National Park and the Shoshone National Forest.

These tentacles of flame reaching north and east from the main body of the Clover-Mist threatened to extend further and bracket the Cooke City area in gigantic pincers of fire. When the southward movement of the Storm Creek Fire was taken into account, it appeared that the area might be encircled by a ring of fire that might then meet in the middle in a flaming denouement. By the evening of Black Saturday, things did not look good for Silver Gate and Cooke City, nor did they look any better for the National Park Service development at the Yellowstone's Northeast Entrance.

Over 50 airline miles to the southwest of the Northeast Entrance, Grant Village was once again threatened by the Red-Shoshone Fire. As the winds of Black Saturday roared at speeds estimated as up to 70 miles per hour, ominous clouds and columns of smoke rose in several directions from Grant. The winds were not only powerful, they were also turbulent, so there was no way to know which way the flames at the base of the columns were going to move. The lakeside development was evacuated for the second time in the summer of 1988, this time for the rest of the season. Doug Ridley, who at the time was the subdistrict ranger in charge of the Grant Village area, was warned over the radio about how dire the outlook was becoming for Grant, and was directed to marshal his resources to protect the location. But Grant had been stripped of most of its firefighting equipment and personnel after the first fire threat had passed in late July. Doug found himself left in an imaginary conversation with a listener who wasn't there, rhetorically asking, "Protect it with what?" Fortunately for Ridley and the structures he had been charged to defend, none of the cells burning in the area made it all the way to the complex that day, and Grant Village lived on.

My friend Diane Papineau worked at Grant Village that summer for TW Services, Yellowstone, the park concessioner with the privilege of providing lodging, restaurant, and other services in 1988. Diane had been evacuated along with everyone else when the Grant complex was threatened by fire the first time, and now she had to evacuate again. The difference was that the first time she had advance notice, and had had time to pack her possessions in an orderly fashion. On August 20 Diane and everyone else had to get out in a hurry, and so had to leave most of their belongings behind. Marti Tobias, Diane's supervisor, also put her in charge of evacuating a visitor who had become separated from her tour group, so Diane had to manage not only herself and her own concerns, but also had to help a stranger escape from the Grant area. Reuniting a large number of tourists with the belongings they left in Grant's lodging units when they departed the complex to tour the park earlier that Saturday morning became a further complication for Diane and some of her fellow TW Services employees. Those visitors couldn't return to pick up their things during the fire emergency of Black Saturday, of course, so it fell to Diane and some others to return to Grant at a later time and retrieve the missing items belonging to the tourists. The items then had to be hauled to Lake where the wayward tourists had been asked to assemble, and there everyone got their possessions back. According to Diane the transfer was successful and all the belongings were restored to their proper owners, except for one bottle of Scotch that somehow went missing somewhere along the way.

On a more serious note, the predicament faced by the Grant Village tourists on Black Saturday when they were separated from their hotel rooms and their belongings is illustrative of the uncountable hardships suffered by park visitors and employees alike through many weeks of the summer of 1988. Abrupt fire movements that led to road closures cut off many people from their hotel rooms or, in the case of employees, from their seasonal quarters. In some cases, people had to drive great distances on roads describing wide outside loops around the perimeter of Yellowstone to access an open route that would allow them to return to where they wanted to be. In other cases, people had to rent additional rooms at other locations in the park, or in one of the park's gateway communities, and simply wait until the road they needed to travel reopened after a fire had passed and burning debris had been cleared out of the way. To say the least, there were difficult challenges for park visitors, and for the park employees who tried to assist them while simultaneously dealing with their own fire-related problems.

Park rangers Bob Duff and Les Brunton mopping up by stomping out hot embers, in the wake of the North Fork Fire along the Madison River Valley, August 1988. © Jeff Henry/ Roche Jaune Pictures, Inc.

While all these actions were going on elsewhere in the Yellowstone area, a new fire started just outside Yellowstone's South Entrance. It was the Huck Fire, named for nearby Huckleberry Mountain, and it started when a tree blew into a power line along the John D. Rockefeller Parkway in front of Black Saturday's gale force winds. Almost all the other fires in Yellowstone made breathtaking runs on August 20, there's no doubt about that, but it's also true that all the other fires already existed when the day began. The Huck Fire, however, started from nothing and then burned nearly 8,000 acres in a 10-mile run during its first few hours. For outright drama involving a spectacular fire run in an unexpected place that immediately posed a severe threat to many lives and much property, the Huck Fire stole the show on Black Saturday.

The Huck Fire started about 4 miles south of Yellowstone's South Entrance, which put it about 2 miles south of Flagg Ranch, a resort complex. Named for an early-day army officer who had been stationed in the area in the late nineteenth century, it is situated along the highway between Yellowstone and Grand Teton national parks just north of where the highway crosses the Snake River. In 1988 Flagg Ranch had a fuel station, a large registration building, several large lodging buildings, and a great many employee cabins and utility buildings. On August 20 it was fully open for business, with many travelers on hand and a full complement of more than 120 employees.

It just so happened that a helicopter with a water bucket was parked at a helibase near Flagg Ranch when the Huck Fire flared to life. The helibase had been set up earlier as part of the effort to fight other fires already burning in the southern reaches of Yellowstone. The helicopter pilot, whose name was Ken Johnson, saw what was happening and attacked the fire almost as soon as it started. Dipping water out of the nearby Snake River and dropping it on the fire as fast as he could fly back and forth made no difference—the fire ran off to the northeast in mockery of Johnson's efforts.

Burning conditions on Black Saturday were off the charts, with fuel moistures at nearly unprecedented lows, humidity almost nonexistent, and temperatures and winds frighteningly high. Nothing Johnson did seemed even to slow the fire's explosive growth, and in no time it had jumped across the Rockefeller Parkway and was on its way toward Flagg Ranch and Yellowstone National Park. So violent and rapid was the fire's spread in the severe winds of August 20 that later when a coworker and I discussed what we might have done had we found ourselves out in front of it, my coworker finalized our discussion by saying, " "You'd have had to shag-ass to outrun it," implying that there probably was no way a person on foot in the forest could have escaped it.

As Ken Johnson watched in dismay from his vantage point aloft, he saw tourists on the parkway drive through forest that was flaming along both sides of the road. Flames were leaping across the road above the cars, just exploding all around, and he couldn't believe people were foolish enough to drive through such an inferno. From their point of view, the tourists were probably confused and didn't know what else to do, but in any event Johnson had enough situational awareness to set his helicopter down in the road and block traffic to keep any more people from driving into the fire zone. By doing so, he may very well have saved lives. As with many other fire situations in Yellowstone that summer all it would have taken was two trees falling across the road, one ahead of a line of traffic and one behind, and tragedy would have ensued. That no one was killed by the 1988 fires in Yellowstone, not a single tourist and not a single firefighter, was nothing short of miraculous. Two firefighters were killed outside the park during the mopping-up period in the autumn, one by a falling snag and another in an aircraft accident, but no one died during the time the big fires were rampaging, either in the park or in the surrounding area.

It was about 1:30 in the afternoon when the tree blew into the power line south of Flagg Ranch. In 1988 Dawn Inafuku was working as the manager of the gift shop at Flagg Ranch, her third year in that job. Dawn was a longtime Yellowstone employee and resident who had married another such person, park ranger Les Ina-fuku. Like me, Dawn remembers having a premonition early in the blustery morning of August 20, that something untoward was lurking out there in the smoky air.

In 1988 Les and Dawn lived at Yellowstone's South Entrance, although by Black Saturday Les had been gone from home for about a month while detailed to fire duty elsewhere. Dawn was shuffling inventory in a storage cabin in the early afternoon when a clerk in the gift shop called her on the in-house walkie-talkie that Flagg employees used to communicate within the immediate area of the resort. "We have fire," the clerk said. "What do you mean 'we have fire?'" Dawn answered, thinking at the time that the clerk might mean there was a structural fire somewhere in the resort. But she could get no further clarification from the clerk, who repeatedly insisted in a panicked voice that Dawn return to the gift shop as fast as she could. By the time Dawn got back to the area of the gift shop, in the front of the complex where she could see to the south, the fire "was right in our faces."

Many people and vehicles milled about in the parking lot by Flagg's fuel sta-tion. No one knew what to do and a wall of flame was fast approaching from the south—escape in that direction out of the question. By this time in the afternoon,

The fearsome mass of smoke rising from the Huck Fire behind RVs and other traffic at Flagg Ranch on the afternoon of Black Saturday, August 20, 1988. Except for the Grassy Lake Road, a dirt road that was little more than a track running 50 miles through the forest to eastern Idaho, visitors and employees were trapped at the resort by the Huck Fire burning just to the south and the Red Fire burning to the north along Yellowstone's South Entrance road. Most people caught at Flagg by the unexpected appearance of the Huck Fire were able to evacuate over the Grassy Lake Road, while by the grace of circumstances the fire veered off to the east and spared the resort, as well as the National Park Service development at South Entrance. © Dawn Inafuku

the road north into Yellowstone had also become impassable because the Red Fire was burning along that road in the area of the Lewis River Canyon. And all but one of the park rangers stationed at Yellowstone's South Entrance were away on other duties, and they couldn't get back to South Entrance and Flagg Ranch because fire had cut off road access.

It was fortunate, however, that there was at least that one ranger present. His name was Nick Herring, and it was Nick who began to make order out of chaos at Flagg Ranch. He circulated through the panicked confusion, trying to get people into their cars and trying to calm jumpy drivers. He next formed up a convoy, which was then evacuated over the Grassy Lake Road west to Ashton, Idaho. So hasty was the departure that most of the Flagg Ranch employees abandoned most of their personal belongings at the resort. According to Dawn Inafuku, many of the employees never returned, and their property went unclaimed. As for the tourists: they had to be experiencing the most unforgettable vacation of their lives.

Thanks to Nick Herring's organizational effort, Flagg Ranch was evacuated, but the evacuees weren't completely out of the woods when they got away from the immediate area of the Huck Fire. There were a great many vehicles in the evacuating convoy, including many large recreational vehicles, and there were also a great many jittery drivers. The Grassy Lake Road is dirt, in some places quite rough and rocky, and only one and a half lanes wide, and it is nigh 50 miles to Ashton. Because of smoke, visibility was an issue, and the Falls Fire had already burned along the

Another photo by longtime Yellowstone employee Dawn Inafuku, this one showing the Huck Fire as it burned up the east side of the Snake River, away from Flagg Ranch and South Entrance. In keeping with the sense of dread she had felt earlier in the day, a macabre face formed by the smoke in Dawn's picture glowers down at Flagg Ranch. © Dawn Inafuku

Grassy Lake Road earlier in the summer. One driver did panic and hit the accelerator when she should have hit the brake, and smashed into a motorcyclist ahead of her in the line of vehicles. Fortunately the motorcyclist's injuries were not major, and the convoy made it all the way to Ashton.

Dawn Inafuku, meanwhile, had left Flagg Ranch and returned the 2 miles north to her home at Yellowstone's South Gate. There she made a quick pass through her house, trying to decide what to pack and haul away—provided, of course, that there would be an open escape route. "Nothing jumped out" at her in the house, however, so she went outside and began hosing down the side of the duplex structure where she and her husband Les lived. Cindy Mernin was simultaneously hosing down the other half of the duplex where she lived with her husband, longtime Yellowstone ranger Jerry Mernin. Both women were dismayed by the low level of water pressure in the garden hoses they were wielding, which was inadequate to reach the eaves of their duplex.

Cindy took time out from wetting down structures around South Entrance to go and fetch park service horses from the barn in the back of the complex. She wanted to tie them close to the house, where she and Dawn were, so they could be released in a quick flick when the fire arrived. Perhaps the horses could run off and have a chance at survival. Cindy actually had observed the very start of the Huck

Fire, when it flashed up while she was talking on the phone in her house. To Cindy, "It looked like a fuel truck explosion," so fast did the fire expand from its beginning. She also heard radio chatter about the tourists who were driving into the fire zone south of Flagg Ranch, and as a professional nurse dreaded the possibility of pulling charred bodies from burned out vehicles. Fortunately, neither Cindy nor anyone else had to face that gruesome duty.

And fortunate, too, was the fact that the Huck Fire unexpectedly veered away from both Flagg Ranch and South Entrance. It blew up the other side of the Snake River from both complexes and no property burned and no people were killed. As pretty much the only ones present at South Gate, Dawn and Cindy, separated from the fire and their homes by just a few hundred yards of the Snake River and its riparian bottom land, had a spectacular if terrifying view of the fire as it burned up the east side of the river. Both women were astonished at how the fire kept burning as "a rolling crown fire," to borrow Cindy Mernin's description, well into the night and a long way up the Snake River.

I remember the radio exchanges I overheard from those involved at the South Entrance when the Huck Fire first started. It was obvious to them and to anyone listening to their transmissions on the park radio what a menace the fire immediately presented. The rest of us around the park had our hands more than full with what was going on right in front of us, but I remember a tangible pause as everyone's attention was diverted to the critical situation at Flagg Ranch and South Entrance. There was a furious fire burning right next to two developed complexes, with a lot of people present and no defense in place.

The radio transmission I remember most clearly was from the South Entrance ranger Nick Herring, who in addition to forming the evacuation convoy at Flagg Ranch was the same coworker who came up with the "shag-ass" conclusion during our conversation about how fast the Huck Fire spread. In a clear and calm voice Nick came over the radio and said, "At this point there is nothing we can do to save Flagg Ranch, and it's not too early to start thinking about what we can do to save South Entrance."

For me, Nick's composed radio transmission summed up a lot—that in spite of everything, in spite of all the chaos and stress and smoke and exhaustion and all the rest, almost everyone in Yellowstone did an exemplary job in the summer of 1988. And that includes every individual, from all the park managers and fire managers, to all the grunts swinging Pulaskis and shovels and running chainsaws. And a tip of the cap also should be made to all the support workers who fed and transported and otherwise aided the firefighters in the field. In addition, a tip of the cap must be made to all the concession workers who did their part to help beleaguered park visitors, and who made very big contributions to help save many of Yellowstone's historic structures. Finally, another acknowledgment has to be made to all the interpretive rangers who tried to help the visiting public understand the nature of what was going on. And so on, to all who were involved in that historic summer. Everyone did very well under very trying and sometimes dangerous circumstances.

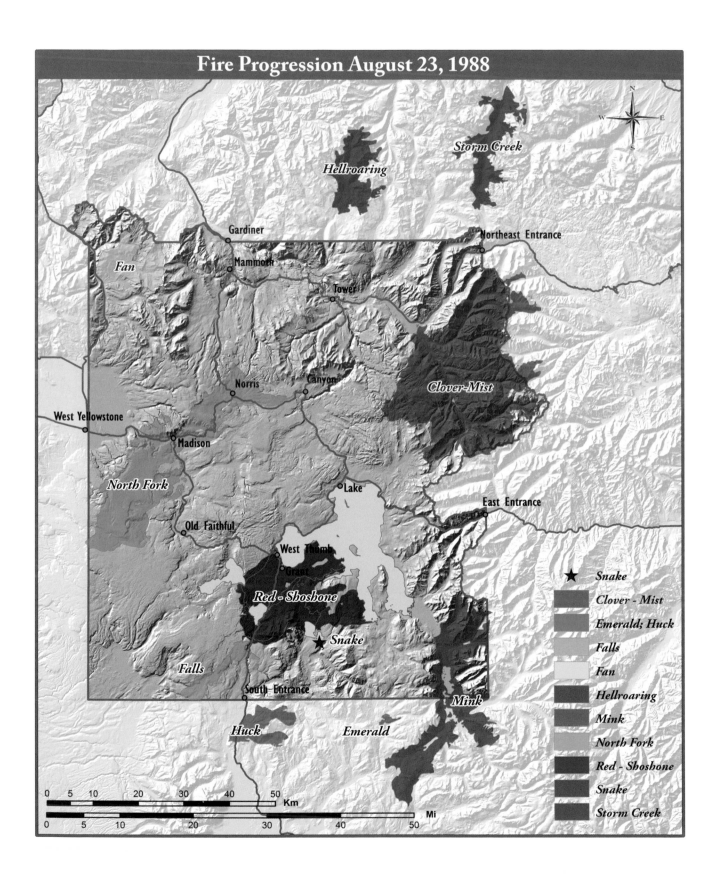

Fire Progression August 23, 1988

Hellroaring

Storm Creek

Fan

Gardiner

Northeast Entrance

Mammoth

Tower

Clover-Mist

Norris

Canyon

West Yellowstone

Madison

North Fork

Lake

East Entrance

Old Faithful

West Thumb

Grant

Red - Shoshone

Snake

Falls

Mink

South Entrance

Huck

Emerald

★ Snake

Clover - Mist

Emerald; Huck

Falls

Fan

Hellroaring

Mink

North Fork

Red - Shoshone

Snake

Storm Creek

0 5 10   20   30   40   50 Km

0 5 10   20   30   40   50 Mi

August 23, 1988

ON THIS MAP from August 23, notice the continued spread of the Clover-Mist Fire outside the boundaries of Yellowstone National Park. The bulge of flame marking where the fire had exited the park on the North Fork of Crandall Creek has lengthened into something of a finger as the fire continued its spread down the creek. Eventually the fire would blow out of the Absarokas and into lower Crandall/Sunlight area, where among other things, it forced evacuation of the massive Crandall fire camp.

Notice how the Clover-Mist had been confined along its northwestern shoulder, along the dividing ridge between Cache Creek and Soda Butte Creek. Much of that ridge is high and rocky, above timberline and largely depauperate of fuel. That was part of the reason that the portion of the Clover-Mist that torched Cache Creek on the 20th didn't cross the ridge into the Soda Butte drainage. But another big factor was a heroic effort made on the ridge by some of Yellowstone National Park's own firefighters, people like Phil Perkins, who in 1988 was in charge of the park's Fire Cache.

This particular crew of Yellowstone firefighters had struggled all day against the flames of Black Saturday, and then had made an epic climb in the dark up the steep slopes of the mountain known as The Thunderer. In the darkness, at the end of their climb, they immediately went back to work fighting not only the flames of the Clover-Mist, but also their own exhaustion. They scratched a line that held, although they had to put out a great number of spot fires that started around them. On the rare times when the smoke cleared from the lofty ridge where they worked near the top of The Thunderer, the crew had a view beyond belief of the surrounding

This is a shot of the forest that blew down just east of Norris Junction as a result of a freak windstorm, possibly a tornado, in the summer of 1984. This photo was shot the day after the trees blew down. © Jeff Henry/Roche Jaune Pictures, Inc.

This photo was shot by District Ranger John Lounsbury shortly after the North Fork/Wolf Lake Fire first established a foothold in the Norris Blowdown. A little flame is visible at the base of the smoke column, and the black smoke in the column indicates that resinous pine needles were burning when the photo was shot. © John Lounsbury

In this photo the beachhead of fire shown in the previous picture has exploded into a wall of flame. © John Lounsbury

country. In almost all directions the vastness below them was aflame, as though they were on an island in an ocean of fire.

The North Fork Fire also showed continued growth, especially in an eastward direction along the Norris-Canyon Road. The North Fork evidently had consolidated its gains south of Norris Junction, an area originally overrun on Black Saturday. The fire also showed signs of a developing finger pointing to the north, not far east of the Norris-Mammoth road. After the huge blowup of Black Saturday, firefighters on the North Fork worked to mop up hotspots in the Norris area, and also continued their efforts to build line along the fire's flanks. In addition, they continued to hope that the weather would give them the break they needed to line off the front of the fire.

Of course the weather did not offer that chance until more than three more weeks had passed. Rather than taking a breather that might have allowed firefighters a chance to put in meaningful fireline, the North Fork actually burned over 10,000 acres on August 22, not much less than the 12,500 it burned on Black Saturday. This was something of a disappointment, because the fire hadn't moved much on the 21st, when humidities were still low but winds had subsided, and fire management

The aftermath of the firestorm in the Norris Blowdown, showing blackened logs and a small twister of ash blowing in the wind in the distance. This photo was taken a few days after the area burned. © Jeff Henry/Roche Jaune Pictures, Inc.

officer Dave Poncin, Sr., optimistically wrote in his diary that "crews . . . were coming within striking distance of turning the corner on the head of the fire."

As it moved east toward Canyon, the North Fork Fire closed in on an area of forest near Virginia Cascades that had blown down in a violent windstorm in July 1984. That storm, which may have been a tornado, uprooted or snapped off virtually all the large trees over a considerable stretch. Then the crisscrossed logs had lain there, drying in freely circulating air for four years. When the North Fork finally did advance to the area of the fallen logs, which was often referred to as the Norris Blowdown, it burned with unusual intensity. Naturally, the media focused on the aftermath of the unusually hot burn in the Norris Blowdown. From their point of view, the blowdown with its many upturned root masses, snapped off tree trunks, and blackened, horizontal logs made for dramatic photographs or film footage. For many in the park service, however, photos taken in the blowdown area amounted to an unfair representation of the postfire Yellowstone, a visual depiction of the media's assertion that Yellowstone had been rendered down to a charred wasteland.

My friend Mike Bader was fortunate enough to be in the right place at the right time to actually see a falling ember—Mike thinks it was a burning pine cone—light in the west end of the Norris Blowdown and ignite the jackpot of fuel. This was after

Ranger Bob Duff clad in Nomex, with his face showing the strain of the summer of 1988. © Jeff Henry/Roche Jaune Pictures, Inc.

four years of saying to himself, and hearing others say out loud, "This sucker is really going to burn someday." Well, it really did burn someday, that day being August 22, 1988. On a day with little ambient wind, Mike saw the fire become so fierce that it generated enough of its own circulation to break off standing green trees around the perimeter of the blown down area.

By August 23 the North Fork Fire had consumed nearly 100,000 acres, and its head was flaring out in what appeared to be a developing two-pronged advance, one heading toward Canyon and the other toward Mammoth. Moreover, the fire camp for the North Fork was located in the Madison Campground, so as the fire burned north and east, it was moving farther and farther away from the base camp of the crews who were trying to control it. Dave Poncin, Sr., the incident commander on the fire, had already figuratively stated that his firefighters and he were so overwhelmed by the North Fork that all they could do was chase it. Now that statement was becoming geographically true as well.

In response to the fire's size and the logistical challenges facing those who were fighting it, a decision to administratively divide the fire was made over the course of several days after Black Saturday. The eastern portion of the huge fire, that which was posing a growing menace to the developments around the Grand Canyon of the Yellowstone River, would be named the Wolf Lake Fire. Most obviously, the eastern fork of the blaze was named for a real place with the same name, a beautiful little lake northwest of Canyon at the foot of the Washburn Mountain Range. But

Fire-darkened conditions along the Canyon-Norris road in late August of 1988, with firefighting vehicles driving down the road with their lights on and a helicopter carrying a water bucket flying overhead. © Jeff Henry/Roche Jaune Pictures, Inc.

given the fact that there are many other natural features in the area that would have provided a suitable name for the fire, and also given the fact that Yellowstone in those years was working toward reintroducing wolves to the park, one has to wonder whether there was an ulterior motive to selecting the name Wolf Lake over all the other possibilities.

Regardless of how the name was selected, the Wolf Lake Fire was assigned its own Type I management team and other resources. Yet another fire camp was set up at Canyon, too, in the commercial campground usually occupied by vacationers. Up to 1,000 yellow-shirted firefighters would be based there, obviously well positioned to keep the Wolf Lake Fire from devouring Canyon Village.

In the northeastern sector, the Clover-Mist Fire continued to grow and to threaten Cooke City and Silver Gate, as well as settlements in Sunlight Basin and around Crandall Creek in Wyoming. A Yellowstone fire crew led by ranger Bob Mahn, then stationed at the park's East Entrance, was dispatched to help with halting the Clover-Mist's spread toward the Wyoming settlement. The crew included my good friend Bob Duff, then a park ranger at Madison Junction. Duff and the others in the crew were assigned to work in the valley of Pilot Creek, down which the fire was rapidly spreading.

It seemed that at one juncture Bob and two other ground pounders were out with another firefighter who was slightly higher up the firefighter hierarchy, and who had been assigned to supervise Bob and the others. The four came to a small tributary running into Pilot Creek, from where they had a good view of the Clover-Mist raging not that far upstream along Pilot Creek itself. The supervisor of the little group announced to the others, "OK. We're going to make a stand right here," indicating the rivulet at their feet with an elongated sweep of his hand as he spoke. My friend Bob looked at the man who had just spoken, looked up at the advancing wall of flame, and then looked at the tiny stream at their feet. Bob considered how he and the others had only a few simple tools with them, just a shovel and a couple of Pulaskis, a backpack pump, and not much more. He turned back to the supervisor and with a good natured smile on his face said, "F—— you, man. I ain't doin' it," whereupon the supervisor blew up and pointed out to Bob that he was the supervisor and the others had to do as he said.

When the man finished his harangue, Bob simply smiled again and repeated, "F—— you, man. I ain't doin' it," which led to an even bigger blowup from the supervisor. This sort of exchange went on for several more salvos, but Bob was resolute and at the conclusion of every tirade from his supervisor, tirades that became ever more vehement, his only reply was the same one he had started with. Fortunately for Bob, the supervisor, and the others, they did not make a stand at the rivulet. Instead, they retreated and survived.

As I wrote earlier, it was a miracle that no one was killed during Yellowstone's great fires in 1988.

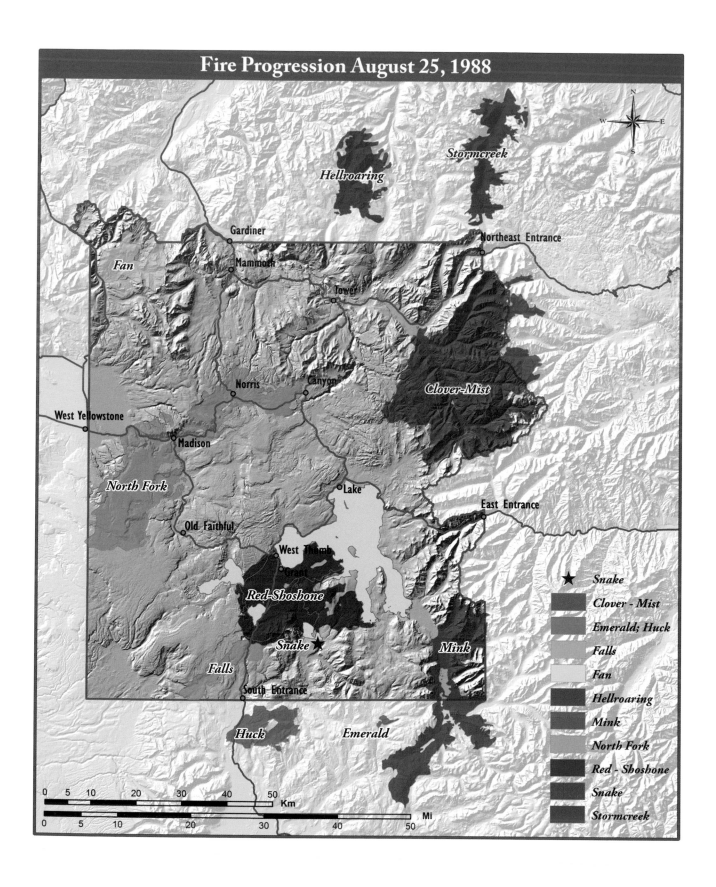

Fire Progression August 25, 1988

August 25, 1988

BY NOW the Yellowstone fires had gained such momentum that there were no more light burning days, even when weather conditions were less than optimum for fire spread. Between Black Saturday on August 20 and the season ending event of September 11, the lowest daily total for newly burned acreage was over 8,000, while the daily *average* was over 61,000 acres. That's an average of over 61,000 acres, or almost 100 *square miles*, burned each day for seventeen days.

This map shows the steady growth of nearly all the major fires in the park and in the surrounding area. The Clover-Mist's growth is marked, as it continued its move to the east toward Sunlight Basin and the settlements around lower Crandall Creek. The Clover-Mist's advance into that part of Wyoming drew the focus of that state's congressional delegation, who in turn put a great deal of pressure on the government agencies involved in trying to stop the fire. The upshot was that a lot of equipment and a great many firefighters were assigned to the Sunlight-Crandall area, amounting to an unfairly disproportionate allocation of resources in the opinion of many in other parts of the Yellowstone region.

The most noticeable growth on this map is that of the Wolf Lake Fire, the renamed portion of the North Fork, that had moved right to the doorstep of the developments at Canyon. As can be seen on this map, the North Fork/Wolf Lake had begun to split into two forks just west of Canyon. To use military hyperbole once again, the splitting of the fire looks like the enveloping move of an attacking army as it nears its objective. In reality, however, the splitting of the fire front in front of Canyon, and probably at some other locations as well, had more to do with the efforts of firefighters working to protect the area than it did with any anthropomorphous move on the part of the fire to imitate the tactics of an attacking military

Another Canyon resident who watched the Wolf Lake Fire move toward Canyon was Dan Beadle. He had not lived at Canyon anywhere near as long as Emma Fuller, but his job and residence at the Yellowstone Park Service Station (YPSS) there were nonetheless important to him. Dan remembers driving the YPSS wrecker out from Canyon when the Wolf Lake was still on the plateau to the west, along the Canyon-Norris road. Dan and a coworker named Kevin Pfeifer drove the company wrecker, probably as a way to gain passage through a roadblock that was restricting travel due to the fire emergency, in order to get a closer view of the approaching fire.

Dan and Kevin found more fire than they cared to see up close, and turned the wrecker around in the middle of the road to head back to Canyon. Later Dan swore that as they were fleeing, a ball of flame flew out from the fire front behind them and actually passed the wrecker. From what I saw of exceptional fire behavior in 1988—how balls of gasified fuel could indeed blow out from fire fronts in front of powerful winds and ignite in midair—I can readily believe there is truth to Dan and Kevin's story.

Partly out of loyalty to his employer, and partly because he was a young concession employee with nowhere else to go, Dan steadfastly stayed at Canyon when the Wolf Lake arrived. He courageously stationed himself at the gas islands in front of Canyon YPPS, and quickly pounded out and hosed down spot fires that started in the belt of trees between the fuel station and the Canyon Junction. Dan's was indeed a bold move, to make such a stand with thousands of gallons of gasoline, propane, and other fuels literally right under his feet. And who can say what might have happened to the Canyon YPS station if the stand of trees in front of the gasoline pumps had torched off?

Yet another Canyon employee was Bill Blackford. Like so many other Yellowstone employees in 1988, Bill's seasonal job at the Canyon Lodge was brought to an early end by the fires. Also like many other employees, Bill was able to find work with the firefighting effort to replace the job he lost, only Bill's job was more unusual than most. Rather than something mundane like cooking in a fire camp, he was hired to guard a helibase that had been set up in Cascade Meadows, along the Canyon-Norris road just west of Canyon Junction.

According to what Bill was told, a bear had molested a parked helicopter sometime earlier in the fire season, and the base managers were especially concerned with the possibility of a bull bison rubbing himself on one of the parked flying machines. Bill worked sixteen-hour shifts to watch over the helibase, having to sit in his parked car in a pullout along the road through the night to do so. Every three hours Bill had to climb out of his car to refuel a generator that powered the spotlights used to illuminate the base. A fringe benefit of the job was that it gave Bill the opportunity to watch fire burning in the night on the slopes of the Washburn Mountain Range to the north of Cascade Meadows.

Of course I spent a lot of time around Canyon during the fire emergency there. In those days long before cell phones, I photographed long lines of firefighters waiting

Superintendent Bob Barbee with his foremost press person Joan Anzelmo at his side, at a press conference at Canyon in late August of 1988. © Jeff Henry/Roche Jaune Pictures, Inc.

for a turn on a pay phone and a chance to call home. During a press conference in front of the old Canyon Visitor Center, Yellowstone Superintendent Bob Barbee, his chief press officer Joan Anzelmo, and Yellowstone's Chief of Research John Varley addressed the media yet again. The three spoke very well, as always, and I was impressed anew at how those three and others in similar positions maintained their composure with all the pressures that were being put on them. And of course, I am certain that I wasn't even aware of many of the pressures and problems that people like Barbee, Anzelmo, and Varley had to face.

Bob Barbee, especially, was unfairly vilified during the fires. He was and is a friendly, well-intentioned man. There was a widespread perception during 1988 in the areas surrounding Yellowstone, and even on a national level, that the huge burns could have been avoided if the park service had attacked the fires earlier in the season. As has been discussed earlier in these pages, I do not believe that to have been the case. A few of the early season fires could have been put out, of that there is no doubt, but in most cases the country those early fires burned would have been consumed by fires that started later in the season and were fought unsuccessfully from their beginnings. With the combination of heavy fuel loads that had accumulated over decades and the unusually hot, dry, and windy weather Yellowstone experienced in the summer of 1988, the park was inevitably going to burn, regardless of what policy was in place and regardless of anything humans could do to try to manage the situation.

Moreover, the policy that the park service had in place at the beginning of the summer was valid, based on a solid interpretation of fire as a necessary, natural element in the ecosystem. The weather and the fires it spawned surprised everyone. As the scientist John Varley pointed out so very well, before 1988 we all thought that fire was like a football game that was played between the two 40-yard lines, but in 1988 we learned that it can be played on a field one hundred yards long. In many ways it was understandable that local people were upset—it was indeed emotional to see familiar scenes in the park so many people loved transformed so radically and in such short

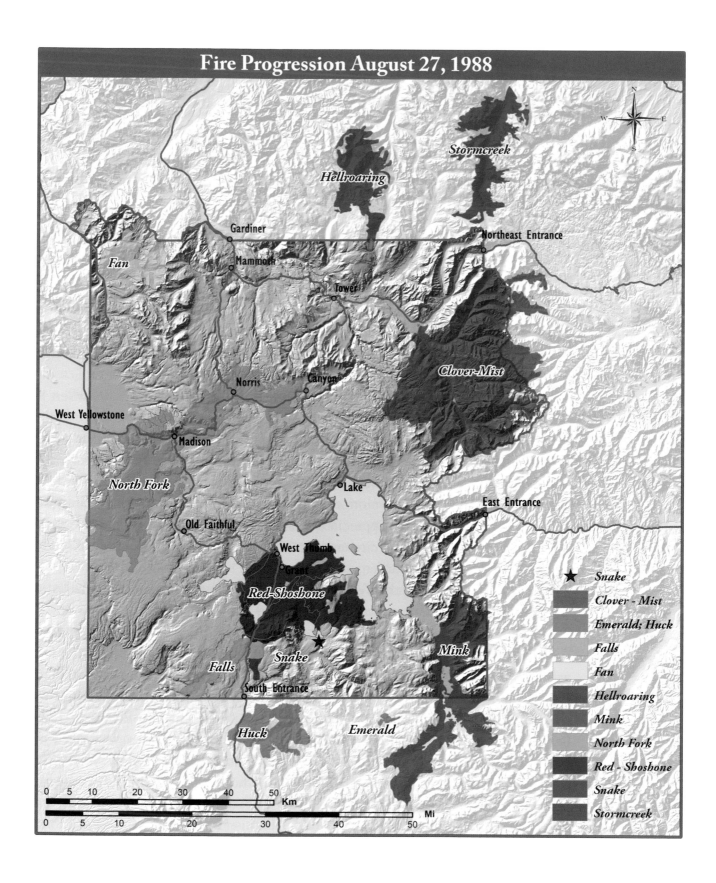

Fire Progression August 27, 1988

Stormcreek

Hellroaring

Gardiner

Northeast Entrance

Fan

Mammoth

Tower

Norris

Canyon

Clover-Mist

West Yellowstone

Madison

Lake

East Entrance

North Fork

Old Faithful

West Thumb

Grant

Red-Shoshone

Snake

Mink

Falls

Snake

South Entrance

Huck

Emerald

★	Snake
	Clover - Mist
	Emerald; Huck
	Falls
	Fan
	Hellroaring
	Mink
	North Fork
	Red - Shoshone
	Snake
	Stormcreek

| 0 | 5 | 10 | 20 | 30 | 40 | 50 | Km |

| 0 | 5 | 10 | 20 | 30 | 40 | 50 | Mi |

August 27, 1988

WITH THE exception of the Fan Fire, which was wholly contained and would spread no more for the rest of the summer, the major fires showed modest growth on this map for August 27, 1988. The two things that jump out here are critical growth areas on Yellowstone's two largest fires, the North Fork and the Clover-Mist. The latter fire had made discernible moves on its unrelenting drive on the east, while the Wolf Lake subdivision of the North Fork had broadened its front into a developing semicircle around the west, north, and south sides of Canyon Village. The Hellroaring Fire, too, had made a significant albeit anomalous move to the south, against the prevailing wind, which had brought it to and beyond the boundary of Yellowstone National Park.

The Hellroaring Fire's move to the south provided a good anecdote illustrating the unpredictability of fire, as well as the acute sensitivity of fire to weather conditions. The story involved Phil Perkins, then in charge of Yellowstone's Fire Cache, and Dan Krapf, who at the time was a seasonal ranger at Tower Junction. Dan was dispatched to protect the park's Buffalo Plateau Patrol Cabin, which was situated near the north boundary of the park a short distance east of Hellroaring Creek. Phil arrived later, after Dan had reduced fuels around the site and then watched as the Hellroaring Fire burned all around the cabin.

In the morning the day after the main fire had passed, the two men could see that with the exception of one stand of trees a short distance away, all the fuel around the cabin had been burned away. They thought if they purposely burned out the remaining stand of trees that the cabin would be safe and would require little if any further attention from Yellowstone's overtaxed staff. Phil, who was an extremely experienced firefighter, set off to burn out the grove of still-green trees

An exhausted firefighter during Yellowstone's summer of fire. 1988 National Park Service photo by Jeff Henry

with a drip torch. Both men thought the intentional fire would explode immediately and accomplish their objective of burning off the remaining fuel around the cabin. But as Phil walked all around the green grove, dripping flaming fuel from the drip torch everywhere he went, the fire he left behind only smoldered, or at most burned low to the ground with only a low level of intensity.

Phil finally gave up and walked back to the cabin, where Dan was waiting and watching. As Phil neared the cabin he looked at Dan and shrugged his shoulders, as if to say, "I can't figure that one out." At almost the same instant Phil shrugged his shoulders, the entire stand of trees behind him burst into a mass of flame. In just the few seconds it had taken Phil to walk back from the grove something had changed—a few points in humidity, a little rise in air temperature, or perhaps the combustion he had started with his drip torch reached a threshold at which it gave off enough heat to tip the balance from smoldering to exploding.

The Clover-Mist Fire at this time provided another illustrative incident, this one illustrating the unusual conditions firefighters had to deal with while fighting fire in Yellowstone. The huge fire burned into a thermal area near Cache Creek, where the flames ignited sulfur deposits around some of the geothermal outlets. The smoke from the resulting sulfur-fueled fire sickened seven firefighters who were working nearby. The firefighters had to be withdrawn from the lines for treatment after they inhaled the caustic gases.

The firefighting effort in Yellowstone by late August was facing a double-edged sword: On the one hand fires were growing and gathering ever more momentum in weather patterns that continued to be drier than anything ever seen before. As fire management officer Dave Poncin, Sr., wrote in his diary, "The fire is still gaining on us, we just cannot seem to turn the corner and gain control." On top of the growing fire problem, fire crews were wearing out from the long tours of arduous labor and the heavy smoke. As another diary entry from the same officer recorded, "A lot of people are sick and tired and need to get away from the smoke to heal up." The problem with exhausted crews was exacerbated by the fact that there was an extreme demand for firefighters on a nationwide level, so finding replacements for crews rotated out to rest was all but impossible.

Equipment was in short supply, too. With so much of the firefighting work carried on in the park's remote backcountry, helicopters were especially important to the Yellowstone firefighting effort. Inevitable fatigue factors with helicopter pilots and crews were an issue, just as they were for hand crews. Mechanical fatigue was an issue, too. In one of the many great anecdotes from the 1988 fires, there was a case of a helicopter that developed mechanical problems while working on the Clover-Mist Fire in the northeastern section of the park on August 19, the day before Black Saturday. The pilot of the stricken machine managed to set his craft down on the ridge between Cache Creek and Calfee Creek, but then the next day the Clover-Mist burned with extreme violence over 56,000 acres in the area of the abandoned helicopter. Probably because the chopper had been parked on a windblown ridge that was vegetated only with fairly sparse grass and forbs, the machine did not burn. A repair crew was flown to the site, fixed the problem, and then the repaired helicopter was flown back to its base.

But by August 27 there was such a general shortage of helicopters that the incident commanders on the Wolf Lake and North Fork Fires contacted Senator Malcolm Wallop of Wyoming in an effort to recruit more of the critically important flying machines. The fire managers hoped that the senator would help with a move to lease helicopters, from oil companies in Wyoming, for use on the Yellowstone fires. When word got out that Yellowstone firefighters were seeking to lease machines from Wyoming oil companies, however, the National Guard in Montana took offense that they had not been contacted first. Long story short, the Montana National Guard did step up and provide some of their choppers to the firefighting effort, so via an indirect route, the proposal to the oil companies through the Wyoming senator succeeded in procuring more flying machines for the firefighting effort.

The most threatened developed area during the last few days of August was Canyon Village. The Wolf Lake Fire first arrived there on August 25. More accurately, in the view of most astute observers, the portion of the Wolf Lake Fire that arrived on the 25th was a backfire that had been unwisely set southwest of the development. In any event, Canyon was under direct siege for about two weeks, with at least some fingers of flame flaring around the development as late as September 7.

In one dramatic moment a fire crew from Mississippi abandoned their position at the edge of the park service residential area, throwing down their gear and running in panic for the government maintenance shop. Fortunately for the firefighters from Mississippi, and for the residential area they had been charged to protect, the flaming front that had driven them from their position inexplicably faltered right at the edge of the development. One observer thought that perhaps an erratic gust of wind had blown the fire back on itself as it neared the park service structures, stalling the fire in one place long enough for it to consume the available fuel there before the normal southwesterly wind came back to potentially move it forward again. Anything is possible in the chaos of wind and flame in front of a big fire, so that very well may be what happened.

Of course there were other dramatic moments in other places around Canyon Village. A considerable grove of trees at the west end of the Hamilton Store dorm behind the Canyon General Store flared with a great blast of heat, but heavy wetting of the adjacent dorm saved the building. Another finger of fire made a run at the back of the building that served as both visitor center and ranger station, and it was halted by some firefighters on a foam-spraying truck—firefighters who had just finished training on the very truck they were using. Other fingers of fire threatened the many tourist cabins and employee dorms in the area south of the visitor center and the general store.

Still another sector of the Wolf Lake Fire burned south of Canyon Village, down to the north side of Alum Creek on the north side of Hayden Valley. A great deal of work was put in ahead of that finger of fire to save the Montana Power transmission line that lead south of Canyon toward the Lake-Fishing Bridge and West Thumb–Grant Village areas. The efforts to save the power line, largely by wrapping wooden poles with old fire shelters, mostly succeeded. A large burnout operation along Alum Creek successfully created what firefighters like to call a "black line," a burned out stretch that ideally stops an advancing fire by depriving it of fuel. The black line along Alum Creek was wide and indeed very black, and it did stop the Wolf Lake Fire's movement toward the south. Arresting its move to the south was seen as important for keeping the developments around Lake and Fishing Bridge secure on their north side.

Lake-Fishing Bridge benefited greatly in 1988 from the huge fire break in its front yard, that front yard being the 140 square miles of open water on Yellowstone Lake. It also benefited from the fact that there were no fire starts in its immediate neighborhood during the summer of fire, as much of the country around the area is heavily forested with old growth timber of the most flammable type. Even given the presence of Yellowstone Lake, and the fact that all the 1988 fires started in locations remote from Lake and Fishing Bridge, there was great concern for the paired developments from late August onward, especially when all the fires flared to a scale approaching Armageddon in early September.

Then there was fear that the greater Lake Area could be threatened by the Wolf Lake Fire from the north, the North Fork from the west, the Clover-Mist from the east, and the various fires in the Snake River Complex to the south. If any of those

The flames of the Wolf Lake Fire exploding in the lodgepole forest just above the Mary Mountain trailhead near Alum Creek, late August 1988 © Jeff Henry/Roche Jaune Pictures, Inc.

fires had approached Lake, the heavy forests in the area would have made a perfect conduit to conduct the flames to the development. As it happened, however, the timely rain and snow of September 10 and 11 halted the fires' spread before they came all that close to Lake.

Also at this time, the Wolf Lake Fire burned up to the edge of the Yellowstone River on the stretch between Alum Creek and Otter Creek, arriving there as a leaping, flaring crown fire. This was less than ideal in the view of fire managers, who had hoped the blaze would arrive at the famous river in the form of a creeping ground fire, which would have made it a lot less likely to cross the river and continue on to the east. As it was, firebrands cast out by exploding trees and turbulent updrafts sailed across the river and ignited the heavy forest on the other side. In yet another inexplicable nonevent, and in spite of the expectations of everyone watching, the fire that ignited on the east side of the river merely burned at a low level and did not build up any kind of a head and run off. The fire on the east side of the Yellowstone continued to burn at a low to moderate level of intensity for almost another month, but never did build up enough momentum to move appreciably away from the river.

I spent several hours at the mouth of Alum Creek on the afternoon the Wolf Lake Fire leapt across the Yellowstone River at the mouth of the creek. Like everyone else present, I was certain that once across the river the fire would quickly take hold and run off. But also like everyone else, I was wrong. I shot a lot of photos of large crown fires on the timbered ridge north of Alum Creek, just above the Mary Mountain trailhead, as well as photos of some firefighters and their trucks from the California Division of Forestry (CDF) who had been staged along the Grand Loop Road in that sector. To help with the fire emergency, the CDF sent a great many firefighters and a lot of equipment to Yellowstone in the summer of 1988. An almost undecipherable number of other agencies around the United States did the same. Once while the CDF people were on standby along the road between Alum Creek and the Mary Mountain trailhead, a small herd of bull bison crossed the road between their trucks, and the California firefighters climbed onto their vehicles to get out of the way.

Firefighters from the California Department of Forestry take to their trucks to get out of the way of a large bull bison crossing the Grand Loop Road just north of the mouth of Alum Creek. © Jeff Henry/Roche Jaune Pictures, Inc.

A lone bull bison grazing on meager forage along the dried-up bed of Alum Creek, while the Wolf Lake Fire burns the ridge beyond, late August of 1988. © Jeff Henry/Roche Jaune Pictures, Inc.

There was another bull bison that afternoon that was grazing a strip of lush vegetation in the middle of the Alum Creek estuary. At this point in the summer of record drought the estuary was all dry, with Alum Creek describing a thin ribbon of wetness down the middle of a dry flat that normally would have been flooded, or at least muddy. I couldn't help but be struck by the juxtaposed expressions of drought—with the lone bull grazing a thin strand of greenery along a grossly receded stream, in the middle of a dry mudflat, positioned in front of a flaming hillside on the other side of the stream.

The most portentous development on this map for August 27, 1988 was how the North Fork Fire was showing growth toward both the west and the south. It was a remarkable phenomenon: the huge mass of the North Fork was expanding in all directions simultaneously. Not only was the fire growing on its north and east sides, where growth could be expected because of the region's normal southwesterly winds, but it was also growing to the south and toward the west. Its westward movement was taking it closer to the gateway town of West Yellowstone, Montana, while its deviant southward spread was taking it to a position exactly upwind from Yellowstone's most famous feature, Old Faithful Geyser.

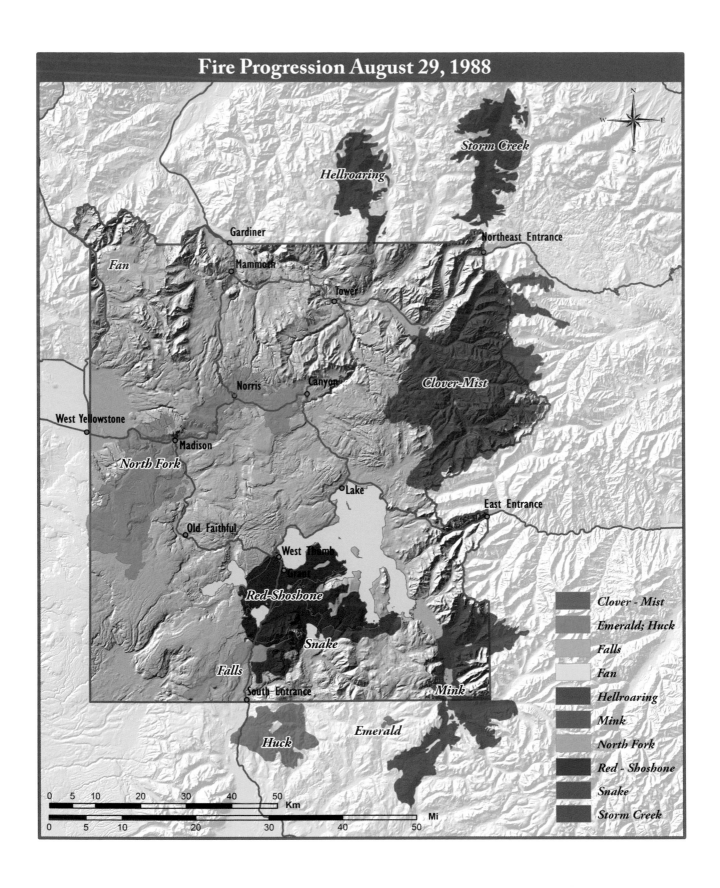

Fire Progression August 29, 1988

Storm Creek

Hellroaring

Gardiner

Northeast Entrance

Fan

Mammoth

Tower

Norris

Canyon

Clover-Mist

West Yellowstone

Madison

North Fork

Lake

East Entrance

Old Faithful

West Thumb

Grant

Red-Shoshone

Snake

Falls

South Entrance

Mink

Huck

Emerald

	Clover - Mist
	Emerald; Huck
	Falls
	Fan
	Hellroaring
	Mink
	North Fork
	Red - Shoshone
	Snake
	Storm Creek

0	5	10	20	30	40	50	Km
0	5	10	20	30	40	50	Mi

August 29, 1988

ON THIS MAP from August 29, the North Fork Fire continued its ominous spread to the west and south, as well the predictable spread to the north and east. Records show that the North Fork was burning about 4,000–5,000 acres per day on these days in late August, modest by the standards of 1988, but still amounting to approximately 7 square miles per day for just that one fire. The Storm Creek Fire showed considerable enlargement in an overall sense, while the Clover-Mist continued to extend to the east. The latter fire developed a pattern of making linear runs along the slopes of the long ridges characteristic of the Upper Clark's Fork country where that portion of the huge fire was burning. The ridge on the south side of the Clark's Fork, on the lower slopes of Jim Smith Peak and opposite Highway 212 east of Cooke City, is one such site. The effects of the fearsomely hot fire that burned there can still be seen today. The lower slopes on the north side of Hurricane Mesa, just south of Jim Smith Peak, burned in a similar linear pattern, and again the aftereffects of the burn can still be seen today.

To replace worn-out fire crews, many of whom had been on the line working as much as fourteen hours a day for weeks, various elements of the United States military began to arrive in Yellowstone in late August. Before the season was over as many as 4,146 (totaling 11,700 different individuals who cycled through during the course of the season) members of the Marines, the Army, the Air Force, the Navy and the Wyoming National Guard would be on the scene at a given time. Arriving in the park with only a modicum of fire training, there was concern for the welfare of the military personnel, but there was also relief that fresh blood was being infused into the firefighting effort. One fire manager noticed, with the dull comprehension of a soldier dazed by extended combat watching replacements arrive at the front,

A member of the United States Army with a contingent from Fort Lewis, Washington using a field radio for communication while dressed in a combination of Nomex and military garb, along the West Entrance Road about 4 miles from West Yellowstone, Montana, late August 1988. © Jeff Henry/Roche Jaune Pictures, Inc.

how clean shaven and eager the fresh military faces appeared. Best of all for the worn-out firefighters, under the clean military uniforms and behind the fresh faced veneer was new energy that could be brought to bear on the fire fronts. The military personnel would primarily be used in fuel reduction work in advance of the fires, and to mop up hotspots in burned out areas after the main fire fronts had passed.

By this point in late August the national news media had established the Yellowstone fires as an ongoing story line on a national level. Every time I talked to long distance friends and relatives around the country, it was apparent that they were following the story of the fires on national news, and I certainly noticed the heavy presence of reporters and camera crews in Yellowstone as I traveled around the park.

And people across the nation were aware of the big Yellowstone fires not just because of the news media. Smoke from the great fires drifted as a cone shaped plume downwind to the east. The plume widened as it spread eastward, and of course it snaked north and south depending on the whims of the prevailing westerly winds, so at one time or another smoke from Yellowstone was visible well north into Canada, south as far as Mexico, and as far east as the Atlantic seaboard.

Naturally, the fires' effects were felt most strongly by those living closest to the park. In 1988 Mike Bryers was a tour guide living near Hebgen Lake just north of West Yellowstone, Montana. As with most everyone else in the Yellowstone area, the beginning of Mike's summer was deceptively normal. Life was good for Mike. His wife Lizabeth was pregnant with their fourth child, and as a long-term resident of the Yellowstone area and a natural showman, Mike was a knowledgeable guide who always showed his clients a good time. The fires grew as the summer progressed, however, and the guide business correspondingly declined. Differing from most others involved in the Yellowstone tourist trade, Mike didn't blame the National Park Service for the decline in business. Instead he blamed the national media for the way they portrayed Yellowstone as a burned out wasteland, an image that Mike figured left readers and viewers disinclined to visit the world's first national park.

In common with many others who were displaced from their normal jobs, Mike Bryers was able to pick up replacement work in the firefighting effort. Also in common with many others who have worked to make the Yellowstone area their homes, Mike was a jack of all trades. In particular, his carpentry skills and his skill with a chainsaw were valuable attributes in 1988. Among other assignments, Mike volunteered to help set up a large-scale irrigation line along the west boundary of the park that was intended to stop or at least slow the North Fork Fire should it spread in the direction of West Yellowstone and other settlements nearby. He and his very pregnant wife also experienced an afternoon of high anxiety late in the fire season, when the great fire did blow out of the park and burned right into the immediate neighborhood of their historic log house. A helicopter, in Mike's recollection operating against a no fly order due to hurricane force winds, dumped buckets of water on and around his house and thereby saved the structure. Mike's wife Lizabeth, for her part, gave birth to their son Sean during the height of the near calamity of fire in early September, and not surprisingly Sean's nickname since birth has been "Smoky."

On the north side of the park another friend of mine was employed in a business similar to Mike Bryers's guide business. He was Dave Poncin, Jr., who happened to be the son of Dave, Sr., the incident commander who was such a major player in the 1988 fires in Yellowstone. The younger Dave made his living as an outfitter operating out of Jardine, Montana, just 5 miles up in the hills above Gardiner at Yellowstone's North Entrance. Normally in the summer young Dave packed dudes into the park, as well as into the Gallatin National Forest north of Yellowstone. When the fires rendered camping and fishing vacations in the backcountry less appealing, Dave switched over to packing firefighting gear into the backcountry on the backs of packhorses and mules. Young Dave even put in one hitch working on frontcountry fire when he helped his dad in the battle to save Grant Village in late July. Other than that one hitch in the Grant Village–West Thumb area, Dave spent most of his time during the summer of fire packing supplies to firefighters working on remote portions of the Fan Fire in the park's northwestern corner.

Mike Adkins was another outfitter in the Gardiner-Jardine area near Yellowstone's North Entrance. Like Dave Poncin, Jr., Mike quickly made the switch from wrangling dudes to packing supplies on horses and mules to backcountry firefighters. Mike also had the foresight to see what was developing with the Yellowstone fire situation in terms of equipment shortages, and early in the summer he invested in two new pickup trucks. In turn he leased the trucks to the region-wide, firefighting effort, and with the money he made from that arrangement paid for the new pickups during the course of just that one summer.

A little farther away from Yellowstone, a medical doctor named Roger Santala and his wife Susan had just moved to Billings, Montana, in 1987. Interested in the area around their new home, Roger and Susan had made trips to both Yellowstone National Park and to the Beartooth Mountains during their first summer of residence here. When they returned to Yellowstone and to the Beartooths in early 1988, they found the country there "crunchy dry," recognizing the unusual drought conditions even without the benefit of long experience in the area. And then not long after their early season trip to the mountains west of Billings the Yellowstone fires started, and soon thereafter the Santalas began to see smoke and ash, even in downtown Billings. As with almost everyone else in the region that summer, Roger and Susan were fascinated by the way ash drifted down from the sky, knowing that the ash had traveled a great many miles on winds aloft to get there. Even more fascinating was how the bits of ash retained the recognizable shapes of individual conifer needles, or even that of small twigs, but when touched with a finger tip the delicate shapes would disintegrate into dust. A further memory for Roger was how ash accumulated on the flat surfaces of his car overnight, and then blew off in small plates when he started his drive to work.

Drawn by curiosity, Roger and Susan made a trip over Beartooth Pass en route to Yellowstone in late summer, hoping to get a closer look at the fires that were the source of the smoke and ash they were seeing in Billings. But unfortunately for the Santalas, the fire emergency on the day they chose to make their trip to the park was such that a road closure was in effect at the junction of the Beartooth Highway and the Chief Joseph Highway, just east of Cooke City, Montana. From there the Santalas had no choice but to return to Billings, which they did via the Chief Joseph Highway over Dead Indian Pass and past the vicinity of Heart Mountain and Cody, Wyoming.

Even farther away from the fields of fire in Yellowstone, Illinois grain farmer Dana Boroughs could see smoke from the Yellowstone fires over his corn and soy beans fields on his farm near Charleston in the eastern part of the state. Dana had a particular affinity for Yellowstone, having visited the park many times through the course of his life. He also planned to move to the park region for his retirement years. In Dana's area, the smoke presented itself as a high haze that was too dispersed and perhaps too high to smell, but that visually reminded the farmer of what he had seen in the sky above his farm after Mount Saint Helens exploded in Washington on May 18, 1980. The haze and the colorful sunsets they engendered were quite similar in both instances. This says something about the magnitude of the Yellowstone blazes—that they could create atmospheric displays over fields many hundreds of miles away that were comparable to displays caused by a major volcanic eruption.

In addition to being a skilled farmer, Dana Boroughs was also an attentive businessman who certified much of his corn crop as fit for human consumption, and who had a lucrative contract with Frito Lay for that high-grade portion of his production. Also an astute observer of agricultural markets, Dana noticed something ominous at the end of the 1988 growing season: Very quietly and probably for the first time in history, the United States as a whole barely produced as much grain as it consumed. It was only because of the massive stockpiles the country had on hand from previous years that consumers did not feel the pinch. As the smoky sunsets over Dana's farm in Illinois were an indication of the magnitude of the Yellowstone fires, the ominous fact that the nation barely grew as much grain as it consumed in 1988 was likewise a barometer of the severity and scope of the drought that affected almost the entire country that year.

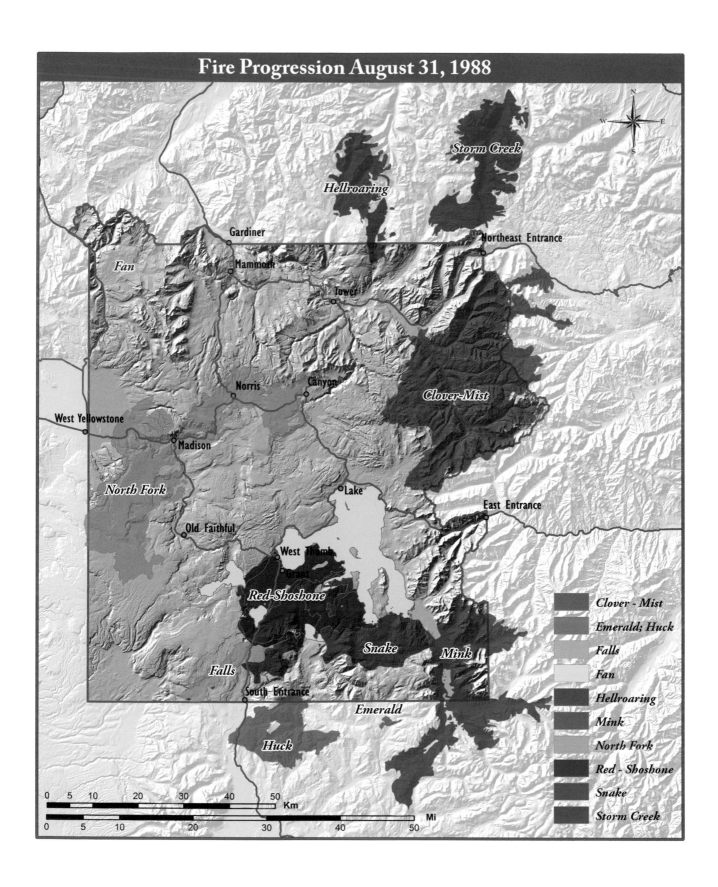

Fire Progression August 31, 1988

Storm Creek

Hellroaring

Gardiner

Northeast Entrance

Fan

Mammoth

Tower

Clover-Mist

Norris

Canyon

West Yellowstone

Madison

North Fork

Lake

East Entrance

Old Faithful

West Thumb

Grant

Red-Shoshone

Snake

Mink

Falls

South Entrance

Emerald

Huck

Clover - Mist
Emerald; Huck
Falls
Fan
Hellroaring
Mink
North Fork
Red - Shoshone
Snake
Storm Creek

0 5 10 20 30 40 50 Km

0 5 10 20 30 40 50 Mi

August 31, 1988

A STRONG WIND event struck Yellowstone on August 30, and some of the area's fires made significant runs in response to the windy conditions. Mysteriously, other fires in the area did not, but the element of mystery is always a factor in the fire equation. On August 30, for example, the North Fork Fire burned more than 18,600 acres, which was about 50 percent more acreage than it burned on August 20, the notorious Black Saturday. The Storm Creek burned more than 13,500 acres, while the fires in the Snake Complex burned nearly 40,000. Paradoxically, the huge Clover-Mist Fire, which had burned a total of 196,000 acres to date and was at the time Yellowstone's largest fire, burned only a little more than 2,500 acres on the same day. The Hellroaring Fire had a modest day, too, torching fewer than 3,000 acres. Overall, however, all the fires in the area burned a total of more than 95,000 acres on the 30th. That's about two thirds of the acreage burned on Black Saturday; yet August 30 didn't receive any special notoriety, either at the time or afterward. Standards of what constituted a big burning day were changing as the fires grew to sizes that were ever more inconceivable, and daily totals of burned acreages escalated to awesome figures as well. In the absence of any significant weather change, the big fires were gathering more and more momentum.

On this map for August 31, much of the growth of the North Fork is on opposite sides of the fire—that is, growth shows on the north side of the fire, northwest of Madison Junction, and on the south front southwest of Old Faithful. Indeed, the North Fork was expanding its occupation of the country upwind from the development at Old Faithful, preparing for the historic run it would make to and through the complex on September 7. As can be seen on this map, a preliminary finger of fire from the southern extremity of the North Fork was already beginning to extend in the direction of Old Faithful.

Incident Commander Dave Poncin, Sr. using a map to brief Director of the National Park Service William Penn Mott on the status of the North Fork Fire, in the Madison Fire Camp in late August of 1988. Dave put in two hitches directing firefighting efforts in Yellowstone during the summer of 1988, the first in the successful defense of Grant Village against the Shoshone Fire in late July, and the second in an attempt to control the North Fork Fire during most of the month of August. Unfortunately for Dave, conditions were such that "the smoke columns and clouds were always bigger when I left the park than they had been when I arrived."
© Jeff Henry/Roche Jaune Pictures, Inc.

This astonishing phenomenon, where one fire made major moves to both the north and to the south on the same day, was seen by most as a manifestation of the erratic winds the fires themselves were creating. In making such inexplicable moves, the North Fork was not alone. All the major fires lurched in unexpected directions at one time or another, sometimes moving in multiple directions simultaneously, as the North Fork did on August 31. The image of fire as a dragon thrashing about in paroxysms of fury occurred to me again. Even on the maps the ragged fringes on some of the fire perimeters suggested the spiny outline of a dragon, and as depicted on the accompanying map some of the fingers that shot out from the main fire masses had the appearance of flaming exhalations.

So many factors influence what fire scientists blandly call "fire behavior." The intensity and rate of spread of a fire is affected by the steepness and compass bearing of slopes, as well as by fire barriers like bodies of water or barren rock outcrops where there is nothing to burn. Fuel types and densities play a big role, too, as some species of vegetation ignite more readily and give off more heat when they burn than do others. Dense vegetation provides more fuel than sparse vegetation, but some vegetation grows so densely that it inhibits the circulation of air, and a fire burning in such a place is likewise inhibited for want of oxygen. And the size and shape of fuels also play a role in affecting fire behavior: Small bits of fuel like leaves or grass ignite more readily, but then burn out more quickly than do large logs. All in all, it's a complicated equation.

And the biggest factor of all, of course, is the weather. Three tiers of weather can be considered as influencing fire. First, long-term weather, what we usually refer to as climate, largely determines what sort of vegetation grows in a given habitat. Climates that are consistently wet through the course of the year tend to grow a lot of vegetation, or a lot of fuel to feed a fire, but because things are always so wet fires are not likely to occur. Extremely hot and dry climates, on the other hand, provide good conditions for burning, but because they are so hot and dry not much vegetation is produced so there is not much fuel around to burn. Climates that are split between wet seasons and dry seasons, classically the so-called Mediterranean climate, tend to spawn frequent fires, as they are wet enough to produce vegetation during the rainy season, but then dry out enough to spark fires during the dry times. Large portions of California can be classified as having a Mediterranean climate, for an example, and of course fires in The Golden State are almost annual occurrences.

Yellowstone falls toward the cool, moist end of the climate spectrum as it applies to fire frequency. It is cool and moist enough in the park to grow trees, grasses, and forbs, and the same cool and moist conditions tend to preclude fire for long stretches of time, sometimes even for centuries. But when the weather does dry out to the point where fires are possible, all that fuel that has accumulated since the last fire is there, ready and waiting to burn.

The second tier to be considered would be long-term weather patterns, specifically drought. Wildfires almost always occur after there has been a drought, usually an extended period of drought. That was certainly the case in Yellowstone in 1988. Historically at least, most of the moisture that falls in the northern Rockies comes in the form of winter snow. The two winters previous to the big fires of 1988 were dry, as was the previous autumn. Yellowstone did receive an above average amount of precipitation in the spring of 1988, but overall the trend for several years had been one of general drying. The drying trend was setting the stage for what happened in the summer of 1988, and that is a pattern that usually occurs before wildfires anywhere.

The third time frame in which to look at weather with regard to wildfire is short term. After the stage has been set by a drought in a climate where there is enough vegetation for a potential fire to burn, the weather in an immediate sense—in the time frame of a day, or even of just a few hours—is what's important. For major burning to occur, the weather pretty much has to be warm (if not hot), with low humidity and strong winds. When all these factors are in place—vegetation that has been dried by drought and is primed to burn, combined with hot, dry, and windy weather conditions—then all that's needed is a source of ignition to create a fire that can explode into a raging conflagration that will continue to burn until it either runs out of fuel or weather conditions change.

As far as the mysterious winds and fire movements in Yellowstone in the late summer of 1988 are concerned, all the above (and more) were factors. Observing what was actually going on was made difficult by the rough and remote country where most of the burning was taking place, and everything was obscured by prodigious volumes of smoke. And then, when you think about it, how mysterious is the weather at any time in a wilderness like Yellowstone, even at times when there is no fire? Even if you're out in the elements, say hiking in the park's backcountry, at best you know what the weather is doing right where you are. How do you know which direction the wind is blowing on the other side of the mountain from where you are? There probably is always some volatility in the winds and other weather

The Wolf Lake Fire burning cooly along the ground in an illustration of one of the manifestations of fire along the continuum of combustion, from the one extreme where conditions of fuel and weather are such that fires won't burn at all, and the opposite extreme where fires explode into all-consuming conflagrations. © Jeff Henry/Roche Jaune Pictures, Inc.

factors, times when winds blow inexplicably in opposite directions, and the other elements of weather vary over just short distances. As it happened in 1988, the big fires left tracings on the landscape that outlined the capricious nature of the winds, the tracings being the scorched forests the fires left in their wakes.

That said, there is no doubt that the Yellowstone fires were so large that they did indeed create their own weather. The physics involved in and around big fires make for a chaotic maelstrom of effects. Numbers of small flames unite to form bigger flames, which then surge upward into the tree tops and beyond. Fire expands from heat radiating outward to combust new material. The ambient wind blows the fire forward, but of course winds are gusty and can have backwashes and eddies, so fire movement is neither steady nor uniform. In 1988 I frequently saw pockets of fire surge up and then fall back, I'm pretty sure for want of oxygen. After a few moments during which the fire literally inhaled a fresh volume of oxygen, the flames would surge upward and forward again.

Literal explosions go off within the fire zone, which are thought by some to be caused by the moisture within the trunks of living trees expanding to the point where they violently burst. Huge volumes of sparks and embers—even big chunks of flaming wood—are cast out explosively or simply picked up by the awesome updrafting of heat. Once up in the air the flaming material is thrown forward by ambient winds, or by winds created by the fire itself as it inhales fresh air in some sectors and exhales smoke and flames in others. As the winds are fickle because of all the varying forces acting upon them, so the direction the firebrands are thrown is also fickle: They can rain down anywhere and in any direction. Once back on the ground, the firebrands start new fires, anywhere from a few feet away from the parent fire to up to a mile or two or even farther away. Each spot fire then takes on a life of its own, some

A red-ball sun shining through copious amounts of smoke hanging over Lamar Valley during the smoky summer of 1988. 1988 National Park Service photo by Jeff Henry

of them only smoldering lethargically while others quickly blow up to become big fires in their own right. And then the spot fires can burn in unpredictable directions, sometimes forward in the same direction as the main fire, sometimes back toward the parent fire, sometimes laterally, sometimes in all directions simultaneously.

Within both the parent fires and the spot fires, trees burn off at their bases and come crashing down in eruptions of sparks. Other trees can snap off like matchsticks, broken by the violent winds within the fire zone. Other trees can be yanked out of the ground like weeds pulled from some giant's garden, pulled upward and out of the ground by the awesome updrafts of heat inside the fire perimeter. The smoke can be so thick that the sun is curtained off and midafternoon can become literally as dark as night. Smoke is choking to the throat and burning to the eyes. Big fires spawn fire whirls and vortexes of flame that go spinning out from the main body of the blaze. In 1988 one of the more frequent, but no less astounding because it was frequent, phenomena I witnessed was updrafting flames that would be caught by the ambient winds blowing aloft, which would then blow the flames forward from the main fire. But after hurtling forward for some distance the wall of flame would be caught by the draft of wind being sucked in to the fire at ground level, which in turn would cause the wave of flame to roll over on itself like an ocean breaker crashing on the beach. The breaking, rolling, waves of flame sometimes rose two or three hundred feet high.

Altogether, the chaos and impaired visibility around a big fire make it tough to tell exactly what is going on. Needless to say, there is also an element of danger involved with trying to get a close look at a big fire. But it is safe to say that the 1988 fires in Yellowstone were so big that they almost undoubtedly did create winds that had impacts on a regional scale. Even though the big fires were often separated by many miles of country that was not burning, the drafts they created probably had an influence on each other, especially in terms of rates and directions of spread.

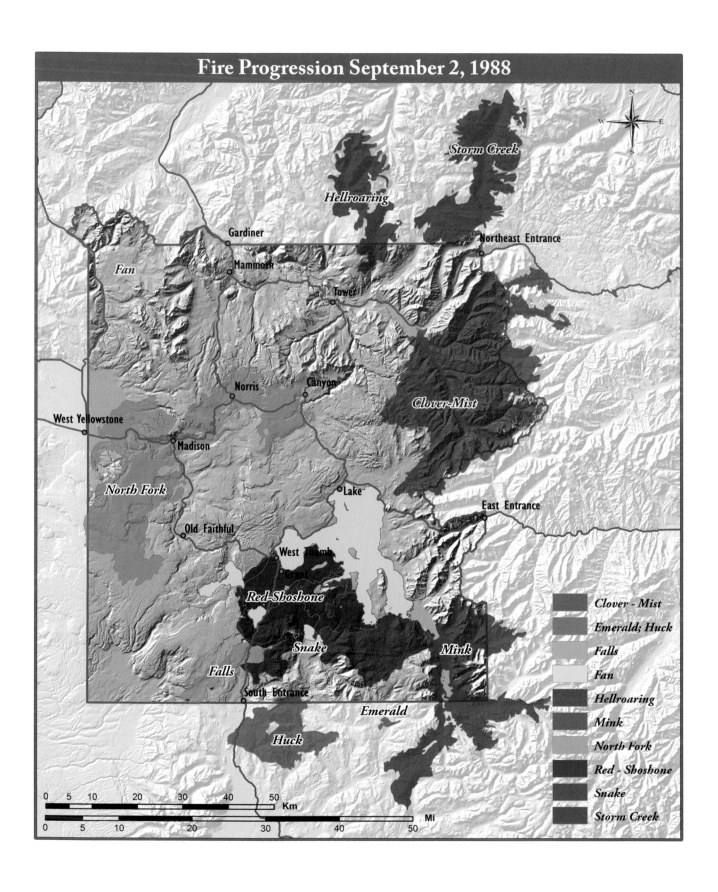

Fire Progression September 2, 1988

Storm Creek

Hellroaring

Gardiner

Mammoth

Northeast Entrance

Fan

Tower

Clover-Mist

Norris

Canyon

West Yellowstone

Madison

East Entrance

North Fork

Lake

Old Faithful

West Thumb

Grant

Red-Shoshone

Mink

Snake

Falls

Huck

South Entrance

Emerald

	Clover - Mist
	Emerald; Huck
	Falls
	Fan
	Hellroaring
	Mink
	North Fork
	Red - Shoshone
	Snake
	Storm Creek

0 5 10   20   30   40   50   Km

0 5 10   20   30   40   50   Mi

A UGUST 31 and September 1 were moderate burning days, and that is reflected on this map from September 2, 1988. Visually, the most striking thing here might be the way the fires in Yellowstone's southeastern quadrant had burned together. On the map they were becoming just one big blob of burned country, and indeed the spread of several of the fires was largely stopped when their fronts ran into country that already had been burned out by other fires.

Both the Hellroaring and the Storm Creek Fires continued their anomalous moves to the south, where both fires presented an ever-increasing threat to the park's Northeast Entrance and the Montana resort towns just outside that entrance. The two fires also threatened the Tower Junction–Roosevelt Lodge area, as well as the National Park Service installation in Lamar. In addition to park service structures along Rose Creek in Lamar Valley, the Yellowstone Association had an old log building there that they used as a classroom for their field institute classes. The association also had moved a number of old tourist cabins from Fishing Bridge to Rose Creek back in 1981 to serve as lodging for students enrolled in Yellowstone Institute field courses. The old cabins were log framed, with ship lap siding on the walls and cedar shingles on the roofs. They were also around fifty to sixty years old in 1988, so they were not only constructed of materials that were known for being flammable, they also had been drying for a long time.

The huge Clover-Mist Fire, by this time somewhere in the range of 235,000 acres, also moved to the south. Eventually it would burn all the way to the south side of Pelican Valley, around the perimeter of Turbid Lake and almost all the way to Yellowstone's East Entrance Road—that's a heck of a long way from the other end of the Clover-Mist, which was all the way up around Cooke City and out into the

Crandall-Sunlight area beyond park boundaries. Outside the park, the Clover-Mist would make it even farther south, burning all the way down the North Fork of the Shoshone River almost to Highway 16–20, the road between Yellowstone National Park and Cody, Wyoming. It almost made it as far south as the Cody Highway, and it almost consumed Pahaska Tepee, Shoshone Mountain Lodge, and some other resorts along the North Fork.

The spectacle of the Clover-Mist Fire burning down the North Fork of the Shoshone was one that those who saw it never forgot. I didn't see it myself, but in talking to some who did, it was described as 400–500 feet high, with whipping flames lashing up at the heavens. Its noise was deafening. With the flames and noise, and with the eerie light made ghastly by filtering through massive banks of smoke, to some it seemed like a preview of the end of the world. It very nearly was the end of the world as they knew it for some of the resort owners along the North Fork, because it seemed that it was nothing short of miraculous that their guest ranches were saved from the firestorm.

Two large tributary streams just upriver from Highway 16–20, Jones Creek and Crow Creek, suffered nearly total burnouts. Both those tributaries of the North Fork of the Shoshone head on the crest of the Absaroka Mountains, along the boundary between the Shoshone National Forest and Yellowstone Park, and both are steep and were heavily timbered. They amounted to a perfect formula for intense burning, and again those who witnessed the conflagrations in the tight stream valleys were left dumbfounded by what they saw. Stories circulated among firefighters and other witnesses that the fire was so hot that Jones Creek and Crow Creek boiled dry. According to all the scientific literature I have been able to find, that is an impossibility, and if the fire around those streams really was that hot I can't imagine how anyone could have been there to witness the water boil away and then lived to tell about it. But I can believe that the fire there was so furious that witnesses would have thought the streams *must* have boiled away. Even if not literally true, the story is informative about the awesome power of the Clover-Mist Fire, as well as the powerful impression the fire made on those who watched it burn its way down the North Fork of the Shoshone.

Most ominous of all, perhaps, was the way the North Fork Fire continued to build strength southwest of Old Faithful, from where it was all but inevitable that it would make a run at the development whenever the normal southwesterly winds returned. Curiously, the park service at this time was still struggling to maintain a sense of normalcy in Yellowstone. All lodging and other businesses were still open in the area, as they were everywhere other than Grant Village.

For a time in early September staying open for business at Old Faithful was probably OK. What was not OK, in my opinion, was how elements of the National Park Service continued to tell people that there was only a slight chance that the North Fork Fire would ever make it to Old Faithful. Up until the day before the fire actually did arrive in the complex, which was September 7, the official word given

An ominous smoke column from the North Fork Fire, emanating from the area around Jackstraw Basin southeast of West Yellowstone in early September of 1988. © Jeff Henry/Roche Jaune Pictures, Inc.

to concessioners and others in the Old Faithful area was that the North Fork Fire had only a one in three chance of ever burning into the village. Such odds did not jibe with what I was seeing when I looked to the southwest and saw two enormous columns of smoke rising into the sky. I remember walking by the weather station outside the Old Faithful Ranger Station in the late afternoon of September 6, the day before the North Fork Fire arrived. A weather vane and an anemometer were part of the station, and the weather vane pointed directly at the twin columns, while the anemometer was spinning so fast that its little wind cups were blurred. I remember thinking that it didn't take a genius to see what was going to happen, at least what was going to happen barring a major change in the weather. And no change was predicted anytime in the near future.

In my view, the problem originated with politicians outside the park, especially the congressional delegations of the states surrounding Yellowstone. They were determined to keep the park open to the visiting public, and applied pressure to the park to make sure that happened. The pressure then filtered down through the ranks of park service employees. Low-ranking employees on the front lines, those who actually dealt with tourists and concessions people on a personal level, had to pass on the information they thought they were required to disseminate—that is, that things were OK and there was minimal danger from the fire. To do otherwise

In a photo reminiscent of the famous picture of General Dwight D. Eisenhower exhorting paratroopers on the eve of D-Day in 1944, fire chief Denny Southerland briefs his firefighters in preparation for the arrival of the North Fork Fire in West Yellowstone, Montana. The picture was taken in early September of 1988. © Jeff Henry/Roche Jaune Pictures, Inc.

would incur the displeasure of their immediate supervisors, and those supervisors in turn were beholden to the next tier of command above, and so on. In the case of Old Faithful in early September of 1988, it was obvious, patently obvious, that the North Fork Fire was going to come. No rational person could have considered the circumstances and concluded otherwise—again, barring any significant weather change that likewise no rational person could have expected at the time.

I suppose it was possible that the rank and file employees who were disseminating the information that they had to know was erroneous may have just been saying what they *thought* their superiors wanted them to say, that in actuality the directive that was being communicated to the public was not exactly what had come down from above. The message also could have gotten garbled along the way, or there simply could have been misinterpretation somewhere along the chain of command. But wars have been lost because of such bureaucratic obsequiousness, and in the case of Old Faithful in September of 1988, devotion to the park service apparently blinded some members of the organization to the reality of the smoke columns to the southwest, and that blind devotion contributed to the near disaster that happened on Wednesday the 7th.

At this point more than twenty-five years after the fact, I am in no way trying to throw rocks at anyone, either in the park service or in any other organization. By now I am sure that it would be all but impossible to even track down the origin of that one-in-three figure that supposedly marked the odds of the North Fork Fire's chances of reaching Old Faithful. But anyone who could read a map, or anyone who could simply look to the west or southwest of Old Faithful during the first few days of September in 1988, had to know that the odds of fire coming to the village were much greater than one out of three. Dave Poncin, Sr., the incident commander on the North Fork Fire until he and his team were rotated out on September 1, had noticed what was developing between the North Fork and Old Faithful as early as August 30, when he wrote in his diary that soon "Old Faithful will be threatened and West Yellowstone is worried and stressed as the fire approaches from the East."

As for the North Fork Fire itself, it didn't care what people thought of it, or what bureaucratic machinations were going on because of it. The big fire could be seen as a living dragon with volatile moods, yes, but it also could be seen as an insentient force of nature that was in its most basic sense an accelerated chemical reaction, wherein organic material was being oxidized in an equation that simply responded to laws of physics that involved moisture, heat, oxygen, and wind. No matter the image in which humans viewed it, the fire was coming, and it also didn't matter what humans might do to try to stop it.

Fire Progression September 4, 1988

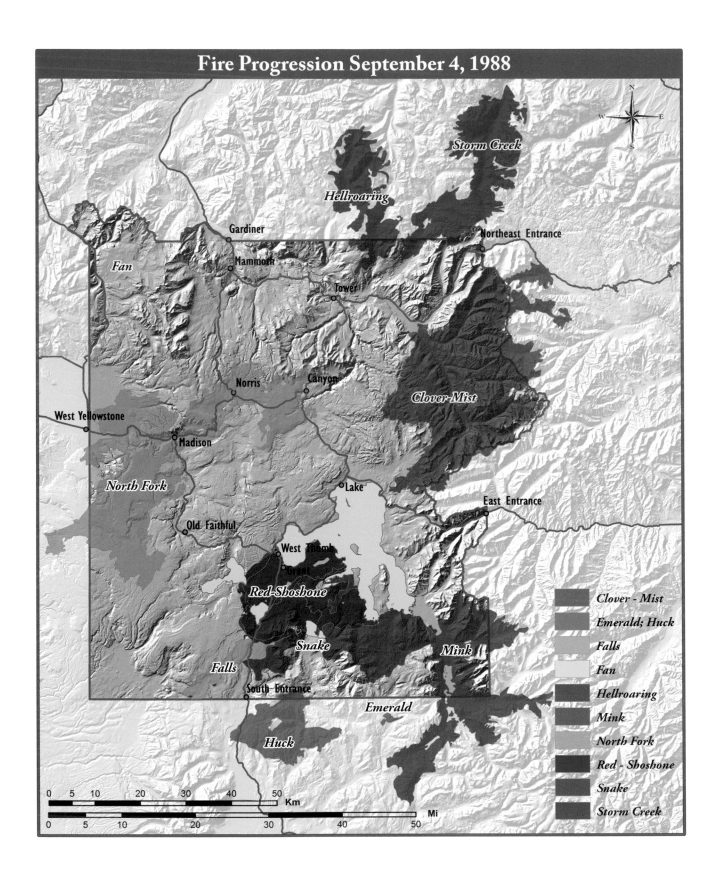

Storm Creek

Hellroaring

Gardiner

Northeast Entrance

Mammoth

Fan

Tower

Norris   Canyon

Clover-Mist

West Yellowstone

Madison

North Fork

Lake

East Entrance

Old Faithful

West Thumb

Grant

Red-Shoshone

Snake   Mink

Falls

South Entrance

Emerald

Huck

Clover - Mist
Emerald; Huck
Falls
Fan
Hellroaring
Mink
North Fork
Red - Shoshone
Snake
Storm Creek

0   5   10   20   30   40   50   Km

0   5   10   20   30   40   50   Mi

September 4, 1988

ON THIS map it is obvious that the Hellroaring and Storm Creek Fires have almost burned together near Yellowstone Park's north boundary, about 15 miles west of the Northeast Entrance. Moving to the south, as both fires were doing at this time, was presenting a growing threat to the Tower-Roosevelt area, the Lamar developed area, and especially to the Northeast Entrance and the two towns just outside the gate, Cooke City and Silver Gate, Montana. Moving to the south was not only bringing both fires closer to Cooke City and Silver Gate, but it was also bringing the fires more in line with prevailing winds that could sweep the fire toward the resort towns. And the normal winds were sure to return sooner or later.

The Clover-Mist Fire was surprisingly quiet for September 3 and 4, burning less than 3,500 acres in total for the two days. It would soon make up for this fairly inactive interlude. The big fires in the southeastern corner of Yellowstone were also comparatively quiet, and that, in addition to the fact that they were burning away from developed locations, rendered them to a lower level of attention. The North Fork Fire, on the other hand, continued to burn energetically. On the 3rd and 4th of September it scorched a total of about 28,500 acres. More important than just the acreages it burned, its movement was putting it in position to pose an ever greater threat to Island Park, Canyon, West Yellowstone, and Old Faithful. Notice how the North Fork had made two significant runs beyond the park's west boundary: One finger was just south of West Yellowstone, while the other, larger breakout was farther south and more in line with the developments in Island Park, Idaho. The irony with this latter movement was that the fire was returning to the very area where it

The smoky and menacing manifestation of the North Fork Fire tight to the edge of the town of West Yellowstone, Montana, during the first week of September in 1988. © Jeff Henry/Roche Jaune Pictures, Inc.

had begun on July 22—one of the more erratic moves in a summer characterized by unpredictable fire spread.

The Wolf Lake portion of the North Fork continued to burn around Canyon Village, describing an ever wider perimeter around the development. With so much more country aflame around Canyon, people feared that just meant there were many more sources for a fire to use to build up a head of steam and make a run at the complex itself. One of the mysteries with the Wolf Lake Fire in the Canyon area was how it jumped the Yellowstone River near the mouth of Alum Creek, and then never moved that far to the east from its beachhead on the east side of the river. When the Wolf Lake Fire first crossed the Yellowstone, and for three weeks or so thereafter, almost all observers thought the fire would take off and burn to the east until it ran into country already burned out by the Clover-Mist. I know that was my personal prediction, but along with everyone else I was wrong, as that anticipated drive on the east never happened—at least not with this portion of the fire.

The North Fork Fire also continued to build strength directly downwind from Old Faithful; the position of that southernmost portion of the great fire was obviously southwest of, and upwind from, the development at Old Faithful. Smokiness in the Old Faithful area began to increase greatly during this time. The North Fork's simultaneous spread in all directions was managerially perplexing and academically fascinating, but to all those with vested property interests in the area, it was most of all frightening. It was as though the ponderous fire could no longer support its own weight, and as it collapsed on itself, flame was squished out in all directions.

The story for these first few days of September, however, was in Yellowstone's northeastern quadrant. The future for the Northeast Entrance, and for Cooke City and Silver Gate, Montana, "did not look good," to quote a fire manager who was involved in that area at the time. The park service maintenance and residential installation at Northeast was only a mile or so from Silver Gate, which in turn was only about 2 miles from Cooke City, so the government's complex was no better off. All three clusters of development were arranged linearly along Highway 212, a road probably best known for crossing the Beartooth Pass to the east. The highway, in turn, followed the valley of Soda Butte Creek. The stream valley narrowed around the three communities, a perfect design for funneling flames. Moreover the valley, in places tight enough to be called a canyon, had an east-west orientation, which put it in line with prevailing winds. In the confidential evaluation of some of the fire managers overseeing the situation, Cooke City and Silver Gate had only a one in five chance of surviving; perhaps only one in ten.

By early September the 4-mile stretch of valley, with Cooke City on the upstream end and the Northeast Entrance on the downstream end, was nearly surrounded by three different fires, each one of them huge. It seemed that one of the most likely scenarios in the gathering storm was that the Clover-Mist would manage to cross the high mountain ridge to the north of Cache Creek and enter the valley of Soda Butte Creek in an upwind location from the developments. Another threatening possibility was that the Clover-Mist would continue burning down the Lamar River Valley, around the southern end of Mount Norris, and enter the Soda Butte drainage that way. Either eventually would have put the fire not only in the same valley as the three developments, but also in an upwind location. Yet another possibility with the Clover-Mist was that it could burn into the upper reaches of the Clark's Fork of the Yellowstone to the east of Cooke City, and then turn to the west, follow topography, and reach Cooke City and the other settlements from that direction. Normally, burning to the west would have been unlikely, but all the fires in Yellowstone by this time in the season of 1988 were behaving unpredictably, so a westward run of the Clover-Mist from the Clark's Fork no longer seemed out of the question.

In fact, the Storm Creek and the Hellroaring Fires had been moving unpredictably to the south for quite a few days by September 4. That movement was putting both fires ever closer to that dreaded upwind position from the Cooke City area. Fire managers decided that the best chance to save the developments around the Northeast Entrance was to construct a massive fireline along the west side of Silver Gate, between that town and the boundary of Yellowstone, and then to burn out the country to the west of their line. The line was constructed with bulldozers, which cleared a wide swath through the forest by first knocking down the trees, and then

Fire trucks staging around structures between Silver Gate and Cooke City, Montana, during the fire emergency of the first week of September in 1988. 1988 National Park Service photo by Jim Peaco

scraping away all organic material down to the level of mineral soil. The burnout to the west of the massive bulldozer line was to amount to another one of the great controversies surrounding the 1988 fires.

It's hard to imagine just how disquieting the situation must have been for residents of Cooke City and Silver Gate in late August and early September of 1988. Almost without exception, occupants of the two towns had settled there because the area was so special to them, and indeed the beautiful location between Yellowstone National Park and the Beartooth Plateau was unique. The two towns were isolated to a degree that was often described as Alaskan-like, and the remoteness was a factor in the tightly knit nature of the communities.

In 1988 Kay King and his wife Ceil had owned and operated the Log Cabin Cafe in Silver Gate for 11 years. Their cafe was exactly that—made out of logs—and it also was filled with a great many taxidermied animals and other interesting knick-knacks. Kay had grown up in the Yellowstone area, in nearby Lovell, Wyoming, but in 1988 he was in the middle of a long career as a professor at the University of Nebraska in Lincoln. For Kay and Ceil, working summers at the Log Cabin Cafe in the mountainous setting of Silver Gate was a perfect way to balance spending the rest of the year on Nebraska's prairies.

Along with most other longtime residents of the Yellowstone country, Kay King noticed how dry things were early in the summer of 1988. And then as the summer progressed, things not only got "drier and drier," they also got "smokier and smokier," as fires began in the region. Following their seasonal pattern, Kay and Ceil left their cafe in late August to go back to Nebraska. The situation in Silver Gate became ever more dire, however, so they flew back to Montana in early September. Landing in Billings, they rented a Ryder truck and drove to Silver Gate, where they found buses "lined up and running, pointed east and ready to leave." The buses were on hand, of course, to evacuate the area. For their part, Kay and Ceil hauled two loads of mementos out of the Log Cabin Cafe in their rented truck, and moved the valuables to a storage locker in Cody, Wyoming. When they left Silver Gate to return to the airport in Billings and fly back to Nebraska, "We didn't know whether we were going to have a building left when we came back."

In contrast to many other property owners in the Silver Gate/Cooke City area, however, Kay did not hold any resentment toward either the park service or the forest service. In Kay's words, "The fire was going to do what it was going to do," and instead of nitpicking about this or that—whether an agency should have done this or that at one time or another—Kay stated "Hey, whatever happened we were fortunate to have survived." It was a good outlook: No matter what else, at the end of the day the Log Cabin Cafe and most of the other structures in Silver Gate and Cooke City were still standing. Everything else, in a very real sense, was detail.

Another longtime resident of the Cooke City/Silver Gate area was Ralph Glidden. He and his wife Sue bought the Cooke City General Store in November 1977, and had run it ever since. Ralph, who was forty-four years old in 1988, was a sharp observer of nature and he, too, noticed 1988's unusual weather. He noticed that the spring of the year was unusually moist, but that early on the summer became abnormally dry. Like Kay King, Ralph watched as conditions got even more dry and the residents of Cooke City began to smell smoke. Ralph really became concerned on August 20, 1988's Black Saturday, when he saw winds the likes of which he had rarely seen before. Of course Black Saturday produced huge volumes of smoke that blew into Cooke City on those strong winds.

As the fire situation became more grim, Ralph was selected to be a community representative entitled to attend fire management meetings at the town fire hall, where he became privy to some of the more confidential information concerning the fires. He was also a member of the Cooke City volunteer fire department, and as such was assigned to a fire hydrant that fortunately for Ralph was located just a short distance up the street from his store. On the one hand, Ralph was pleased that his historic store had been placed on the National Register of Historic Places just a short time before, in March of 1986, because he thought that might entitle his building to an extra level of protection. But on the other hand, he also had concerns that if indeed his structure did receive extra attention and survived while his neighbors' property did not, he and Sue might end up living an existence isolated by community resentment. Happily, no one's property burned in the vicinity of the

National Park Service (NPS) firefighters using drip torches to start a backfire to burn out fuel around the NPS compound at Northeast Entrance. This backfire was successful and controlled—it accomplished the objective of burning out fuel around the park service area at Northeast, but did not run off out of control and become a dangerous fire in its own right. © Jeff Henry/Roche Jaune Pictures, Inc.

Cooke City General Store, so no one had to feel guilty that his or her property survived while someone else's did not.

Ironically, the big fires that seemed so certain of invading Cooke City and Silver Gate never got there. Instead, the fire that burned past the two little towns was a result of the backburn that was set on the west side of town with the intent of depriving the big fires of fuel. The backfire got away, jumped the wide bulldozer line, and then burned along the face of the ridge north of the towns. The fire first started from an ember that landed up the hill behind the Range Rider Inn, on the west side of Silver Gate. From there it quickly exploded and ran east. By the time it got to Cooke City, it was after midnight, in the early hours of September 7, 1988. As with the other big fires in Yellowstone in 1988, the sight of the fire at Cooke City made an indelible impression on those who saw it. The flames were hundreds of feet high, and its sound was deafening, variously described as a "freight train" or a "fleet of jets." Those who resort to such comparisons usually complete their statements by saying that no hyperbole could adequately describe the infernal roar of the big fires. For those on duty in Cooke City when the fire raged by just north of town, the huge flames leaping into the dark of night must have added even greater impact to the hellish din.

Watching from his store on the south side of street in Cooke City, Ralph Glidden was comforted by the fact that a detachment of firefighters from another part of Montana was on hand to help him protect his building. He also was glad that his wife Sue had evacuated the fire zone. When the commander of the firefighters in his sector reminded Ralph that he had informally been assigned to his unit, and that the commander wanted Ralph to promise to not stay behind if an evacuation order was issued, the store owner made no argument. The big worry, as Ralph and the others discussed, was that both sides of the narrow valley where Cooke City was situated would burn simultaneously. If that happened, the air down in the center of the valley, where Cooke City and Silver Gate had been built, would be "like the wrong end of a blow torch" in Ralph's words—so hot that buildings might spontaneously ignite just from radiant heat and in spite of anything that firefighters could do to defend them. With this threat in mind, Ralph was relieved when only one side of the valley burned. With the fuel on that side of valley removed, at least Cooke City couldn't be caught in such a flaming crossfire.

Like Kay and Ceil King, Ralph and Sue Glidden were grateful that their historic general store survived. Ralph points out that those who were most critical of the park service in the way the agency handled the fires were those who were predisposed to be critical of government agencies in the first place. At the extreme, some people in the Silver Gate/Cooke City area (and elsewhere in the Yellowstone region) thought the park service had let the fires grow, or perhaps even kindled them, in order to burn out property owners around Yellowstone as part of a strategy

Some of the results of the backfire set around the NPS compound at Northeast Entrance.
© Jeff Henry/Roche Jaune Pictures, Inc.

to annex neighboring lands into the park. Other critics, a little less outlandish, believed the park service and the forest service had been too slow on the uptake, that the agencies should have switched to full fire-suppression mode earlier in the summer than they did. Ralph has observed, however, that the resentments of the less vitriolic critics "have cooled with time," while the attitudes of "the sagebrush rebels" have remained as they were both before and during the fires.

Ralph and Sue Glidden's store was a remarkable old building dating back to 1886, and its interior furnishings and artifacts were no less remarkable. When the fire danger in Cooke City became undeniable after Black Saturday, a friend in Billings offered to bring a truck and evacuate the historic fixtures and artifacts from the old store. After they thought it over, the Gliddens declined the offer: They saw their holding as a complete package, and they wanted the whole package to either survive the fires or to not survive, intact one way or the other. Theirs was an interesting response to what was an exceptionally stressful situation.

On a final note, Ralph Glidden acknowledges that while it was an escaped backburn that came closest to the Cooke City and Silver Gate communities, those responsible for defending the towns had to try to do something, and the wide fire-line/backfire strategy was the one that seemed most likely to succeed. Furthermore, if one of the big fires actually had moved into the area, the burned out zones west and north of the towns would unquestionably have been an advantage to those trying to defend the place. The burned out sectors would have done exactly what a burnout is supposed to do by denying fuel to a larger fire.

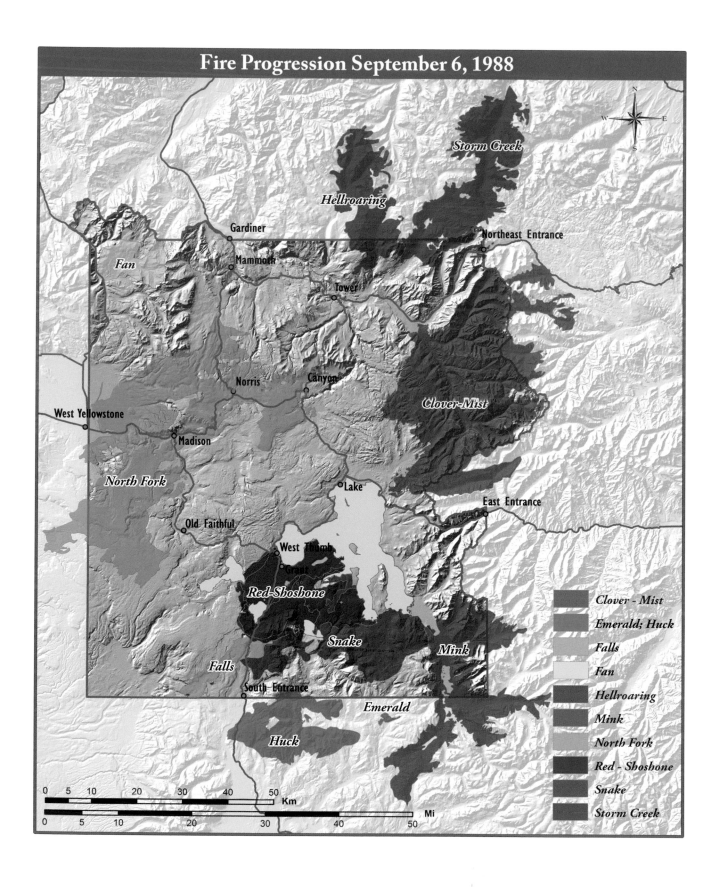

Fire Progression September 6, 1988

Storm Creek

Hellroaring

Gardiner

Fan

Mammoth

Tower

Northeast Entrance

Norris

Canyon

Clover-Mist

West Yellowstone

Madison

North Fork

Lake

East Entrance

Old Faithful

West Thumb

Grant

Red-Shoshone

Snake

Mink

Falls

South Entrance

Emerald

Huck

0 5 10 20 30 40 50	Km
0 5 10 20 30 40 50	Mi

Clover - Mist

Emerald; Huck

Falls

Fan

Hellroaring

Mink

North Fork

Red - Shoshone

Snake

Storm Creek

September 6, 1988

THE PARK service conducted its own burnout operation around its installation at the Northeast Entrance on September 5. (This backburn was not a contributing factor to the backburn that eventually ran past Silver Gate on September 6 and 7.) The park service backburn was conducted by ranger Nancy Clemons and others, and their operation was the principal reason I traveled to the Northeast Gate on that date, which in 1988 was Labor Day. The backburn at the Northeast Entrance seemed to be attended with great risk. After all, burning conditions were extreme, as evidenced by the wild fire behavior displayed at the time by so many big fires in the region. But the drip torches used to start the backfire at Northeast started fires that burned with only moderate intensity. As always, fire remained mysterious and unpredictable, even by those who knew it best. As it was, the backfire at Northeast worked ideally. It burned out a lot of fuel around the development without flaring into a conflagration in its own right.

I spent most of the day on September 5 photographing Nancy Clemons and the others start and then monitor their backburn around the Northeast Entrance, after which I drove back to my summer home at Madison Junction. My route from Northeast took me down Soda Butte Creek to Lamar Valley and Tower Junction, then over Dunraven Pass to Canyon, and then on to Madison via Norris Junction. I was in or near fire for the entire 75-mile trip, and I was never out of smoke along any portion of the route.

The portion of the trip through Lamar Valley was especially surreal. The road there was closed because of the fire emergency, so there was no tourist traffic. There were no firefighters or equipment about while I was driving there, either, so I was completely alone on the road. The valley was smoked in, with the distant ridges and mountains visible only in silhouette through the haze. The overriding feeling was one of being in front of an approaching juggernaut—that the fires that had burned so far, as large as they had been, were increasing almost exponentially in both size and intensity and were about to overwhelm everything in front of them.

Of course it was just temporal happenstance that it seemed to me that I was alone in Lamar Valley. There were other people in the area, firefighters and other park employees who were at duty stations working to protect key points from the advancing fires. But with no traffic on the road, a large part of my mind was free to think about other things, principal among which were the stories I had heard about the fire drama at the Silver Tip Ranch that had happened just two days before.

The Silver Tip Ranch was and is located along Slough Creek, which is a major tributary of the Lamar River. Slough Creek begins north of Yellowstone, in the Absaroka-Beartooth Wilderness portion of the Gallatin National Forest, and then flows south into the park. Early day settlers homesteaded along Slough Creek and that is how some of the land in the area passed from government ownership into private hands. The Silver Tip Ranch was built on some of that privately held land in the 1920s by the Guggenheim family, and the development soon became an ultra-high-end and exclusive resort for the super wealthy. For all of their history since the 1920s, the well-connected owners of the Silver Tip Ranch have been able to retain the right to use a dirt track running from Yellowstone's Northeast Entrance road north along the Slough Creek corridor to their property, which is only about a quarter mile outside the park boundary. Unfortunately for the Silver Tip Ranch, the Hellroaring Fire started not far to the west on August 15, 1988. Soon afterward, on August 19, weather conditions breathed life into the Storm Creek Fire, which had been nearly dormant since it started on June 23 not far east of the ranch. At the same time the gigantic Clover-Mist Fire was moving toward the Silver Tip from the south, so the expensive ranch found itself nearly surrounded by fire. Possibly because the owners of the Silver Tip were wealthy and well connected, two full fire crews and other firefighting resources were assigned to protect it from the advancing fires. In preparing for whichever fire might arrive first, the crews followed the usual regimen of clearing combustibles from the close proximity of ranch buildings, setting up pumps and sprinklers, and scratching firelines around the perimeter of the development.

It was the Storm Creek that won the race with the other two fires and blazed into the area of the Silver Tip Ranch, doing so on the afternoon of Saturday, September 3. When the fire struck, there were about fifty people on hand at the Silver Tip, including the two twenty-person fire crews, some Gallatin National Forest rangers, and a few ranch hands who had stayed to help with fire protection. The fifty people watched as the Storm Creek blew in with winds topping 40 miles per hour and enveloped the ranch on three sides. Flames rose hundreds of feet high, and the two helicopters that had been assigned to help defend the Silver Tip by dropping 200 gallon buckets of water on and around the ranch had to give up and fly away,

A furious smoke column, emanating from the Storm Creek Fire, over mountains to the north of Lamar Valley on September 5, 1988. © Jeff Henry/Roche Jaune Pictures, Inc.

out of the turbulent danger zone. So furious was the firestorm that burned over the ranch that those observing from a distance figured the people caught in the inferno would perish, or at the very least some on the crews would suffer injuries. In fact, as one of the helicopter pilots flew away to escape the firestorm, he radioed a notice to fire commanders that they should prepare for medical evacuations from the area of the Silver Tip Ranch. Privately the pilot feared that many of the firefighters down below would die.

But thanks to a large meadow near the ranch complex, and to the preparation work done in advance of the fire, no buildings burned and no firefighters were injured. I do remember the long and apprehensive pause in radio traffic, however, while the firestorm burned around the trapped crews and everyone else put aside their immediate concerns to listen for the outcome of the burnover. The area around the ranch suffered a nearly complete burnout, but thankfully the helicopter pilot's grim forecast of injuries, along with his private fear that there would be fatalities, did not turn out. There were moments of doubt, however, among some of the people trapped by the firestorm around the Silver Tip Ranch. Predictably, response to the situation ran the gamut of human emotion, with some individuals thinking their time had come while others responded more matter of factly and simply moved to zones of lighter fuel and rode out the storm. Some of the firefighters felt compelled to deploy their fire shelters, and that's where they chose to ride it out.

Two firefighters look toward the approaching Storm Creek Fire beyond the buildings of the Silver Tip Ranch on September 3, 1988. This and the following photos were taken by Thomas Williams Munro, Jr., a longtime employee of the Silver Tip Ranch who loyally stayed at the ranch to help with the fire emergency. The photo gives an idea of the inconceivable fury of the Storm Creek as it bore in on the ranch. © Thomas Williams Munro, Jr.

Continuing my drive down the Lamar River Valley I eventually came to Tower Junction, where I turned left and continued toward Dunraven Pass on my route back to my summer home at Madison Junction. As I drove up the long grade toward the Dunraven notch west of Mount Washburn, I had several different views of the basin formed by Carnelian Creek, the deep declivity on the west side of the road. Way up at the top of the basin, along the crest of the Washburn Range west of Dunraven Peak, I could see puffs of smoke rising from a few spot fires. The smoke signaled that the Wolf Lake portion of the North Fork Fire had crossed the Washburns on its way north. The Wolf Lake/North Fork had established a beachhead north of the mountains from which it would soon break out to race across the northern range of Yellowstone Park.

The day after my trip to the Northeast Entrance, I stayed closer to home and only traveled as far as Old Faithful. I was certain the North Fork Fire would burn into the location soon, and I wanted to be sure to not miss it. As exciting as backcountry fires were, I figured nothing could be more important than to be on hand to document fire burning around Yellowstone's most famous feature. And of course, Old Faithful was home to the Old Faithful Inn, certainly the most known building

A second photo by Tom Munro that conveys a sense of the violence of the firestorm that burned up to the Silver Tip Ranch on the afternoon of September 3, 1988. One of the ranch buildings is visible as a faint silhouette at the lower right. Munro remembers that the Storm Creek Fire was so violent that one of the windows of the Silver Tip lodge broke, and flying embers started a fire inside the building. Firefighters were able to put out the interior fire before it got out of hand. © Thomas Williams Munro, Jr.

in Yellowstone, and perhaps the most well-known structure in any national park anywhere.

As things unfolded, on the morning of September 6 I was taken away from my photo documentation work and detailed to circulate through the Old Faithful area to deliver the official park service message that there was only a one in three chance that the North Fork Fire would ever arrive there. My friend and fellow ranger Bonnie Gafney was detailed to work with me in making the rounds to concessions managers, to whom we delivered our official message, at the various properties in the Old Faithful area. Bonnie and I did as we were instructed, but for my part, after our official spiel was finished, I took aside certain people I knew and quietly gave them my personal view of the fire situation. My view, of course, was that fire in town or at least on the outskirts of Old Faithful was all but inevitable, and probably imminent.

After Bonnie and I had concluded that assignment, she went off to do something else while I resumed my photo work. I roamed the Old Faithful area, shooting some pictures of the Inn silhouetted against a smoky sunset to the west, and also shooting some other pictures of the weather vane and the anemometer in the

Sunset over the Old Faithful Inn on the afternoon of September 6, 1988. The huge smoke column behind the Inn is coming from the North Fork Fire, burning directly downwind from the historic Old Faithful complex. © Jeff Henry/Roche Jaune Pictures, Inc.

weather instrument compound by the Old Faithful Ranger Station. All the photos I shot, and everything else I saw, seemed to support my view about the fire future of the area, at least in my mind. The weather vane pointed directly at two large fire columns that were rising from the Madison Plateau to the west. And not only was it windy, as evidenced by the blurred whirligig in the weather station, it was also very warm for so late on an early September day in Yellowstone. On top of that, the smoky air was very dry, feeling almost as harsh as a fine-grit sandpaper when it blew past my face. I didn't know it at the time, but later I learned that the two huge smoke columns I saw to the southwest of Old Faithful were not illusions; the North Fork Fire burned 55,615 acres on September 6. Much of the fire's new growth was on its west front, where it posed a growing danger to Island Park and West Yellowstone, and southwest of Old Faithful, where it was poised to make a run right at the historic complex.

During the whole fire season in 1988 there was never a time when I felt fear for myself—I was young and tough and macho, so I suppose that was part of it, but

The weather station beside the Old Faithful Ranger Station silhouetted against the sunset on September 6, 1988. The two huge smoke columns from the North Fork Fire can be seen behind the weather station—the vagaries of the wind have merged the two columns in their upper reaches. Note that the weather vane is pointing in the direction of the smoke columns, while the wind cups on the anemometer are spinning so fast they are blurred in the picture. © Jeff Henry/Roche Jaune Pictures, Inc.

I always rationally figured that no matter what happened, there would always be something I could do and somewhere I could go to save myself. And further, I always made sure that I never put myself in a situation where things could develop such that there would be no escape. That said, however, I did feel a deep worry for the Old Faithful complex on the evening of September 6. I distinctly remember how I thought the wondrous old buildings, where I had spent so much of my adult life and which consequently were so important to me, as they were to so many others, were in very real danger. In addition to the big smoke columns that were near and directly upwind, it seemed to me that fire defense around the Old Faithful area was meager, and the relative absence of firefighters and equipment heightened my concern. I knew for certain that I would be back in the Old Faithful area the next day, which would be Wednesday, September 7, 1988.

Fire Progression September 8, 1988

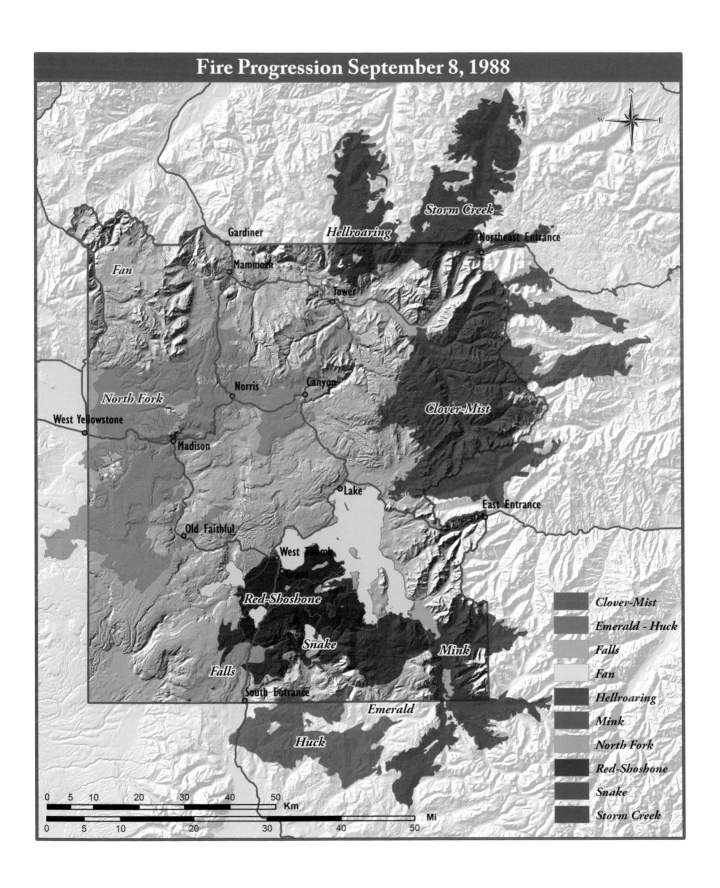

September 8, 1988

THIS MAP, based on information collected on the morning of September 8, reflects the explosive growth made by nearly all the Yellowstone fires the day before. The North Fork alone burned nearly 28,000 acres, which is about two and a third times as much as it burned on Black Saturday (but only half as much as it burned on September 6). The Clover-Mist was also busy, burning its way through almost 33,500 new acres. Collectively, all the area fires burned nearly 126,000 acres on the 7th, which is not far from Black Saturday's total of something more than 150,000. Inexplicably, however, the Mink Fire burned exactly zero new acres, even though weather conditions around the Mink must have been very similar to those in place around all the other fires that did blow up.

September 7 was the day the backfire set near Silver Gate, Montana (to deprive the advancing Storm Creek Fire of fuel), ran out of control, and burned the area immediately north of both Silver Gate and Cooke City. That episode has already been discussed under the heading of September 4, 1988. The 7th was also the day the Clover-Mist Fire put on spectacularly fearsome displays around Yellowstone's East Entrance, again as has been discussed previously. Wednesday the 7th, which did not receive a special moniker like "Black Saturday" but probably should have, was also the day when the North Fork Fire made a major advance to the north to threaten park headquarters at Mammoth Hot Springs, as well as the town of Gardiner just 5 miles north of Mammoth. Yet another front of the North Fork pushed on from the spot fires I saw smoking on the north side of the Washburn Range on the evening of September 5, and burned very hot along a considerable segment of the road over Dunraven Pass. This latter front of the North Fork now seemed certain to carry on

Official photographer Jim Peaco of the National Park Service shot this picture of fire burning on the ridge behind the Range Rider Inn and the Pine Edge Cabins in Silver Gate, Montana, in early September of 1988. 1988 National Park Service photo by Jim Peaco

to the north and east, where it probably would link up with the Hellroaring, the Storm Creek or the Clover-Mist Fires—perhaps even with all of them.

Of course, September 7, 1988, will forever be remembered as the day the North Fork Fire finally arrived at Old Faithful. The arrival of the fire came with great bureaucratic irony. Earlier in the summer, in late July, the park service had taken advantage of the then nascent fire to stage a media event at Old Faithful, even though at the time it was not that likely that the fire would make it to the area, at least not for some time. And then, after a period of anomalous winds had moved the fire to the south and left it almost inevitable that it would burn to the complex whenever normal southwesterly winds returned, the park service reversed its stance and steadfastly denied that obvious likelihood.

September 7 dawned warm and smoky. It was also windy at an early hour. I began my day at Madison Junction, but shortly after I arose I drove from Madison to Old Faithful in a large, stake-bodied dump truck that had been issued to me for the summer. If I remember correctly, and I think I do, I was pretty sure this was the day the North Fork was going to make it to Old Faithful. After all, the smoke columns had been so very close the evening before, and were undeniably upwind from the location.

Once I arrived at Old Faithful I set to work with a few others removing park service signs from an old log building the area rangers used as a sign cache. The old building had been constructed by the Civilian Conservation Corps in the 1930s, so it was not only well constructed, it was also historic. The log structure was situated

A huge Columbia helicopter carrying a 1,000-gallon bucket flying over the North Fork Fire. The large water bucket was never filled to capacity in Yellowstone, as the park's high, thin air reduced the flying machines' lifting capacity. Water drops from helicopters and slurry drops from fixed-wing aircraft were ineffective in stopping the advance of the North Fork Fire toward Old Faithful on Wednesday September 7, 1988. © Jeff Henry/Roche Jaune Pictures, Inc.

on the west side of the Grand Loop Road near the base of the timbered ridge above the park service housing and residential area. Perhaps because of its proximity to heavy forest, it was thought that the building was indefensible, or that defending it would take too many resources away from other priorities. In any event, it had been decided to remove the signs from the building to save them in case the building burned. We hauled the signs in my stake-bodied truck to a graveled parking area near the Old Faithful Ranger Station, where we simply dumped them on the ground, hoping that the lack of combustible material around the spot would keep the signs from burning when the fire came.

After completing the sign moving assignment, I drove my truck back to the residential area, where I commenced loading some firewood that was stacked near a new government housing duplex. The duplex had just been built during the previous year, and trees that had been felled to make space for the construction had been blocked up and left on site for the occupants of the new duplex to use as firewood. The duplex was occupied by personal friends of mine, and I'm sure that factored into my decision to use my time and my park service truck the way I did that morning.

Fire spotters used infrared scopes to see focal points of heat through obscuring smoke. The spotters and their communications person with the radio were positioned on top of the Old Faithful Inn when the North Fork Fire made its move on Old Faithful on the afternoon of September 7, 1988. The images in the infrared scopes became so bright the spotters could no longer bear to look through them, at which point they suited up with fire protective clothing of all sorts and asserted their opinion that the Old Faithful area was doomed. © Jeff Henry/ Roche Jaune Pictures, Inc.

The truck I had at my disposal was large, its bed probably seven feet wide and sixteen feet long, with stakes about four feet high around its sides. We neatly stacked all the wood onto it that we could, so when we were done it amounted to a big load. By the time we were finished, it was late morning, and the wind and smoke had both intensified. I parked the truckload of firewood in the large lot behind the Old Faithful Inn and in front of the Old Faithful Ranger Station. I hoped the load of firewood would survive the fire, but whether it did or not the time had come for me to begin using my cameras.

I figured the best vantage point in the area was the widow's walk on top of the Inn itself. The great building was eighty-four years old in 1988, and was arguably the most iconic structure in any national park anywhere in the world. The widow's walk was approximately ninety feet higher than the ground, so it offered a good view of the Old Faithful area and of the timbered country to the west. When I reached the top of the roof via the stairways that rose above the interior lobby, I found two fire spotters positioned there with infrared scopes, which allowed them to see heat through smoke. The two men were looking, of course, at the fire that was burning on the Madison Plateau off to the west and southwest. Other observers came and went while I was on top of the Inn, including a variety of concessions and park service employees. To all who came up, it became apparent that the fire to the west and southwest was rapidly building momentum and that it was on its way toward us.

As usual, most of the time the large volumes of smoke the fire was belching forth obscured the actual flames. And general visibility by this point in the summer was obscured by the dense level of ambient smoke. But we could hear the flames, and on the rare occasions when the walls of smoke opened for a moment we could see them, too. The fact that the flames were usually out of sight made them seem more menacing, not less. After a while, the two lookouts could no longer bear to look through their infrared scopes because the heat-based images were too intense. Then the two men put down their scopes and began donning fire-proofed clothing of every description—fireproof gloves, fireproof face masks, fireproof bandanas, you name it, they had it and they were putting it on. While they were suiting up, both men resorted to nonstop strings of nervous profanity, the meaning of which could be distilled down to their view that the Old Faithful area and most of the people in it were doomed.

But an infrared scope wasn't necessary to see that the fire had built up a huge head of heat. Looking at it gave one the sense that the firestorm was swelling like a tsunami at sea, and that it was about to surge forward and break over us. Numerous helicopters with water buckets and fixed wing slurry bombers were dropping their loads in front of the fire, but to no discernible effect. Seeing what was coming, I tried to get on the park radio to tell people down below what was happening, but radio traffic was so constant I never could find an opening. A fire officer of some description—I have forgotten his name and his exact title—was also on the roof by this time, and on a fire-specific radio channel he was able to get through to people down below and try to alert them to the approaching danger that was not yet visible from their lower vantage point.

Incredibly, officials at ground level answered back that what we were seeing was only a finger of fire and not a meaningful risk to the Old Faithful location. At about the time we were told that what we could see was only an insignificant finger, the fire topped the ridge to the southwest of Old Faithful, around the upper reaches of Iron Spring Creek. As soon as it topped the ridge I could feel its radiant heat from my perch on top of the Inn, even though the fire was in the neighborhood of a mile and a half away.

The wind on the roof of the Inn by now was up to hurricane strength. At least that's how it seemed to me—my camera tripod would have blown over a number of times if I hadn't caught it, and tripods have a widely braced stance and not much sail area. Ever since that September 7 there has been much debate about the wind speed and direction at Old Faithful that fateful day. Some sources have estimated that the wind blew in excess of 80 miles per hour, while other estimates put the speed at considerably less. The records of the official weather station by the Old Faithful Ranger Station put the top wind speed at only 17 miles per hour. I would find it very

Flames from the North Fork Fire as it burned over the ridge to the east of Fern Cascades on one of the upper forks of Iron Spring Creek. In spite of their tremendous size, the flames were almost always hidden by dense smoke. Even in this photo, the flames are almost invisible in the haze. © Jeff Henry/Roche Jaune Pictures, Inc.

hard to believe that anyone who was there that day would accept the claim that the wind speed topped out at 17 miles per hour. Everyone who was there has superlatives to describe not only the firestorm but also the wind speed as a separate entity note-worthy in its own right. Other evidence indicates the wind speed was exceptional, such as videos shot of the fire where much of the audio intended to accompany the footage is drowned out by powerful winds blowing across recording microphones.

As for wind direction, there has been a widespread belief since the Old Faith-ful firestorm that the buildings in the complex and the people present at the time survived because of a last minute wind shift. I could not disagree more strongly with this contention. Official weather records (records I believe rather than discount) from that afternoon show that wind direction was fairly constant, varying from about 250 to 300 compass degrees, or from west southwest to west northwest, during the entire afternoon burning period. In my opinion, the Old Faithful complex was saved by the rather large firebreaks that were situated between the development and the oncoming fire. The paved parking lots and the wide geothermal expanses that were mostly barren of fuel were the biggest factors. Other firebreaks included the network of roads in the area, the power line along the west side of the development, and the high volume irrigation line that had been set up along the power line by a

A photograph by ranger Bonnie Gafney, taken along the Grand Loop Road during the evacuation of leftover tourists and employees from Old Faithful after the North Fork Fire had burned through the area. Note the open flames along the road, probably just north of Biscuit Basin. © Bonnie Gafney

team of good hearted Mormon farmers from Idaho. All those breaks took a lot of punch out of the main fire front that advanced on Old Faithful, and the segment of the front that would have intersected the complex stalled out for want of combustible material as it neared the development.

But millions of sparks and embers rained down on the area as the firestorm struck. The embers swirled around the parking lots as thick as swirling snow crystals in a winter ground blizzard, yet another indication that the wind continued to blow from the main fire into the development. So thick were the firebrands and so dry were conditions that isolated bits of fuel—things like remnant stumps on islands in the parking lots and tufts of grass sprouting through cracks in the pavement—burst into flame as though exhaled upon by some fire-breathing dragon. In what is perhaps the most telling evidence of all that the wind was indeed blowing from the main fire directly toward Old Faithful, a firebrand leapt completely across the development, right over our heads, and landed near Observation Point on the other side of the Firehole River. Within seconds of landing the firebrand had spawned a new fire, and within a minute or two the new fire had flared into the trees, where it took off as a running crown fire in its own right.

Back down in the area of the Inn, sparks and embers continued to swirl around my ankles, as by this time I had descended from the roof after deciding that it wasn't

The menacing smoke cloud of the North Fork Fire rolls into the Old Faithful complex on the afternoon of September 7. The picture was shot from the top of the Old Faithful Inn, while the structures in the foreground of the photo are maintenance buildings associated with the Inn. 1988 National Park Service photo by Jeff Henry

exactly the safest place to be. When I passed through the doors of the Inn on my way out, I remember thinking that I might be leaving the great building for the last time in my life. Earlier, when I was still on top of the Inn and could see the fire coming at us, I had been dismayed by the contrast of what I could see below. On one side of the Inn, I could see a collection of tourists on the boardwalk around Old Faithful Geyser. Oblivious to what was coming, the tourists were using their instamatics to shoot pictures of the famous geyser. In the parking lot on the other side of the Inn sat their parked cars and recreational vehicles, while beyond the parking lot and other smaller buildings the fiery waves of the North Fork Fire were rolling down on all of us.

When the full effect of the firestorm hit, there was so much smoke and turbulence that things became literally as dark as night. The wind was buffeting and the smoke choking, and we were so immersed in the infernal cyclone that it felt like we had entered an unknown realm, as different in atmosphere as the contrast between free-flowing air and the fetid air of a cave. The deciding moment was at hand, and I think everyone present must have experienced an interval of feeling closed in by the smoke and alone in the dark, an individual realization that the Old Faithful area really might burn. Only the very dull could have escaped the enveloping sense that the issue was in doubt.

The flames were stupendous. When the smoke parted so that the fire was visible, I could see that it was at least twice the height of the trees in the forest, so

The fiery waves of the North Fork Fire as it rolled by Old Faithful. The buildings and vehicles in the foreground are nearly hidden in smoke. 1988 National Park Service photo by Jeff Henry

probably more than 200 feet high. Fire whirls and swirls, some of them looking very much like honest-to-god tornadoes of flame, spun out of the superheated head of the fire. Orange tongues of flame licked up at the sky, but when they reached a certain height above the trees the ambient wind caught them and blew them forward. Then, after blowing forward from the main fire, the tongues of flame would be caught in an inward rush of wind that was being sucked into the inferno at ground level. That would cause the flames to roll over on themselves in a wavelike motion. The effect was very much like tremendous, breaking waves of fire, a phenomenon known to firefighters as a "rolling crown fire," but this rolling crown fire was gigantic in scale. In addition to the rolling, breaking waves of flame, it was also apparent that fuel within the fire's maw was being gasified but not igniting. The dark balls of superheated gas were flung forward ahead of the front, where they ignited in mid-air and become flaming fireballs. I think that the pockets of gasified fuel formed in the oxygen-deprived environment inside the firestorm, so they couldn't ignite until they had blown far enough forward to reach fresh, unconsumed air, at which point they exploded into open flame. The noise was deafening beyond belief—as loud as a fleet of jet engines close at hand.

When the firestorm burned up to the very edge of the development, we were caught right in the fount of the smoke. We were probably as close to the heart of a firestorm as anyone can be and live to tell about it. The smoke was so thick and dark that the vehicles in a small convoy that was crawling to a safe zone in the large parking lot in front of the Inn repeatedly banged bumpers, in spite of the fact that

Another view of the North Fork Fire from the top of the Old Faithful Inn. The head of the fire in this photo is behind the Hamilton Photo Shop and the original Old Faithful Snow Lodge. Patrick Povah of Hamilton Stores is using the fire truck in front of the Photo Shop to wet down the roof of the structure. The Photo Shop was originally a Haynes Picture Shop, and has now been moved closer to the Old Faithful Lodge and is operated by the Yellowstone Park Foundation. 1988 National Park Service photo by Jeff Henry

the drivers all had their headlights on. Above the roar of the fire there were numerous explosions. I thought at the time, and still do, that cabins that burned behind the old Snow Lodge and the old Hamilton Photo Shop caused at least some of the detonations. My thinking, which was shared by at least some others, was that air inside the burning cabins expanded to the point where the internal pressure could no longer be contained and the structures blew apart.

Another explanation was that green trees within the firestorm were heated to the point where the moisture in the their trunks flashed to steam and blew up. But I have been around many other forest fires that were burning away from developed areas and have not heard such explosions, so I rather doubt that exploding green trees caused what we heard at Old Faithful. Another possible explanation, and an ironic one, was that the explosions we heard were caused by the superheating of fire extinguishers mounted on the outside walls of cabins that burned. This last possibility was suggested to me by Dan Tompkins, who was the 1988 Old Faithful area maintenance manager for TW Services, Yellowstone, the park's hotel concessioner at the time. Dan was an experienced maintenance person, and he was also present the day of the Old Faithful firestorm, so his insights had merit. The thought of exploding fire extinguishers, and of the attendant possibility that they were expelling shards of metallic shrapnel in the proximity of firefighters, is a scary one.

A close-up view of the same building with the rolling flames of the North Fork Fire right behind it. 1988 National Park Service photo by Jeff Henry

The cabins that burned included a number of rental units associated with the Old Faithful Snow Lodge. Some other utility buildings and a few vehicles burned, too, almost all along the south side of the complex. In my view, buildings burned in that portion of the development because they were situated proximal to combustible forest. I wasn't in that sector of the complex when the cabins burned, but I further suspect that because those structures were not a high priority they were not that well defended. Elsewhere in the development, again in my opinion, I believe the buildings survived because of heavy wetting from sprinklers and firefighters wielding hoses. That's what kept the buildings from igniting in the blizzard of sparks and embers that fell on the area as the firestorm blew past.

The burned buildings also included a number of employee cabins that were situated directly behind the Snow Lodge that existed in 1988 (not today's Snow Lodge, which came into service in 1998). One of the cabins that burned was assigned to a food and beverage employee named Amy Beegel. I did not know Amy at the time, but I did come across her burned belongings in the cabin where she had lived that summer. A mass of melted coins especially caught my eye—the large volume of coins told me the cabin probably had belonged to a tipped employee. I was intrigued by the way the silver coins had melted in the fierce heat when the cabin burned, while the copper pennies had not. The result was a mass of recognizable pennies welded together by the silver coins that had been rendered molten in the fire. I shot several photographs of the welded mass, but never got to know Amy well until she did me an enormously good turn twenty-three years after the fires. After Amy and I

A fire investigator holding a mass of melted silver coins twisted around some unmelted copper pennies in the wreckage of a burned employee cabin that had housed the belongings of TW Services, Yellowstone employee Amy Beegel. © Jeff Henry/Roche Jaune Pictures, Inc.

became friends during the time when she was doing me the big favor, we were having a discussion about the 1988 fires one day when we compared notes and figured out that the burned wreckage in the Old Faithful Cabin that so intrigued me in September of 1988 was actually the remains of her personal belongings.

Many fascinating personal stories came out of the Old Faithful firestorm. Dan Tompkins, the maintenance supervisor who theorized that the explosions that went off in the middle of the conflagration were caused by overheating fire extinguishers, personally put out fires that started on several structures in the Old Faithful area. One of the potentially most consequential was a fire that started on the upper gas station, with its thousands of gallons of stored fuel. Dan also put out other spot fires that started on cabins behind the Old Faithful Lodge. Dan, who had evacuated his wife Jill and their three-year-old daughter Lindsey before the firestorm arrived, remembered later that hose nozzles were at a premium. "Once you got hold of a nozzle, you didn't give it up. You held on to it, and carried it with you from hose to hose." Other maintenance employees who helped Dan fight spot fires in the development included Randy Boardman, Tim Dalathower, and John Lauderbaugh.

Firefighters Ken Hansen and Nick Ricardi struggle to save the Old Faithful Inn on the afternoon of September 7. Ken and Rick were two of a great many firefighters who deserve the credit for saving the great building from the North Fork Fire. © Jeff Henry/Roche Jaune Pictures, Inc.

Another concessions employee who helped the TW Services maintenance men fight spot fires was Mark Watson. In 1988 Mark worked as a park-wide food and beverage supervisor, and his assignment during the fires was to remove perishable foods from locations that had been evacuated and closed. That's why he was at Old Faithful on the day of the firestorm, and after he was cut off by the fire, he worked to save cabins in the area behind the Old Faithful Lodge. That was the same area where Dan Tompkins and his maintenance employees spent most of their time, too, and it was well that they did.

No professional firefighters were on hand in the cabin area, which apparently had been assigned a lower priority. The TW Services people hosed out a large number of spot fires, many of which started on the sill timbers of the externally framed cabins, where duff-like debris had accumulated over time. More accurately, the workers other than Mark Watson hosed out spot fires. For his part Mark, who is better known by his nickname Doc, could not find a hose nozzle, so he beat out spot fires with a broom he retrieved from a janitor's storage room. Again, it was well that Doc and the others did what they did. The Old Faithful Lodge cabins were all made of wood, and all were roofed with highly flammable cedar shingles. In the absence of any firefighters, if even just one of the cabins had become fully engulfed in flame, it certainly would have ignited adjacent cabins, and then the fire would have surely moved to the next cabin, and to the next, and so on. While Doc Watson was beating out spot fires in the Old Faithful Lodge cabins, he was astonished to see big firebrands, some as large as chunks of logs, whizzing by overhead on the fiery winds.

Earlier in the day, Mark Watson had been corralled by members of the National Park Service when they rounded up concessions employees and tourists and forced them to move to a safe zone on the boardwalk around Old Faithful Geyser. On that boardwalk Mark paired up with Darren Kisor, a friend of Mark's who worked for TW Services as a warehouse manager at Old Faithful. For his part, Darren had already put out a significant fire on the roof of a building that in 1988 housed maintenance shops and other facilities and stood adjacent to the Old Faithful Inn. In retrospect, Darren remembers that he simply reacted without conscious thought when he saw the spot fire start on the roof of the building next to the Inn. He leapt inside a door to where he knew from previous observation that a fire hose was stored, recruited another employee to help handle the hose, and sprayed the fire out. Then Darren, too, was herded to the boardwalk by Old Faithful.

Resentful that they were being controlled and contained by people who were less experienced and less capable than themselves, Mark and Darren bolted away from the makeshift compound on the Old Faithful boardwalk. They moved in the direction of the Old Faithful Lodge, where they came upon a female ranger struggling to open a fire hydrant. Frustrated and frightened, the ranger was in tears from her inability to turn the tight valve on the hydrant. The valve was indeed tight, but together Mark and Darren were able to twist a wrench and open the water flow, whereupon the ranger officiously demanded to know why they had left the boardwalk by Old Faithful Geyser, and further ordered them to return to the designated safe zone. One more time, it was a good thing that Mark and Darren did not return to idleness by Old Faithful; they played a significant role in saving cabins behind the Old Faithful Lodge and by extension, probably other structures as well.

In 1988 George Bornemann was the bell captain in the famous Old Faithful Inn. In connection with his job, George was entitled to live in a large room inside the great building, in an area reserved for the bell staff known as Bats' Alley. On the day of the firestorm, George was busily packing his possessions in his room when the order came to evacuate. Taking what he could, George and his friend Tom Robertson drove their vehicles to the Old Faithful overpass, where a convoy

Another unidentified firefighter who had bravely stationed himself on the roof of the East Wing of the Inn and was spraying water onto the roof of the Old House. © Jeff Henry/Roche Jaune Pictures, Inc.

of evacuating employees was forming. While waiting in line for the convoy to get underway, George and Tom talked to each other on CB radios.

They decided that what was about to happen was huge, in their view the biggest event at Old Faithful since the August 1959 earthquake that shook Yellowstone and surrounding areas, and that as longtime employees they couldn't afford to miss out on history in the making. They pulled out of the convoy, drove across the median strip between the egress and access roads, and returned to the area of the Inn. There they parked their cars and walked into the Upper Geyser Basin, where they reckoned no one would find them and tell them they had to leave the area. Then that evening, after the main fire front had passed, George and Tom walked back to the front of the Inn, relieved that the unique building had survived. As they were walking past the front door, Inn manager George Helfrich came out and asked the two friends what they were still doing at Old Faithful, that they were supposed to have evacuated hours before. Before they could formulate an answer to Helrich's first question, he asked them a second: Would they come back to work in the Inn, serving as security guards for the building in the absence of the security people who had been evacuated?

George Helfrich's story is unquestionably one of the more important stories from that Wednesday at Old Faithful. George is a considered, thoughtful man, who today works for the National Park Service as Chief of Concessions Management

National Park Service interpretive rangers rounded up wayward tourists and concessions employees and staged them on the boardwalk between Old Faithful Geyser and the Old Faithful visitor center during the height of the firestorm on September 7. © Jeff Henry/Roche Jaune Pictures, Inc.

in Yellowstone. George prefaces his recollections of the events leading up to and including September 7, 1988, at Old Faithful with the insightful caveat that we all structure our stories to present ourselves in a positive light, even in the guise of a "hero," to use George's word. That said, George's memory is that for the few days previous to the Old Faithful firestorm, up to and including the morning of the day the North Fork Fire arrived, he was told by park service sources, and by fire managers, that there was only a slight chance that the fire would ever make it to his location. One of the fire managers, in fact, told George it would be a bad idea to evacuate the Old Faithful Inn, especially of its employees, because it might be difficult to retrieve the employees after the fire danger had passed and therefore it might be impossible to reopen the property for the remainder of the season.

Because of what he had been told by other, unofficial sources, and because of what he could see with his own eyes, George became progressively more skeptical about the official line that was being presented to him. In the interest of being thorough, however, he called and consulted Jim McCaleb, who in 1988 was vice president in charge of operations for TW Services, Yellowstone, with his office located in Mammoth. On the phone Jim agreed that once closed, the Inn probably would not reopen for the 1988 season, and he pointed out that such a closure would result in the loss of a great deal of revenue for the company. To Jim's credit, he also allowed that he was not the one on scene at Old Faithful, whereas George was, and therefore George should be the one to make the final call. On the evening of September 6, George made the decision to evacuate guests from the Inn early the following morning.

The early morning evacuation of hotel guests went "smoothly," but for the remainder of the morning of the 7th George did not follow up with an order to evacuate employees—he still held on to hope that a major fire danger would not materialize and that he still might be able to reopen the Inn if he kept his employees around. In the meantime, he put his employees to work doing tasks not easily accomplished while guests were present, such as deep cleaning public spaces. As the morning progressed, however, George could see that the situation was deteriorating, and around noon he made the call to evacuate employees. George made the decision largely "because employee behavior is so unpredictable." By 1:00 o'clock or so almost all of the employees were gone. Those who did not have their own cars were bussed out to West Yellowstone on company buses. Sharon Chuba, who was George's assistant manager at the Old Faithful Inn, reluctantly assumed the duty of accompanying the evacuating convoy. For her part, Sharon would have preferred to stay at Old Faithful to witness what was about to happen.

When the firestorm hit at sometime around three or four in the afternoon, George oversaw some of the few TW Services employees still left in the area as they used hoses to wet down the roof and walls of the Inn, so George and the others made a major contribution to saving the great building. Later in the evening, after the front of the North Fork had passed and the immediate danger had lessened, George circulated around the Inn, checking on things and worrying about the lack of security now that his security staff was gone. When he came to the employee cafeteria he found a scene reminiscent "of a science fiction movie where the people had instantaneously vanished." Because the employees had been evacuated on very short notice during lunch hour, they had stood up and simply left their food trays and half consumed beverages on the long institutional tables. Cooks and servers had left abruptly, too, so bins of food were still steaming on the serving line. Everything was as it would be during a normal lunch hour, except George happened upon the scene in the evening and, most importantly, all the people had disappeared.

Most of the Old Faithful Inn employees who were evacuated in midday on the 7th made their way out to West Yellowstone, Montana. En route, they were met by tourist traffic heading in toward Old Faithful. Because of bureaucratic ambivalence, guests were evacuated from the Old Faithful Inn in the morning. They were followed by an evacuation of employees later in the day, but at the same time employees were being evacuated, tourists were allowed back in to the Old Faithful area. That's how some tourists ended up present at Old Faithful when the firestorm hit. Some of the tourists who were left, along with some lingering employees, were convoyed out at the last minute, but some remained stranded at the complex when the North Fork Fire showed up and for quite a while afterward, until burning debris could be cleared from the roads leading out of the area. During the firestorm, National Park Service interpretive rangers gathered some of the wayward tourists and many of the wayward employees on the boardwalk around Old Faithful Geyser, an area considered to be a safe zone.

Of course law enforcement rangers at Old Faithful had their hands full on September 7 as well. One such ranger was Lee Whittlesey, who by 1988 had already worked in Yellowstone for seventeen summers and six winters. By early afternoon on the 7th, Lee, who is now Yellowstone National Park's official historian, found himself manning a barricade on the road leading out of Old Faithful toward West Thumb. Stationed nearby was a fire crew with twenty-five members from Texas, a group who called themselves "Texas Two." As the afternoon progressed, Lee and the Texas firefighters could see some flames in the distance, and for a time thought the main fire front was going to bypass the Old Faithful area—at least that's how it looked from their perspective. Then Lee heard the radio transmission from the fire official on top of the Old Faithful Inn, the one who was standing near me when he radioed his warning to other fire officials in the Old Faithful area. The fire official's report about what he could see from the roof of the Inn worried Lee a bit, and soon thereafter his worry turned to raw fear as the massive flames of the North Fork Fire suddenly appeared very close to Lee's barricade, moving with frightening speed toward him and the Texas Two firefighters.

The commander of the fire crew on station with Lee yelled, "Texas Two, abandon the line! Run! Run! Every man for himself!" Lee and the Texas firefighters ran as fast as they could toward the big parking lot in front of the Old Faithful Ranger Station. As he ran, Lee radioed to anyone who could hear "The fire is here! It's huge! I'm abandoning the barricade!" Also as he ran, Lee thought to himself, "So this is it. This is how I die."

Fortunately Lee and the others made it to the large parking lot, and while they had to gasp for air in the oxygen-starved atmosphere during the height of the firestorm, they survived. As the afternoon progressed, Lee observed some of his park service coworkers put out a spot fire on the roof of the ranger station, and also watched "about 35 of what I took to be TW Services employees, all frantically beating spot fires out [on the roof of the Old Faithful Inn]." Then still later, he partnered with ranger Gary Youngblood and cruised the Old Faithful area helping with whatever situation they found. Lee found Youngblood exuberant, exclaiming "Can you believe this, and we're right in the middle of it!" Others were not at all exuberant, but instead were terrified: Ranger Youngblood spent part of his afternoon attending to a woman "who had collapsed from the shock of it all."

Another Old Faithful ranger involved in the Wednesday firestorm was Bonnie Gafney. Early in the afternoon on the 7th, at what turned out to be an inopportune time, Bonnie's supervisor Debbie Bird had insisted that Bonnie accompany her on a reconnaissance of the road toward West Thumb. Bonnie did not want to leave the Old Faithful area at what she saw as a crucial juncture; she was quite sure the North Fork Fire was about to arrive at the location. As it turned out, of course, Bonnie was correct. She and Debbie drove a short distance on the road toward West Thumb, on what turned out to be a meaningless reconnaissance into an unimportant area, when they found themselves cut off by the advancing fire front that burned across the road behind them. As things unfolded for Bonnie and Debbie, they couldn't get back to Old Faithful during the critical time when the firestorm exploded, and moreover they had to wait things out on a road that was heavily timbered along its sides and therefore not a completely safe place to be.

Bonnie also remembers resentment toward higher ups in the park service, not only for their insistence that there was only a remote chance that the North Fork Fire would ever burn its way to Old Faithful, but also for the way that the upper-level bureaucrats commandeered so much firefighting equipment and so many fire-fighters to protect park headquarters at Mammoth Hot Springs. In this resentment Bonnie was not alone.

By the time the North Fork Fire burned to Old Faithful, park headquarters at Mammoth was indeed threatened. But Mammoth was seen as the most defensible, developed location in the park, what with its wide, irrigated lawns, stone buildings with tile roofs, and a relative paucity of forest in proximity with the development. Bonnie and others saw the situation as one in which the generals of the army were taking care of themselves first, with the enlisted people in the field be damned. By this point in the summer of fire almost all developed locations and most gateway communities were simultaneously threatened, and a more equitable allocation of resources would have seemed to have been in order. But such was not the case: Bonnie's perception seemed accurate to me, that there was indeed an unfair distribution of firefighters and equipment in favor of Mammoth. In Bonnie's personal case, she had particular worries about her residence at Old Faithful, where all of her personal belongings were stored. Most especially, she worried about the welfare of her pets when the firestorm struck. It wasn't until later, after she had managed to return to Old Faithful, that she learned that her home and her pets had survived.

Yet another personal story from September 7, 1988 involved Dave Thomas, who was a fire behavior analyst for the North Fork Fire from mid-August until mid-September. As it turned out Dave was fortunate enough to be at Old Faithful himself on the day of the firestorm, so he had a chance to see things up close and personal. One of his memories is that some people present "displayed panic in the confusion and chaos." There was a woman who came running up to Dave and the other fire officials accompanying him, frantically screaming "How the f—— do you open this thing?" while holding up a folded fire shelter in front of her. Dave said later that the woman looked like someone who would not normally use such profanity. Dave has also observed that the situation that day at Old Faithful, in his opinion, had the potential to embark on a cascading "chain of events that could have had disastrous, fatal results." In Dave's mind, all it would have taken would have been a "car wreck, helicopter break down, an overly panicked tourist, or a hotter building fire" for things to unravel.

I couldn't agree more, and can think of several other scenarios where disaster would have ensued, such as flaming trees falling across and blocking roadways ahead of and behind an evacuating convoy. And most catastrophic of all, in my mind, would have been an interruption of water supply to the Old Faithful area at the critical time—an interruption that any number of eventualities could have precipitated. To place things in overall context, Dave Thomas wrote on the twentieth anniversary of the Yellowstone fires that they "were so uncommon, so unique, that many of us [firefighting professionals] became mesmerized just by their power and beauty."

As it was, there were a great many people who did panic at Old Faithful that day. There were many who broke down in tears or prayer, and even some professional media people who did not perform their jobs. In the height of the firestorm, I myself thought that the buildings in the Old Faithful area might well be incorporated into the conflagration, and that the best I would be able to do at that point was to take one or two families of visiting tourists by the hand and lead them to the Firehole River, to one of the barren geothermal plains in the area, or to some other safe zone, there to weather out the holocaust.

For me, one of the more revealing moments of the day came in the evening, when a press conference was held on the porch of the Old Faithful Ranger Station. By this point in the summer, the Yellowstone fires had become big news, and many high-powered reporters were on the scene, reporters who at other times in their careers had covered stories in a lot of different hot spots around the world. Several reporters in the assembled crowd told me they had covered stories in places like Saigon and Beirut, but what they had gone through that day at Old Faithful left them more frightened than anything they had previously experienced anywhere else in the world.

For my part, I just couldn't bring myself to leave Old Faithful. I spent the rest of the daylight hours walking around the area, shooting almost all the film I had with me, which was a lot. After dark, I went to the home of my friend Dan Tompkins, the Old Faithful area maintenance manager. His house was a historic old cabin above the Firehole River and behind the Old Faithful Lodge, in the same cabin area where he and Mark Watson and the others had put out so many spot fires and probably saved most all the Lodge cabins earlier in the day. Several others were gathered there, and without specifically saying so, we all knew we had a commonality from the day's events, that we had witnessed and been a part of something extraordinary that none of us would ever forget.

I wandered on, stopping once at a phone booth in front of the Upper Store to call my parents in Maryland to tell them that I had made it through the day's events OK. Then, walking on, I could see the silhouette of the Old Faithful Inn looming up out of the smoky darkness. Earlier in the day I had similarly seen the Inn rising up out of the smoke shortly after the furious firestorm had blown past. As I wrote in my 2004 book about the Old Faithful Inn, a book I coauthored with Karen Reinhart,

The venerable Old Faithful Inn on the early evening of September 7, 1988, still standing after the North Fork Fire had come and gone. © Jeff Henry/Roche Jaune Pictures, Inc.

the scene of the Inn rising up out of the smoke reminded me of Herbert Mason's famous photograph of St. Paul's Cathedral looming out of the smoke of the London Blitz on 29 December 1940. As Londoners must have been relieved to see that their great cathedral had survived Nazi bombing, so also was I relieved to see that the Old Faithful Inn had survived the blitz of fire on September 7, 1988. I was further relieved when I considered that no other major structures in the area had burned.

I lingered until late that night at Old Faithful, until sometime well after midnight, before I finally left the area to return to my seasonal home at Madison Junction. The trip down the Firehole River Valley was unforgettable. I drove the big, stake-bodied truck, the same one some of my cohorts and I had heaped with firewood many hours before, on the morning of the 7th. There was absolutely no one else on the road. I drove though fire most of the way to Madison, and was continually mindful that I was hauling a load of firewood. I tilted my external mirrors to an acute inward angle, the better to keep an eye on my flammable load. My plan was to simply pull the hydraulic lever in the cab of my truck and dump the wood on the highway should it catch fire from the sparks and embers that were arcing like tracer bullets though the darkness. In several places I had to stop to manhandle smoldering debris out of the road before I could continue. But of course I made it to Madison, where I spent a long time with my mind buzzing with sounds and images of fire before I finally fell asleep.

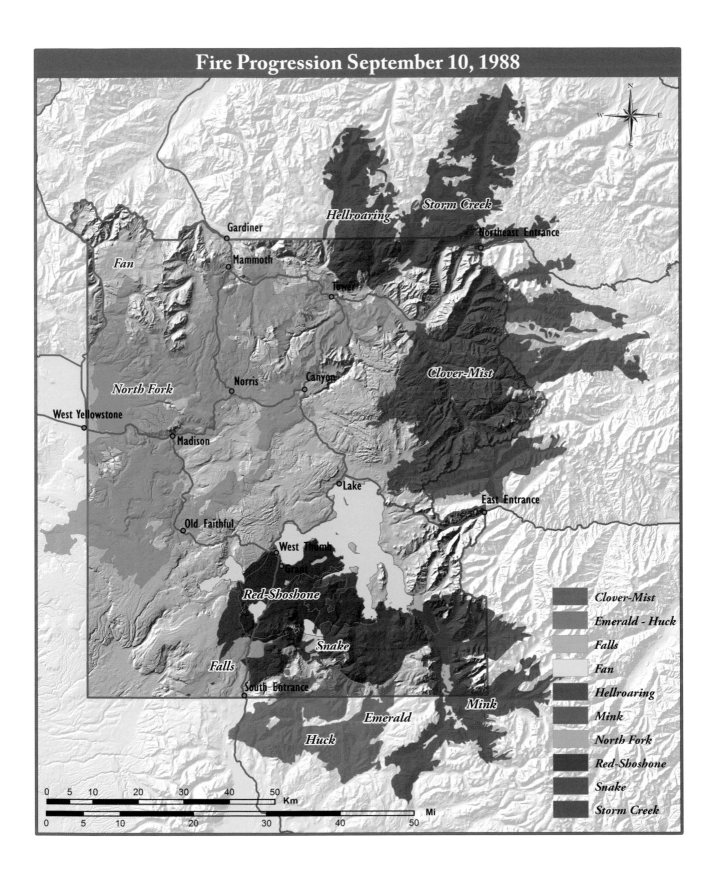

Fire Progression September 10, 1988

Fan

Hellroaring

Storm Creek

Gardiner

Mammoth

Northeast Entrance

Tower

North Fork

Norris

Canyon

Clover-Mist

West Yellowstone

Madison

Lake

East Entrance

Old Faithful

West Thumb

Grant

Red-Shoshone

Snake

Falls

South Entrance

Mink

Emerald

Huck

	Km
0 5 10 20 30 40 50	
0 5 10 20 30 40 50	Mi

Clover-Mist
Emerald - Huck
Falls
Fan
Hellroaring
Mink
North Fork
Red-Shoshone
Snake
Storm Creek

September 10, 1988

AS COMPARED to the map from two days earlier, the unbelievable growth of the North Fork Fire presents the most striking change on this map for September 10. On September 8, the day after the North Fork burned through Old Faithful, it charred only a little over 19,000 acres, but on the 9th it burned almost 150,000. In just one day the North Fork by itself burned almost as much acreage as all the fires combined burned on Black Saturday. In total, the Yellowstone fires combined to burn a dumbfounding 228,137 acres on the 9th, which was about 50 percent more than the total burned on Black Saturday. It was also an area equal in size to approximately 10 percent of the total acreage of Yellowstone National Park, although much of the country that burned on the 9th was on land outside the park's boundaries. Another illustrative comparison is that 225,137 acres amounts to an area well over one third the size of the entire state of Rhode Island. Friday the 9th of September did not receive a special moniker the way Black Saturday did, perhaps because people in Yellowstone were running out of metaphors, and perhaps because they were also running out of creative energy to come up with any new ones.

On the map it is possible to see the North Fork's rapid and long-reaching spread toward the northeast, beyond Old Faithful—the long tentacles of burned country depicted on the map are quite literally fire-etched tracings made by the wind on the landscape. So far reaching was the finger of fire that blew past Old Faithful on the 7th that it very nearly linked up with the Wolf Lake Fire, which of course was simply another sector of the same fire. The near reunion of fire can be seen just to the west of Hayden Valley, in the approximate center of Yellowstone National Park.

A shot of Firehole Lake in the Lower Geyser Basin, with the long view above the lake illustrating how smoked in all of Yellowstone was during early September of 1988. © Jeff Henry/Roche Jaune Pictures, Inc.

In terms of acreage burned and distance covered, the North Fork's biggest gains were on its northern fronts. Some sources record runs of as much as 17 miles in a single day by the huge fire. One flaming tentacle moved so far north that it burned into country already burned earlier in the season by the Fan Fire. Of course, the progress of that finger was arrested when it intersected the already-burned-out forest left in the wake of the Fan.

Another major spearhead of the North Fork ran north along the Mammoth-Norris road corridor, a run that brought it right to the doorstep of park headquarters at Mammoth Hot Springs. In fact, the fire continued its northward movement on both the east and west sides of Mammoth, bracketing the development, and so inexorable seemed its spread that the town of Gardiner, Montana, at Yellowstone's North Entrance was placed on pre-evacuation notice.

Aside from the thrusting spearheads of fire, the entire north side of the huge blaze made a major frontal move to the north. But perhaps most significantly of all was the way the North Fork moved to the northeast, across the Solfatara Plateau and the Washburn Mountain Range. That portion of the fire burned across Black-tail Plateau, blew across the Mammoth-Tower road, and then continued on to the Yellowstone River's Black Canyon. From there it seemed all but certain that the fire would move out of Yellowstone and into Montana's Gallatin National Forest, a move that would have put it in the heavily forested Absaroka Mountain Range on the east side of the Yellowstone River Valley.

The Absarokas north of Yellowstone offered a virtually unbroken progression of fuel that might allow the North Fork to run all the way to Livingston, Montana. A further possibility was that the fast moving fire could cross the Yellowstone River somewhere along the way, perhaps on the steep and timbered slopes of Yankee Jim Canyon, a situation that would have put it in the forested Gallatin Mountain Range. The Gallatins, in turn, would then offer the North Fork a burnable corridor leading almost all the way to the town of Bozeman. Given the rate that the Yellowstone fires were spreading, particularly in the case of the North Fork, such a scenario did not seem far fetched during the first week of September in 1988.

By September 10, for the first time in its history all of Yellowstone was closed to the public. A pall of dense smoke hung over everything and everybody. All around the park wind-battered and smoke-abraded employees stood lonely vigil at road barricades, on duty to prevent unauthorized entry. Except for a few government vehicles engaged in the firefighting effort, roads beyond the barricades were deserted. Peculiar winds blew improbably in opposing directions, but even more peculiar pockets of still air were present in other places. Another peculiar sensation was how the air could feel alternately hot and then cool, hot near the fires and cool with the feel of early autumn elsewhere.

Everywhere, everyone was exhausted from weeks of unsustainable effort with little or no time off. I think everyone felt beaten down and small, and there was a sense of being overwhelmed by fires that were so big, and burning on so many fronts in burning conditions so extreme that the flames were now inarguably far beyond anyone's control. By now all attempts to fight the fires in the backcountry had been abandoned—all firefighters and all equipment had been pulled back to developed areas, there to make a last ditch attempt to protect structures.

It's hard to describe the impending weight of the fire situation by the 10th of September. Stark newspaper headlines in bold black print made pronouncements like, "Yellowstone Braces for Fire D-Day," and a confidential communication predicting the immediate future of the Yellowstone fires was issued on September 9 by the so-called Area Command, the bureaucratic entity headquartered in West Yellowstone that was in overall charge of the firefighting effort in the Yellowstone area. Its dire forecast was illustrative of the outlook at the time, and in part it read:

> The noteworthy issue now is that the dramatic fire behavior on September 7—flame lengths 100–200 feet above the tree canopy, fire whirls, crowning and torching runs, fire-induced tornado-type winds—is only a prelude to conditions that are getting in place to produce a whole new magnitude of fire behavior on Saturday, September 10. We know the fuels are cocked and primed. Added to the explosive fuel situation on Saturday will be southwest winds of 20–40 miles per

National Park Service employees Betsy Mitchell and Jeanne Peterman watching over a road barricade at the edge of Mammoth Hot Springs, amidst dense and choking smoke on September 9, 1988. © Jeff Henry/Roche Jaune Pictures, Inc.

hour with gusts to 60 miles per hour at the ridges. [Fires] will be massive in scale with tornado-like winds, fire whirls, and the potential for long-distance spotting up to 6 miles. . . . The merging of independent fires or fire fronts will greatly accelerate burning rates above that characteristic of an individual fire . . . . Direct structure protection [will be] totally untenable . . . . The only good safety zone will be a large black one.

One of the first frontcountry presentations of the fiery prelude to September 10 was at Tower Junction. The development there consisted of a small park service maintenance and housing compound. Immediately next door was Roosevelt Lodge, which derived its name from the fact that President Teddy Roosevelt had camped in the vicinity while on an early twentieth-century tour of Yellowstone. It consisted not only of the main lodge, but also a large number of wooden cabins, horse barns, and other outbuildings. Two miles farther up the road toward Dunraven Pass was another development at Tower Falls. A public campground and a large Hamilton general store were located there, along with a number of associated structures. Especially in the case of Roosevelt Lodge and the Tower Falls area, heavy timber was present right up to and within the developments.

The North Fork Fire burns violently along the Dunraven Road between Tower and Canyon, just south of the turnoff to the Chittenden Road. 1988 National Park Service photo by Kathy Peterson

The Tower-Roosevelt developments were far removed from the starting points of all the major blazes, and through the early and middle portions of the summer it didn't seem that likely that the area would ever come under fire. As the summer progressed, however, the Storm Creek Fire and the Hellroaring Fire flared to life just north of Yellowstone. By late August both those fires had made major moves to the south, in the direction of Tower-Roosevelt. And then in late August and early September the North Fork Fire made its extraordinary runs across north-central Yellowstone. Over the course of just a few days, the North Fork transformed itself from the status of being merely a huge fire to one that was epically vast, ending up covering an area more than twelve times the size of the District of Columbia. Its rapid movement to the northeast made it seem likely that it would merge with the Hellroaring, the Storm Creek, or the Clover-Mist, perhaps even with all three. As the early autumn unfolded, the North Fork did link up with the Hellroaring just

The incredible smoke column rising from the Hellroaring Fire burning on the Buffalo Plateau along Yellowstone's north boundary. Note the angry spiral of energy in the column in this photo shot from the Chittenden Road on Mount Washburn in early September of 1988. © Jeff Henry/Roche Jaune Pictures, Inc.

north of Tower Junction, and it did indeed come very close to country encompassed by the Storm Creek and the Clover-Mist.

Of course the North Fork's northeasterly movement put it on a collision course with the developments at Tower Junction and Tower Falls. More than simply being downwind from the rampaging fire, the complexes were also situated at the end of an almost continuous tract of heavy fuel that led from the advancing fire right to the developments. Many heavily foliated trees also stood right around the buildings at both Roosevelt Lodge and the Tower Falls. At Roosevelt Lodge the trees were mostly Douglas firs. At Tower Falls, which was situated at a somewhat higher elevation, there were likewise many Douglas firs, but the forest there also included a component of lodgepole pines. Both species are known for their flammability in drought conditions.

By early September it was apparent to all involved that the North Fork Fire would inevitably overrun the Tower-Roosevelt area, and if it happened to collide

Another shot of the smoke column from the Hellroaring Fire, perhaps shot at about the same time and on the same day as the previous photo. This photo was taken by ranger Kathy Peterson, obviously at the road junction at Tower. 1988 National Park Service photo by Kathy Peterson

with one or more of the other big fires in the immediate neighborhood, might even pinch the twin developments in an apex of flame.

By September 9, rangers and other personnel had been working to prepare Tower-Roosevelt for fire for several days. One of the principal players at Tower was ranger Dan Krapf, who had started working in Yellowstone as a seasonal ranger in 1973. Dan and others, including a detachment from the United States Army, had followed the usual regimen of removing flammables and trimming trees to reduce fuel around the developments. They had also set up sprinkler systems around the buildings, with a pump situated in Lost Lake above the Tower Junction and Roosevelt Lodge providing a good portion of the water used to charge the sprinklers.

On Friday, September 9, Dan and others in the park service contingent at Tower decided that it would be wise to evacuate as many of their nonessential vehicles as possible. Checking with fire behavior analysts who were present in the area, Dan and the others were told that it would be another 24–48 hours before the North Fork showed up at their location, so they figured there was plenty of time for four Tower residents to drive four vehicles to a safe zone at Mammoth and then for all four to ride back to Tower in one vehicle. Aside from Dan Krapf, the drivers were Randy King, who was the Tower subdistrict ranger; Bob Flather, a longtime Yellowstone aficionado working the summer of 1988 as a volunteer for the Tower rangers; and Ellen Petrick, an interpretive ranger stationed that summer at Tower.

Before leaving Tower to take the little convoy of unnecessary vehicles to Mammoth, ranger Dan took it upon himself to make an additional reconnaissance of the

Another shot of the incredibly smoked-in conditions around Gardiner at the North Entrance to Yellowstone National Park during the first few days of September in 1988. Nothing can be seen of Mount Everts and other elements of the scenery that normally would be visible from this angle just outside the entrance station. © Jeff Henry/Roche Jaune Pictures, Inc.

approaching fire. To do so, he drove from Tower to the east end of the Blacktail Plateau Drive, a one way dirt road running south of and parallel to the Mammoth-Tower road. Dan entered the Blacktail Drive from the east end, which normally would have had him driving against traffic, but since all roads in the area were closed to everything other than fire vehicles, oncoming traffic was not a problem. What was a problem was the nearness of the North Fork Fire. From his vantage points along the Blacktail Road, probably in the vicinity of The Cut, Dan was able to see that the flames were quite close, so close that the 24–48 hour estimate was probably much too generous. But Dan thought there was still time to remove the surplus vehicles to Mammoth, so after he returned to Tower all four drivers loaded up and departed on their mission.

The four made a smoky but otherwise uneventful trip to Mammoth, where they parked their three extra vehicles and then started back toward Tower. No sooner had they had begun their return trip, however, when they received a distressed radio call from Kathy Peterson, a ranger who had been left behind at Tower, who urgently related that flames were now visible on the ridges immediately above the Tower complex. Subdistrict Ranger Randy King was driving the return vehicle, and he raced the 18 miles back to Tower in a remarkable fifteen minutes. It was a good thing the four raced back to Tower as fast as they did. A large grove of very large Douglas firs along the road just above Tower, between the junction and the Petrified Tree road, burned spectacularly hot that afternoon just after Randy, Dan, and the others passed through. Ranger Dan remembers looking back up the road toward Mammoth, at that stand of big Douglas firs, and realizing that "the road had become impassable just five to ten minutes" after they got back to their home enclave.

Dan and the others assumed their defensive positions around the park service area at Tower. The North Fork Fire burned toward them, but fortunately late afternoon came on with its lower temperatures and somewhat higher humidities, and the flames slowed. Dan also remembers feeling the fire suck air into itself as it neared, and because of the copious sprinkling of the Tower complex that had been done beforehand, the air the fire inhaled was cool and damp in front of the development. Dan and the others could feel the cool, humidified air blowing across the backs of their necks as the fire pulled it in.

The inflow of cool moist air seemed to change the burning equation in the approaching flames to the point that they noticeably diminished, and the immediate threat to Tower Junction abated. That evening, after the heated moment of decision had passed, Dan and his park service compatriots continued their vigilance but had seated themselves in lawn chairs in order to ease their weariness. Wayward embers were still falling around them, however, and the park service people were alternately amused and annoyed by an army NCO who also was still on hand and who insisted on yelling "Incoming!" with the landing of every spark, no matter how insignificant.

Efforts put forth by Dan Krapf, Bob Flather, and others at the park service compound at Tower were matched by other firefighters at nearby Roosevelt Lodge and Tower Falls. Because of their efforts, along with a measure of good fortune, no significant losses of structures occurred at any of the developments. As with so many other parts of Yellowstone, however, the appearance of the Tower-Roosevelt area was greatly altered by the North Fork Fire, and those who lived and worked there had to adjust to a new natural.

Postfire reconnaissance of the area that revealed the first snapshots of its new look also revealed that the pump that had been placed in Lost Lake had burned during the fire. In a fortunate twist of fate, the pump had lasted long enough to help the Tower area survive the flames. Making a further reconnoitering around the area, the Tower contingent discovered that some of the sprinklers in the area, including those near Roosevelt Lodge, had been so forceful they had stripped the bark off some of the tree trunks within range of their fields of fire. Some of the trees were completely girdled and died as result, and in subsequent years they had to be removed as hazards.

Meanwhile, out in Lamar Valley where I had been struck by the lack of human presence and the eerie calm just a few days before, two other park rangers were having a similar experience. Scott Beattie and Mike Robinson were working to prepare the Lamar Ranger Station and associated buildings for fire, whichever fire might be the one to finally arrive at their duty station. Mike Robinson, it might be recalled, was the backcountry ranger who six weeks or so earlier had been so spellbound by the Clover-Mist Fire when it was burning in the dark of night around Frost Lake, along the crest of the Absaroka Mountain Range. Now he and Scott were grubbing out sagebrush in the area of the ranger station, and were also setting up an old water pump mounted on a trailer to pull water out of nearby Rose Creek. The rangers were attaching hose lines and sprinklers to their pumping system to wet down the lawns surrounding the buildings at Lamar, as well as the buildings themselves.

As it seemed to me that I was alone when I drove through Lamar on the afternoon of September 5, so it also seemed to Scott and Mike on the afternoon of the 9th. Their supervisor, Lamar Subdistrict Ranger Joe Fowler, had gone to Mammoth to pick up another trailer-mounted water pump, and there were no other people around the Lamar Station. Unaccountably, the smoky air around the rangers was completely still, as it had been in the same area when I drove through two days earlier. In a summer marked by powerful winds, and on a day when Mike and Scott and everyone else knew that the huge fires were rampaging and undoubtedly there were strong and blustery winds in the vicinity of the fires, it was eerily calm in the valley. The stillness of the valley seemed out of context, knowing as they did that huge fires surrounded them in all directions. Somehow the air in Lamar Valley was calm even though it was in the middle of a tempest of wind and flame, and Mike and Scott must have felt like they were in the eye of a hurricane of fire. That's how it had felt to me when I drove through the area two days before.

The effect was magnified for Mike and Scott when they turned off the pump for some reason and they gradually became aware of a muffled, distant rumble. It dawned on the two rangers that they were hearing the infernal roar of the Wolf Lake/North Fork Fire as it was moving from the Washburn Range toward Lamar Valley. When the two Nomex-clad rangers realized what they were hearing was fire, it was probably 15 miles away to the southwest, on the far side of Specimen Ridge.

The impact of the atmospheric peculiarities was stunning, that there could be a pocket of still air as large as Lamar Valley in the midst of so much wind and fire, and that a fire could be so loud that its noise was audible 15 miles away. The fact that the roar of the distant fire was faint in no way diminished its impact on Mike Robinson and Scott Beattie. In fact, its subtlety heightened the effect of the distant roar.

Another tongue of the North Fork Fire burned north along the Mammoth-Norris road on the 9th. That portion of the fire burned with exceptional ferocity, most especially in the area along Obsidian Creek. In several places along the stream, such as the area around Brickyard Hill, the Grizzly Lake trailhead and Willow Park, the fire was so fierce that it snapped off mature trees like matchsticks and pulled others out of the ground by their roots. In some places all the broken or uprooted tree trunks pointed in the same direction, as though they had been blown down by a powerful frontal wind, or perhaps by the violent rush of air drawn to the chimney-like

A Montana Power Company power line in Yellowstone, protected from the North Fork Fire by heavy sprinkling from a large irrigation system. Many such irrigation systems were brought to Yellowstone in 1988 by generous farmers from eastern Idaho. © Jeff Henry/Roche Jaune Pictures, Inc.

updraft in the center of the firestorm. In other places, however, broken and uprooted trees were strewn helter-skelter, left crisscrossed in the wake of what appeared to be have been fiery tornadoes. Some of the piles of crisscrossed logs were higher than the head of the tallest firefighter who ever lived. Lined up on the ground or chaotically arranged, all of the logs were black, as was everything around them.

There is a story about a contingent of park employees who were on the Norris-Mammoth road when the North Fork Fire exploded on September 9. As the story goes, the little group was caught in close proximity to one of the firestorms that blew up that day, and because of some sort of disturbance presumably caused by the intensity of the fire, their park radios would not work. Because of their last radio communications, it was known that the park service group was close to violent fire, and of course there was only the one road on which to escape, so when they faded from radio contact it was feared for a time that they had been lost. I have not been able to substantiate this story, but even if it is not literally true, in my mind it illustrates the ferocity of the North Fork Fire on September 9, as well as human reaction to that ferocity. The fire was so fierce and so fast moving, it seemed believable, even probable, to observers that it likely would trap someone somewhere. As for the interruption of radio service, again the fire was so fierce that it seemed believable that it could somehow adversely affect radio waves or electronics. As linemen working for Montana Power Company in Yellowstone had already noticed, indeed something about the big fires caused breakers in their substations to trip, even when nearby power poles did not burn down and nearby electrical wires were not severed.

One of Montana Power's linemen actually was out on the main power line feeding Yellowstone Park on the 9th, when the North Fork Fire blew up so spectacularly along the Norris-Mammoth corridor. Tor Pederson was walking the line along the west side of Willow Park to evaluate what might be done in the way of fireproofing the wooden power poles and copper/steel wire along the line. Montana Power had already lost a great many power poles and a great many miles of wire to the fires, especially to the North Fork, and they had decided to try to be more proactive in defending their infrastructure. Wrapping power poles with old fire shelters had proved marginally successful—poles often just burned off at a level above the fire shelters. What had worked the best was setting up large volume, agricultural irrigation systems to sprinkle the power line corridors and adjacent forest before a fire arrived, and to continue irrigating while the fire was burning past.

Tor was in the Willow Park area, looking for the best place to set up an irrigation pump, and otherwise how to set up the whole irrigation system so as to best protect the power line. Of course Tor thought there was adequate time not only to scout things out, but also to construct the irrigation line, before the North Fork Fire burned that far north. But like everyone else, he underestimated just how fast the fire was going to move during those first few days of September. More suddenly than he could believe, Tor found himself right next to a forest exploding with fire. He had to run as fast as he could through the bogs and bushes in Willow Park to get back to the road, where a coworker waited in a pickup vehicle. An understated man, Tor said later, "It wasn't exactly a close call, but it was the closest thing possible to being a close call without actually being one." Tor made it to the road, where his coworker and he managed to drive out of the fiery danger zone.

South of Willow Park, at Norris Junction, rangers John Lounsbury and Andy Fisher were waiting to meet five park service dump trucks that had been recalled from Old Faithful to Mammoth. The trucks were needed to haul flammable materials away from the developed area at Mammoth, in the interest of reducing fuel around park headquarters before the North Fork Fire arrived there. Viewed from a

Ranger Andy Fisher directing traffic and trying to explain the fire situation to a befuddled tourist, at Norris Junction during one of the many fire emergencies in the summer of 1988. © Jeff Henry/Roche Jaune Pictures, Inc.

certain perspective, the recall of the dump trucks from Old Faithful could be seen as yet another move by officers at park headquarters to strip the rest of Yellowstone of firefighting resources in the interest of protecting their own home turf.

Be that as it may, rangers Lounsbury and Fisher were on hand to escort the dump trucks through the fire zone along the Norris-Mammoth road en route to their destination at Mammoth. The trucks arrived at Norris, and the convoy of the two rangers in a pickup truck and the five huge dump trucks headed north. They made it only a couple of miles, however, before encountering fire so intense that Lounsbury and Fisher, who were leading the convoy, thought it prudent to stop and reconnoiter ahead on foot. Very quickly it became obvious that it would be most unwise to continue toward Mammoth, so John and Andy decided to turn everyone around and head back to Norris while the getting was still good.

They effected the turnaround in two small pullouts at Frying Pan Spring— Andy Fisher stood behind each dump truck and directed the driver in making the six-point turn necessary to turn the big vehicles about. In this Andy was well qualified, as he had driven the exact same trucks earlier in his park service career, before he had entered the ranks of the rangers. All the while super hot fire was burning all around, and John Lounsbury said later, "I don't think we would have gotten cooked

Ranger John Lounsbury using two radios in a struggle to keep up with communications. So much was happening and so many people had something to report that radio channels were frequently overwhelmed with the volume of traffic. © Jeff Henry/ Roche Jaune Pictures, Inc.

if something had gone wrong, like if one of the trucks had backed off the road and gotten stuck. We could have gotten away somehow. But I do think we would have cooked some dump trucks." As it was, the entire convoy turned around successfully and made it back to Norris, an area that had burned out earlier in the summer and by September 9 was safely black. Talking things over after they got back to Norris, Andy said to John, "What we just saw was a ballet of dump trucks." For Lounsbury, it was one of the most memorable statements in a most memorable summer.

It was also about this time when Mark Haroldson of the Interagency Grizzly Bear Study Team trapped a grizzly bear that was raiding apple trees near the town of Gardiner, Montana. From a point of view more than twenty-five years later, a bear pirating a few apples would seem to have been a minor problem when compared to the awesome juggernaut of fire that was bearing down on Gardiner at the time, but somehow it was arranged for the bear to be trapped and hauled away. Mark was transporting the bear in a culvert trap, which was simply a large piece of corrugated steel pipe fastened on a trailer and outfitted with a guillotine-like trap door. Mark intended to haul the bear in the trap to a site near Yellowstone Lake, there to release

Ferocious flames from the North Fork Fire burning along the Grand Loop Road near Frying Pan Spring just north of Norris Junction, September 9, 1988. © John Lounsbury

it and hope the site's remoteness from Gardiner would keep the bear from returning to his apple-marauding ways. Mark made it as far as the wooded stretch of Yellowstone's Grand Loop Road between Otter Creek and Alum Creek, just a few miles south of Canyon Junction. There he found the road ahead blocked by fire, with other flames disconcertingly close both alongside and behind him. With the bear trap bearing the bear attached to the back of his pickup truck, there wasn't enough room to turn around in the middle of the road, so Mark had to disconnect the trailer, turn the truck around, and then seesaw the trap around by hand. Mark found he had "superhuman strength" when he turned the trailer around, probably brought on by the closeness of the flames.

Lake Hotel and other properties in the Lake Area were evacuated at this juncture, too, some of the last tourist facilities to be abandoned during Yellowstone's summer of fire. Though not yet directly threatened by fire, Lake Area was located in heavily timbered country, and some of the wildfires were moving closer to its location. Given the rapid and erratic nature of fire movement in late August and early

Longtime ranger Mark Marschall shot this picture of fireline construction near the park boundary at Jones Pass in early September of 1988. In the ballpoint notation Mark penned on the mount of his slide, he lamented "Just a few minutes before it had been untouched wilderness." The unfortunate thing was that most such firelines were constructed with the full knowledge that they weren't going to work, and with the further knowledge that the wilderness was being cut up solely to mollify critics of the park who believed park service mismanagement was the reason Yellowstone was burning. © Mark Marschall

September, it was not much of a stretch to think that Lake might soon be directly threatened. Beyond that, pretty much everything else in the way of visitor services in Yellowstone had been closed by early September anyway, so there wasn't much for any tourists to do elsewhere in the smoked-in park during a potential stay at Lake. As it was, fire danger at Lake was considered near enough at hand to justify reducing fuels in the area, as well as near enough to justify setting up a number of irrigation lines around the complex.

In another sector of the park, Old Faithful was threatened yet again by the North Fork Fire. Two days after the firestorm of the 7th had blown through the area, a different part of the same fire built up a head of heat and made a run at the development from the north. This fiery advance burned most dramatically around the north end of the Upper Geyser Basin, in the neighborhood of Riverside and Daisy geysers, and did not come as close to the buildings in the Old Faithful complex as the fire run on the 7th had done. Nevertheless, it was close enough to give the defenders of Old Faithful yet another memorable adrenaline rush.

Late in the evening on the 9th, Elenor Williams, who worked as a landscape architect for the park service at Mammoth, drove out the Bunsen Peak Road just

Firefighters wetting down the roof of the dining room at the Mammoth Hot Springs Hotel, September 9, 1988. © Jeff Henry/Roche Jaune Pictures, Inc.

south of Mammoth on a fire reconnaissance. Unfortunately for Lori, as she was often referred to in 1988, she backed off the road and became temporarily stuck when she tried to turn around after discovering that fire had already crossed the road in front of her. Fire was quite close and burning hotly in spite of the lateness of the hour, so a few minutes of high anxiety ensued for those listening to Lori's predicament on the park radio. Naturally, anxiety was highest of all for Lori herself, especially when at first it seemed there was no one available to help extricate her vehicle, which was a lightweight, two-wheel-drive, pickup truck.

Elenor decided that the best course under the circumstances was to abandon her park service rig and hike out in the dark. After all, she was familiar with the area and was appropriately clad in fire retardant Nomex and had other firefighter gear on her person. After hiking a short distance, however, she met three firefighters on their way to help. The three, one of whom was park researcher Gillian Bowser, picked up Eleanor and returned to the stuck vehicle, where together they were able to push it out.

After extricating the stuck pickup truck, Elenor and the others received a dire warning from a fire lookout posted on top of nearby Bunsen Peak, who told them that fire was fast approaching their location. The four did not need to be warned a second time—they quickly drove out to the Grand Loop Road, and from there down

Firefighter Gillian Bowser with a shovel on her shoulder and light rays beaming through thick smoke over her head, while she looks up and considers the impossible nature of fighting Yellowstone's 1988 fires. © Jeff Henry/Roche Jaune Pictures, Inc.

to the relative safety of Mammoth Hot Springs. As for the lookout on Bunsen Peak: he, too, had to be evacuated from his post later that same night.

Of course anxiety was high for everyone in the Yellowstone area on the night of September 9. People were exhausted, and the incredible growth of the fires on the 9th far exceeded anything seen so far during Yellowstone's summer of fire. The fires threatened virtually all developments in the park to a greater or lesser degree— mostly greater—as well as most developed districts outside the park's boundaries. Most mind-numbing of all was the fact that what we had seen on the 9th was "only a prelude" to what was predicted to happen on Saturday the 10th. All of the fires, and especially the North Fork, had grown to such a size that in a sense they were no longer single fires. Each of the big fires had any number of "heads," or focal points of heat, any one of which was capable of picking up and making a major run in its own right. No one could predict which of the hot spots would develop and make runs, or which directions those runs might take.

I had been directed on the 9th to move a piece of equipment from Madison to Mammoth, and as a result did not shoot many photographs of the holocausts that developed that day. The rig I drove to Mammoth was a small tractor with a trailer-mounted water tank I pulled along behind. I drove the tandem rig through the fearsome firestorms along the Norris-Mammoth road, so I got a chance to see that fire show from a perspective that was quite up close and personal. The top speed of the tractor was only about as fast as an average person jogs, so that was a bit of a worry. But the fact that I had several hundred gallons of water in the tank I was towing, and could use the water in my own defense if I had to, was a bit of a consolation for my lack of speed.

Because I ended up at Mammoth after I drove the tractor and the water tank from Madison, I decided to spend the night in Gardiner. Before dark I affixed some lawn sprinklers to the roof of the house I rented in Gardiner at the time, and strung some garden hoses from the ground up the roof to charge the sprinklers. To paraphrase John Varley, who at the time was Yellowstone National Park's head of research and who similarly was hosing down the roof of his park service house at Mammoth at about the same time: You have different perspective when its your own house that's in front of the flames. In my case, I did not own the house I was preparing for fire, but it did contain the bulk of my worldly possessions. And beyond all that, I thought the best place to be for photographs the next day was going to be Mammoth Hot Springs, just five miles away from Gardiner.

While I was setting up the sprinklers on the roof of my rented house, the smoke in Gardiner was so thick it was impossible to see from one end of the Highway 89 bridge to the other, and by bull horn announcements from sheriffs' deputies repeatedly rent the smoky air and announced that the town was on pre-evacuation notice.

True to prediction, the next day dawned insanely windy, as so many other days had done that summer. There was a difference, however. The salient sensation on the other windy days had been that the air was hot and abrasively dry. But on Saturday September 10 the air was quite cool, and perhaps more importantly, it felt moist on exposed skin.

The wind continued to blow hard all day, buffeting all who were exposed to it, to the point where most people perceptibly cowered in front of it and took any excuse they could to take a break from it by getting inside a vehicle or a building, even if just for a short time. And the fires did burn hot and hard, consuming almost another 100,000 acres, but they did not explode to "a whole new magnitude of fire behavior," as had been forecast.

On Saturday the 10th, Roy Renkin, who in 1988 worked for the park service as a biological researcher with a known expertise in fire, was stationed as a lookout on the bridge over the Gardner River just out Mammoth on the road toward Tower. Roy's assignment was to watch for fire moving toward the Youth Conservation Corps (YCC) Camp on the south side of the Mammoth development, especially for fire

Flames of the North Fork Fire torching a Douglas fir on the slopes above Africa Lake, just above Mammoth Hot Springs, in the night of September 9, 1988. © Jeff Henry/Roche Jaune Pictures, Inc.

moving up and out of the Gardner River Canyon. He was to report what he saw to firefighters positioned in the YCC Camp for structural protection.

Mostly, Roy remembers having a long day in the buffeting wind that was actually quite chilly. It was a long day because not much happened on his watch. Only late in the day did the fire in the river canyon below build up a bit of a head and make something of a run toward the southern extremity of the Mammoth complex. That finger of fire burned up to the vicinity of the park service repair garage, as well as fairly close to the dormitory in the YCC compound. This was in spite of the fact that the strong frontal wind was topographically enhanced by the alignment of the river valley below Roy's lookout post, an alignment that should have favored the fire's spread toward the YCC Camp.

The wind was so strong that it maxed out the wind gauge Roy had with him. The little gauge was calibrated to 50 miles per hour; the wind speed was something in excess of that. Even with wind of that velocity, the fire in front of Roy's position didn't respond that much, so something had to be different.

That difference became even more pronounced late in the afternoon on the 10th, when unbelievably a few drops of rain began to fall out of the wind-driven air. I spent the day shooting photos around the Mammoth area, but there really wasn't much to shoot in the way of dramatic fire. I mostly shot close-up pictures of the faces of beleaguered firefighters and their lookouts. As the afternoon waned and evening came on, the raindrops became a bit more frequent and the wind began to abate. After dark, when I returned to my rental home in Gardiner, the rain continued— still by no means heavy, but striking after an entire summer of almost no rain at all. I felt a sense of relief and also excited anticipation, but I tried to keep a lid on both emotions for fear of being disappointed.

But the next morning when I woke up and looked out the window the ground outside was wet. More than that, there were a few snowflakes in the air. If it was snowing in Gardiner, at an elevation just over 5,000 feet, it had to be snowing a lot more up on the higher plateaus of Yellowstone, and the fires had to be taking a hit. To celebrate the weather, I decided to take the morning off, and went out for breakfast with five friends at the Best Western in Gardiner. On the welcome sign outside the restaurant someone had arranged plastic letters that read, "Let It Snow, Let It Snow, Let It Snow."

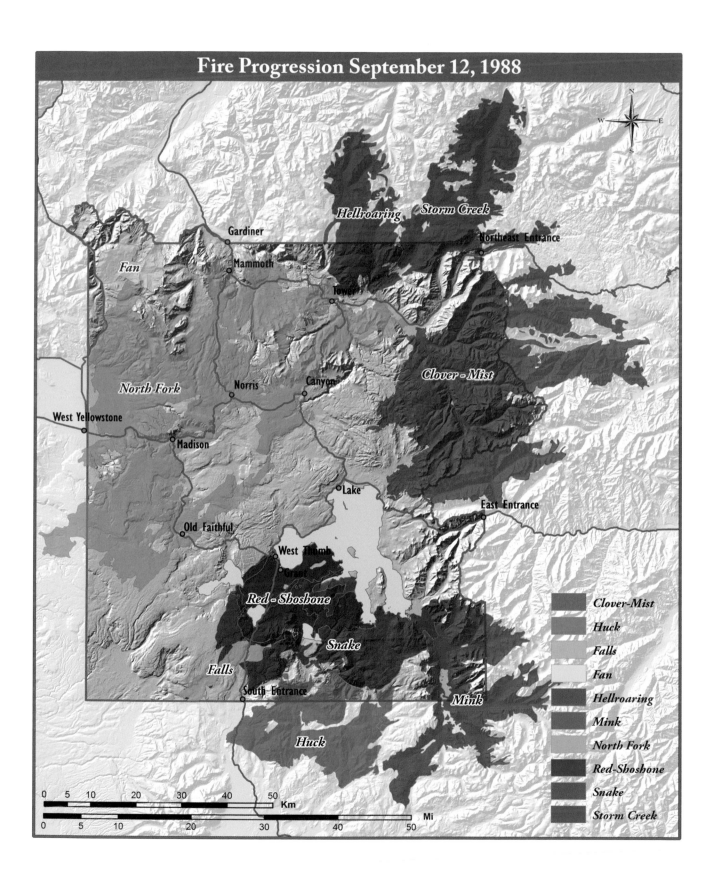

Fire Progression September 12, 1988

ONE HAS to look closely to discern the fire growth that had occurred since the map of September 10. Remembering that close to 100,000 acres burned on the 10th, it speaks to the magnitude of the Yellowstone fires that a 100,000-acre increase in extent seems like a subtle addition to the map. Most of the burning that took place on the 10th was on the northern front of the North Fork Fire, especially in the southern end of the Gallatin Range. Significant burning also occurred on the Clover-Mist Fire in areas outside the park, and in remote sections of the Mink Fire outside the southeast corner of Yellowstone National Park.

Late in the morning on September 11, I left Gardiner and drove into the park. As I drove south beyond Mammoth, I did indeed encounter ever more snow as I climbed in elevation. There was even a little accumulation on the ground in places. In Gibbon Meadows I found some young bull elk browsing in charred forest near Sylvan Springs. It was still snowing when I photographed the young bulls, and I liked the way the falling snow made slanting lines in front of the animals. The streaks of falling snow were especially stark in front of the blackened tree trunks behind the bulls. Everywhere a surprising amount of smoke rose from uncountable millions of still smoldering hot spots. The falling drizzle and snow sizzled and steamed when it landed on the hotspots. There really was a lot of smoky steam rising everywhere, the way a stovepot puts off a pronounced puff of vapor the instant the heat is turned off on the burner underneath.

Elsewhere in the Gibbon Meadows/Elk Park area I found a swale that burned, probably on the Black Saturday of August 20, that was already sprouting a growth of green grass. With no significant rain other than what had fallen the night before, the new grass had sprouted less than three weeks after the area had been incinerated.

A young bull elk feeding on unburned vegetation in front of a fire-blackened forest, near Sylvan Springs on the west side of Gibbon Meadows. Note the fire-season-ending snow falling around the bull in the foreground of this photo, as well as around his companion in the background. Photo shot on September 11, 1988. © Jeff Henry/Roche Jaune Pictures, Inc.

The green blades seemed especially fresh and hopeful with droplets of water on their tips, and with traces of snow falling around them. I marveled at the droplets of moisture that just a couple days earlier had been salt water in the Pacific Ocean.

Around the grassy swale stood endless ranks of blackened trees. Many other trees had burned off or had blown over, and their blackened trunks lay on the ground. As I had been taken so many times already, I was fascinated by the vertical and horizontal patterns the logs made, but now there was the extra dimension of the contrasting white snow—literally the ultimate contrast between elements that were very black and others that were absolutely white.

The light fall of snow and rain was general, extending across the park and beyond. Looking at records from automated SNOTEL sites that existed in 1988, it can be seen that precipitation amounts for the storm that began on the 10th varied from only about one tenth of an inch (of water equivalent) in the northeastern section of the park to about seven tenths of an inch at sites in the high country south of Yellowstone Lake. But everywhere there was at least a little precipitation, and given the lateness of the season with its shorter days and cooler temperatures, I think most realized with relief that we had experienced what is known in firefighting argot as the "season-ending event."

Green grass sprouting around a piece of charcoal in the aftermath of the North Fork Fire near Elk Park. Remarkably, the grass was sprouting without the benefit of any significant precipitation since the area burned in late August. © Jeff Henry/Roche Jaune Pictures, Inc.

Mike Bader, the ranger at Canyon who had figured so prominently in so many fiery theaters of operation in 1988, remembered later that everyone at his location "was pretty happy that the longest fire season was over." Mike organized a celebratory party in a mess hall at Canyon, where someone mounted a homemade sign on the wall with big block letters that read "SNOW!" The very next day, Mike and his coworkers began working to demobilize and close the big Wolf Lake Fire camp in the Canyon Campground.

At the Old Faithful Inn, bell captain George Bornemann, who was working as a security and fire guard since the building had been closed, felt a "huge sense of relief" that the summer "that had dragged on for so long" was finally over. The maintenance and security employees still present at the Inn shared George's sentiments, and many repeated a one-word statement—"Finally"—over and over again. As with most young park employees, George and his coworkers were prone to partying, but on September 11 they "took it up a notch." The most outstanding memory for George during the immediate postfire period was of park geologist Rick Hutchinson picking burned debris out of the runoff channel from Morning Glory Pool about a mile down basin from Old Faithful. George remembers that Rick was still clad in fire-retardant Nomex, in spite of the cool and damp weather that had quieted the

The charred and ashen-gray forest-scape left in the wake of the fierce North Fork Fire in Secret Valley north of Madison Junction. Remarkably, almost all such places, dubbed "moonscapes" by many in the media, regenerated profusely in the spring of 1989. © Jeff Henry/Roche Jaune Pictures, Inc.

fires, and was so engrossed in what he was doing that he never did notice George's presence.

Another Old Faithful Inn employee, manager George Helfrich, remained at the historic property in his charge for only a short time after the snow and rain that began on September 10. After he left Old Faithful he took a six-day contemplative backpacking trip in the Gallatin Mountain Range north of Yellowstone, and later in the fall took an even longer and more contemplative trip through Nepal. Helfrich never worked for the hotel company in Yellowstone again, and instead embarked on a career with the National Park Service in concessions management, a career that eventually led him back to Yellowstone to oversee the same concessions that had once employed George himself.

At Mammoth Hot Springs Joan Anzelmo breathed an exceptional sigh of relief. As Yellowstone's public affairs officer, Joan had been particularly besieged by the national press during the great fires of 1988. Now, with snow and rain falling on the area, she "wandered around Mammoth in a giddy daze." In her relief it didn't matter to Joan that she was getting thoroughly soaked by the cold rain and the wet snow that was drifting down like manna from heaven.

Bob Duff, a seasonal ranger based at Madison and one who had been present when the North Fork Fire had blazed its way past his home station, was on detail

A shot of a calf elk nipping at burned browse in a forest blackened by the North Fork Fire near the Firehole Canyon just south of Madison Junction. © Jeff Henry/Roche Jaune Pictures, Inc.

to fight the Clover-Mist Fire when the merciful snow and rain fell on the night of September 10–11. Actually, Bob had spent quite a few days away from home that summer, dispatched to fight the Clover-Mist Fire in and around the northeast corner of the park with a Yellowstone fire crew headed by ranger Bob Mahn. After the storm, Bob and his fellow team members had to wade through a considerable depth of snow on the ground to make their way to firelines they were constructing to contain the Clover-Mist, and it was well that they did. Probably because of its size, the Clover-Mist had enough forward inertia to burn through another 31 square miles of country before it finally stopped, the snow-covered ground notwithstanding. As an avid outdoorsman, Bob not only shared the general sense of relief that the fires were on their way out, he was extra pleased that the end of the fire season would allow him to get back to the fishing and hunting he loved to do in the autumn.

Back home at Madison, Bob's good friend Les Brunton was so worn out, even at age twenty-five, the only statement he could formulate in his inner monologue was, "I'm tickled pink."

Another Madison ranger, Subdistrict Ranger Rick Bennett, had also played a major role in defending his home area when the North Fork stormed through on August 15. Rick was at home at Madison when the blessed snow came down. Exhausted like everyone else, Rick drove his patrol car to the home of his friend and fellow law enforcement ranger Steve Sarles in West Yellowstone, where together they

Another view of burned-over country, this one in the Washburn Range just opposite the entrance to the Chittenden Road. This area was also burned by the huge North Fork Fire, the largest fire to burn across Yellowstone during the summer of 1988. The hazy profile of Cutoff Mountain looms out of the smoke in the distance. © Jeff Henry/Roche Jaune Pictures, Inc.

watched an NFL football game on Park Service time. An Internet search showed that the Washington Redskins beat the Pittsburgh Steelers 30–29 in the game that Bennett and Sarles watched. Given the extreme effort that Rick and Steve and everyone had put forth during the summer of 1988, I think the two were entitled to a little downtime on the company clock. While relaxing during his downtime, Rick felt an overwhelming sense of relief that "Finally, it was over." As a longtime park resident who was weary of Yellowstone's wintry interior, Rick further remembers that "It was one of the few times I didn't dread seeing snow in September."

Out in Lamar Valley, ranger Mike Robinson remembers thinking, "Finally, the unstoppable fires" had been halted by what "had to be the season-ending event." Mike and his coworkers were so tired, they had no energy for any sort of celebration to observe the season ending event; they just felt relief that the "period had been printed at the end of the sentence." Always conscious of their backcountry concerns, Mike and his coworkers had almost immediate thoughts about how much trail clearing work there was going to be in the aftermath of the big fires.

Blackened snags in the Washburn Mountain Range, in late September of 1988. © Jeff Henry/ Roche Jaune Pictures, Inc.

Across Yellowstone and in many places beyond, thousands of firefighters had similar feelings of finality and relief. In yet another ironic twist, workers in the fire camps now had to deal with being cold and wet, this after months of suffering from fiery heat and arid air. Probably the best thing of all for most firefighters was the realization that soon they would be able to go home, where they could look forward to the chance to recuperate from their arduous labors and to recover from their smoke-induced ailments.

Personally, for some reason I found myself pondering the firefighting system of evaluating fuel moisture content of organic fuels. Potential fuels are classified by size, and correspondingly by the length of time they theoretically take to dry out in periods of drought, as well as how long they take to rehydrate when moist conditions return. So-called ten-hour fuels, for example, are classified as pieces of fuel less than a half inch in diameter, and because of their small size are supposedly apt to adjust to a new level of humidity in the air in just ten hours. One-hundred-hour fuels are one to three inches in diameter, and correspondingly take ten times as long to dry out or to remoistureize with a change in ambient moisture. The next gradation is one-thousand-hour fuels, which are considered to be logs three to eight inches in diameter, and which take more than forty days to rehydrate after they have dried out. It occurred to me that I was like a one-thousand-hour fuel: It had taken me a long time to get as tired as I was, and it was going to take a long time for me to recover.

The big fires were down but they were far from dead out. The North Fork and the Clover-Mist Fires, probably because of their enormous size, respectively had enough momentum to burn through another 10,000 and 20,000 acres after September 11. In any year before 1988, either one of those comparatively minor totals would have qualified as a major fire. Beyond that, all the fires would smolder for another eight weeks, until the lasting snows came in early November. But there would be no more big flare-ups, firestorms, or dramatic long-distance fire runs. The big show of 1988 was over.

In Closing

TWENTY-FIVE thousand firefighters had cycled through Yellowstone during the summer of 1988, and several thousand of those stayed on until the real snows came. For the first couple of weeks or so after the storm of September 10–11, firefighters continued doing their namesake work—building firelines, extinguishing hot spots, and so forth—all to make sure there was no chance the fires would pick up and run again. After all possibility of further fire spread had passed, many of the same firefighters were put to work rehabilitating the firelines they had constructed just a few weeks earlier. Other impacted areas were "rehabbed," as the firefighters like to say, places like backcountry spike camps and helicopter bases.

For my part, I discontinued my photo documentation work shortly after the snow and rain storm of September 10–11. At that point I was given authorization to hire a crew to work at postfire rehabilitation, and I found most of my hires in the ranks of park employees whose regular jobs had been short circuited by the fires. My crew reached a maximum of twenty-eight during the course of the autumn, and a major part of our work consisted of cutting burned off trees out of cross-country ski trails in the Old Faithful area in preparation for the upcoming winter season. We cleared many other trails in Yellowstone's West District as well, cutting well over 5,000 fallen logs by the time our rehab season was concluded by wintry weather in early November. We also raked organic debris back onto firelines that had been dug in the Madison area, and cleaned up large amounts of litter that had been left behind at firefighter campsites and helibases on the Madison Plateau. Working as we did in omnipresent soot and ash, we ended our work days plastered with black smudges on our faces and clothing that made us look like West Virginia coal miners, but we were young and fit and greatly enjoyed our tasks. We spent a great deal of

A cow moose along Aster Creek (near Lewis River Falls) browsing on burned twigs left in the wake of the Red-Shoshone Fire. The cow, as well as a bull that was nearby at the same time, seemed to be selecting in favor of the burned browse over other browse that was still green and available in the same area. © Jeff Henry/Roche Jaune Pictures, Inc.

time hiking trails, flying in helicopters, and camping in the backcountry, so a fringe benefit was that we got to see a lot of Yellowstone in its new successional stage.

A further fringe benefit for me was that I was assigned to spend several days flying in a helicopter to look for the carcasses of animals that had died in the fires. We found one group of about a dozen elk that had been burned over by the North Fork Fire along the upper reaches of Grayling Creek, near The Crags in the Gallatin Mountain Range. The fascinating thing about the dead elk was that, because they had been burned, they were exactly the same color—a charcoal gray/black—as the surrounding charred forest. Even from our overhead vantage point, we never would have spotted the monochromatic carcasses in the monochromatic landscape had it not been for the fact that each carcass was streaked with whitewash from the droppings of scavenging birds.

Almost all the members of my crew were housed in hotels and motels in West Yellowstone, 14 miles west of my seasonal base at Madison Junction. Hundreds, perhaps thousands of other firefighters were similarly housed in West while they worked on rehabilitation projects in the area, and all of them were fed in local restaurants. Both the housing and the food were paid for on United States government accounts, with a certain amount allotted for each firefighter for each night of lodging and for

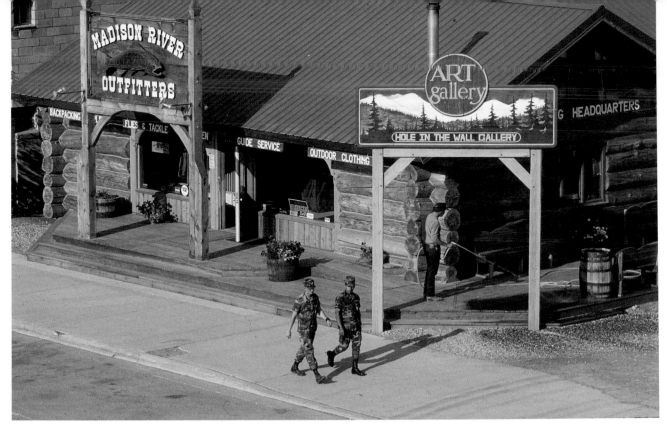

United States Army troops, brought in to fight fire and to work at fire rehabilitation, walking the streets of West Yellowstone, Montana, while on leave from work in Yellowstone. © Jeff Henry/Roche Jaune Pictures, Inc.

each meal of the day. Extending as it did well into November, the fire rehab season must have gone a long way toward compensating business owners in West Yellowstone, as well as in other gateway communities, for the losses they had incurred from the great fires during the normal business season. This was particularly true in 1988, when the masses of firefighters stayed late into the autumn, long past the point when the tourist season normally ended in those days.

Meanwhile officials in the tourism and travel bureaus of the states surrounding Yellowstone were hard at work trying to change the public's perception of Yellowstone as a burned out wasteland. Other officials with Yellowstone concessioners were doing the same type of work. They were aided by photographs of shoots of green grass already sprouting in areas burned by the conflagrations of just a few weeks earlier, shoots that miraculously had sprouted without the benefit of much precipitation other than the light storm of September 10 and 11. Cinematographers were able to find moving subjects, too, that illustrated the fact that Yellowstone was still alive. Among other subjects, film footage was shot of moose browsing on the scorched twigs of trees killed by the fires, and of elk rutting in front of backdrops of burned forest. Travel to Yellowstone in the fall of 1988 did experience a bit of a surge as a number of visitors came to the park to see for themselves what had happened during the fires. A disproportionate percentage of these autumn visitors came from the immediate region around Yellowstone.

A large bull elk in the black near Madison Junction. In an unfortunate twist of fate, this large bull was observed by some firefighters stationed for a time during the fire emergency at the Madison Campground. Later in the fall two of the firefighters returned to Madison and poached the bull along the Madison River near National Park Mountain. The two poachers were foolish enough to enter the head of the bull in a trophy contest in nearby Island Park, Idaho, which led to a case being made against the poachers by National Park Service rangers, as well as by agents from the United States Fish and Wildlife Service. 1988 National Park Service photo by Jeff Henry

At the same time, public affairs professionals with the National Park Service were trying to disseminate similar messages that Yellowstone was still viable, in spite of how some in the media had presented the 1988 fire story as being the ultimate ruination of the world's first national park. The park service message stressed how the fires could be seen as part of a natural progression, a system in which plant communities initially pioneered new habitat and then evolved through successive stages of development until they reached a climax state, at which point they were cleared away by fire to start the cycle over again. As the park service message was refined, it became one in which fire was seen as neither good nor bad, but rather as just a single stage in a natural cycle. A further point was that each stage of plant succession tended to support a certain coterie of wildlife, and a mix of habitats along the continuum of vegetative succession was seen as a healthier state than a monoculture of plant communities in a moribund, climax state, as in a situation where fire had been absent for a long period of time.

Some of the thousands of carcasses of animals that starved during the severe winter of 1988–1989. These winterkills were found on a geothermal flat near the mouth of Rabbit Creek in the spring of 1989, in the Midway Geyser Basin. © Jeff Henry/Roche Jaune Pictures, Inc.

As the winter of 1988–1989 unfolded, that natural cycle included the die off of a very large number of Yellowstone's iconic ungulates. The first factor contributing to the huge winterkill was the general drought of the previous summer, in which comparatively little forage had grown. And then, of course, much of the forage that had been produced burned in the summer's great fires, which ended up covering an area of almost 1.7 million acres both inside and outside Yellowstone's boundaries. On top of that, snowfall during the winter of 1988–1989 was heavy, as it almost always is following a summer of drought in the Yellowstone area. A repeated pattern of abnormally mild temperatures punctuated by unusually harsh cold snaps compounded the problem of heavy snowfall for the park's herbivores. In this pattern, a succession of ice layers froze into the snowpack and rendered access to what meager forage there was very difficult.

A tidbit illustrating the harshness of the winter following the great fires of 1988 was my own experience with the carcass survey I did for the Interagency Grizzly Bear Study Team beginning in 1984. In the first five springs of the carcass survey

Botanist Don Despain points out some of the subtleties of postfire regeneration to his coworkers while doing a study transect in the Washburns in the early summer of 1993, five years after the area was burned with stand-replacing intensity by the North Fork Fire. © Jeff Henry/Roche Jaune Pictures, Inc.

I found a combined total of about 175 winterkilled elk and bison in the Firehole River valley. Then in the spring of 1989, I found 489 such carcasses in the same survey area. In many places there were the carcasses of up to ten or so ungulates in just a small area, in some cases almost touching each other, and usually located in a small oasis of warm geothermal ground where the animals had bedded down for the last time before succumbing to starvation and exposure. Needless to say, all that carrion was a bonanza of meat for Yellowstone's scavengers. I noticed that the park's famous bears had so much to choose from in the spring of 1989 that they selected only the choicest options in the way of winterkilled ungulates.

Scientific researchers scrambled to cash in on a bonanza of grant money that was made available to investigate the 1988 fires. More than 250 different research projects were initiated in Yellowstone in the twelve years after 1988, with about fifty-eight of those designed to investigate matters specific to fire. Many of the other research projects were primarily focused on nonfire subjects, such as particular species of wildlife, but even a good many of those projects somehow related their primary objects back to the subject of fire. The fire-specific research revealed much about the nature of the elemental force in the world's first national park, a lot of which had to do with just how well the area's vegetative communities were adapted to fire. Some species, such as Yellowstone's signature lodgepole pines, were actually somewhat dependent on periodic burning. In the case of the lodgepole, the tree's serotinous cones (amounting to 50 percent or more of the cones of an individual lodgepole) were designed to open in the heat of a forest fire, and consequently seedling counts of up to several hundred thousand per acre were observed in burned areas in the years after 1988. In most cases, most of the seedlings sprouted in the spring of 1989, only half a year or a little more after their parent forests had been torched. No reseeding or replanting of burned forests was done in Yellowstone. That is, no restoration was done by humans, but trees naturally returned to virtually all the forested areas that were burned in 1988.

Concomitant with the profusion of tree seedlings that sprouted in the spring of 1989 was an even more profuse display of wildflowers. Fireweed, of course, was one of the most conspicuous flowers, but many other species of forbs and grasses sprang to life in the wake of the fires. The heavy snows that fell during the winter following the fires provided abundant water for the regrowth, as did the unusually large amounts of rain that fell during the summer of 1989. Many of Yellowstone's famous grazing animals died as a result of 1988's drought and fires, and especially from the harsh winter that followed. But those who survived benefited from the bounty of fresh vegetation that burst forth in phoenix-like renewal the following spring. The surviving herbivores and their offspring benefited not only from the well-watered regrowth, but also from the fact that so many members of their own species had perished and therefore intraspecific competition was reduced. Many individuals of competing species had died as well, so interspecific competition likewise was reduced.

Fascinating research into Yellowstone's fire history revealed that big fires had burned in the area many times before, the last time being in the early to mid-1700s. This research involved clever techniques of looking at such evidence as tree-ring growth patterns, as well as pollen depositions in the bottoms of ponds and lakes. This sort of research revealed that large wildfires have burned through Yellowstone to renew the cycle of plant succession as many as several dozen times since the ice of the last period of glaciation melted away. Delving still deeper, researchers improved their knowledge of how frequently fires occurred in various habitats in Yellowstone. Grasslands on the park's northern range, for example, probably burned historically on the order of every couple of decades, perhaps even less, while the more moist coniferous forests at higher elevations had fire intervals of two or more centuries.

Contemplating this information on the historic frequency of fire in Yellowstone's predominant coniferous forests leads to an interesting point. There is a contention that part of the reason the fires of 1988 were so all consuming was because fire suppression over the previous one-hundred-odd years had contributed to an unnatural buildup of fuels. Considering that the fire interval in some of Yellowstone's higher elevation forests can be as much as 400 years, and that the last big fires in the area were only 200–250 years before 1988, it might be fair to say that it just wasn't the right time for Yellowstone to burn before 1988. Further consideration of

Dense regrowth of lodgepole pines in an area burned by 1988's North Fork Fire near Gibbon Falls. This photo was shot on July 1, 2008, almost exactly twenty years after it burned. © Jeff Henry/Roche Jaune Pictures, Inc.

weather records collected since the park was created additionally reflects that there were very few years during that time when conditions were dry enough to support widespread fire. So with inadequate fuel loads and unfavorable weather conditions, big fires simply weren't in the equation for Yellowstone during its first one-hundred-plus years of existence as a national park. A further counterargument against the idea that fuels had accumulated to unnatural levels in the years before 1988 is that for most of the park's history—that is, in the days before helicopters and airplanes and other technological capabilities that enhanced human ability to suppress fires— efforts against wildfire probably didn't make much of a difference in terms of wildfire spread and acreages burned.

The national media returned to Yellowstone in great numbers in the spring of 1989. It seemed that they all wanted to do the rebirth story on the first national park. To me and to many others it seemed that the intense media presence might have been something of a makeup or a do over on the part of reporters, firstly because they had missed the magnitude of the Yellowstone fire story until the season of 1988

The blackened snags of a stand of whitebark pines along the crest of the Absaroka Range near Mount Chittenden, silhouetted against a hot and dry sunset in late September of 2007. © Jeff Henry/Roche Jaune Pictures, Inc.

was fairly far advanced, and secondly because they realized that in many cases they had overstated the view that Yellowstone had been reduced to a smoking wasteland by the end of the fire season in 1988. The increased level of media attention carried well beyond 1988 and 1989, and Yellowstone as a seasonal backwater was never quite so quiet again. For one example, closer scrutiny on a national level that at least in part could be traced back to attention brought on by the fires probably became a factor in the vehement controversies over winter management of Yellowstone that erupted in the 1990s and 2000s.

The great fires of 1988 had profound managerial implications for national parks, and for the management of wildfire in the jurisdictions of other land management agencies. For the first century or so after they were created, national parks, national forests, and other preserves for the most part suppressed all fires on their property in a sort of Smoky the Bear reaction. This mania to put out all wildfires intensified after the Big Blowup of 1910 in Idaho and western Montana, in which several towns were destroyed, as many as 200 people were killed, and approximately three million acres of timber were burned and pretty much lost to commercial use. The official attitude toward fire could be summed up with a quote from a United States Forest Service manual that was written in the early part of the twentieth century, and that read in part: "Each succeeding day will be planned and executed with an aim, without reservation, of obtaining control [of a wildfire] before ten o'clock of the next morning." Understandably, this philosophy was often referred to as "the ten o'clock doctrine."

As the decades of the twentieth century passed, however, more and more observers became aware of fire as an integral force in natural systems, and gradually recommendations made by those who recognized fire's place were incorporated into areas that ostensibly were managed for their natural values. In the case of Yellowstone, in 1972 the park instituted a revised fire policy that allowed some fires to burn in some portions of the park. This revision was followed by another in 1976 that expanded the area where natural fire would be allowed to include nearly all of the park. Exceptions to the policy were made and fires were fought if they threatened human life or property, or if fires were determined to have been caused by humans. At no time was the park's policy simply one of "let it burn," as so many critics of the park and its fire policy facilely claimed in 1988 and at other junctures.

Yellowstone's policy of allowing most natural fires to burn was suspended in the wake of 1988 firestorms, pending exhaustive review. The updated fire policy that evolved as a result of the post-1988 review was similar to the earlier one in that it allowed for naturally ignited fires to burn if they did not threaten people or property. Additionally, parameters were adopted that required even naturally caused fires to be suppressed under certain conditions. These so-called "trigger points," upon which control efforts were to be initiated, involved considerations of fuel moistures, weather conditions, and the availability of firefighting resources on the national level. If weather and fuel conditions were judged to be so extreme that fires might explode out of control, or if there were insufficient resources available to deal with fires that grew too large, nascent fires were to be attacked and controlled before they could spread. These new management directives were aided by improved technology that utilized in-depth evaluations of factors entering into the fire equation, as well as by sophisticated computer models that analyzed the information and predicted future fire behavior.

As always, however, there are unknowns and unknowables that enter into the question, and fire science remains imprecise. To a very great extent fire prediction involves weather prediction, something that is notoriously uncertain, and the most fundamental point of all is that there is only a very fine line between conditions where fires won't burn at all and conditions where fires can explode and quickly blow out of control.

One prediction that has not come to pass is that parts of Yellowstone that burned in 1988 were bound to reburn. Yellowstone's homegrown scientists, people like Don DeSpain and John Varley, never did buy into the idea that the 1988 burns were likely to retorch. But many non-Yellowstone observers, mostly firefighting professionals who had been brought in to work on the 1988 fires, were quite certain that reburns were inevitable. They looked at the large amount of woody material that remained in the burned areas, considered how reburns are common in other habitats

Red needles on a stand of lodgepole pines that were dying from an infestation of pine bark beetles. Forests in the Rockies are much more susceptible to disease and insects when they are stressed by abnormally hot and dry conditions. This particular stand of lodgepoles was photographed in the upper reaches of the Gros Ventre River in Wyoming, not far south of Yellowstone National Park, in the summer of 2005. © Jeff Henry/Roche Jaune Pictures, Inc.

around the nation, and figured it had to happen in Yellowstone too. Many areas charred by the Big Blowup in Idaho and Montana, for example, reburned in the years following 1910. So far, however, nothing significant has reburned in the aftermath of 1988 in Yellowstone. Now most of the dead snags that remained standing after the big fires have fallen, and generally much of the leftover fuel has rotted into the ground and is no longer available to power a reburn. As time goes on it becomes less and less likely that any of the 1988 acreage will burn again. It won't burn again, that is, until decades have passed and plant communities have grown enough new material to fuel the next generation of fire.

There is no question that in the past fire was a natural element that got rid of dead wood and cleared the way for new growth. Fire intervals were specific to habitats, and were determined by how long it took to accumulate organic material sufficient to carry a fire, and also by the frequency of drought periods dry enough to enable the organic material to burn. The wild card today is, of course, the Earth's

A road sign photographed near Old Faithful in the wake of 1988's powerful North Fork Fire. The sign indicating a pedestrian crossing might be seen symbolically as representing humankind at a crossroads, where we all face an uncertain future of a warming and destabilized climate. © Jeff Henry/Roche Jaune Pictures, Inc

warming climate, and specifically what that warming climate will mean to forests in the northern Rockies. Forests in Yellowstone and surrounding regions have always been limited by the amount of available water, which in turn depended on the amount of winter snowfall, summer rainfall, and seasonal temperatures. Without any question, winters are shorter in the Rockies now than they were not that long ago. Snowpacks are lighter, begin to accumulate later in the autumn, and melt off earlier in the spring. Temperatures at all seasons of the year are warmer, and consequently drought conditions tend to commence earlier in the summer than they used to and to persist later into the fall. Water from any source, be it snow or rain, evaporates more readily and leaves arid soil and parched vegetation behind. Gigantic fires around the western United States are much more common, and they are not only larger in extent, they are often more violently intense. From a perspective of more than twenty-five years after the event, many now see the 1988 fires in Yellowstone as a threshold that marked the beginning of a new fire regime in a new era.

In the new regime, trees die directly from drought and heat, or can be so stressed by underlying conditions that they fall victim to insects or fungus. With warmer temperatures and drier conditions present in a fire season that is as much as two months longer than it used to be, the probability of ignition at some point during that longer season is much greater, and fires once started have a higher probability of exploding to radical intensities and extents.

In short, forests are stressed from heat and drought, and fire can be seen as the agent that removes the ailing forests. Some sources already predict that forests burned by wildfire in the American Southwest might not ever grow back in the warmer, effectively drier world that we all now face in the Mountain West. As time goes forward and the Earth continues to warm incrementally, the zone of arboreal inhospitability will inevitably move northward and someday will probably arrive in the Yellowstone area. Fire will still respond to the age-old conditions of fuel and weather, but given the warming climate of a changing world that is almost unequivocally the result of enormous numbers of human beings burning enormous amounts of fossil fuels, it might no longer be properly viewed as an altogether natural force or part of an altogether natural system.

In another, cultural sense, the 1988 fires unquestionably ushered in a new regime in terms of fire management and fire awareness. Park managers pay much more attention to phenomena like snowpack depth and water content, the date of snowpack melt-off, stages of plant phrenology, and the rate at which organic fuels dry out through the spring and summer seasons. Massive amounts of fire data are collected, analyzed, and inordinately reanalyzed by high-powered computers, and elaborate fire action plans are written, evaluated, and then rewritten. Over any discussion of the upcoming fire season, either in Yellowstone or elsewhere, and whether it's just a couple of guys leaning on a pickup truck while on a coffee break or a confidential discussion at the highest levels of park management, a specter hangs in the air. The question is sometimes spoken, sometimes not, but it's always in the minds of all concerned: "Could this year be another 1988?"